9/1 1

FASTER CHEAPER
BETTER

FASTER CHEAPER
BETTER

The 9 Levers for Transforming
How Work Gets Done

Michael Hammer
and Lisa W. Hershman

CROWN
BUSINESS

Library of Congress Cataloging-in-Publication Data

Hammer, Michael, 1948–2008.
  Faster, cheaper, better by Michael Hammer and Lisa W. Hershman.
    p. cm.
  1. Reengineering (Management). 2. Workflow. 3. Organizational effectiveness. 4. Performance. 5. Management. I. Hershman, Lisa W. II. Title.
  HD58.87 H3624 2010
  658.5'1—dc22   2010040792

ISBN 978-0-307-45379-2
eISBN 978-0-307-45979-4

Printed in the United States of America

DESIGN BY PHILIP MAZZONE

10 9 8 7 6 5 4 3 2 1

First Edition

In Memoriam

Michael Hammer
April 1948–September 2008

Even the most mundane work can be given meaning and value for those who perform it if they understand how it benefits, even in the simplest of ways, the lives of others. Process-centered work can help satisfy everyone's hunger for connection with something beyond themselves and their own needs. It widens our horizons and connects us with others—with our teammates, with our organization, with our customers. In the process-centered world, dignity is restored to work, the dignity that was lost to workers who only performed repetitive tasks.

A late classical Jewish text contains a paean to the spiritual value of work: "Precious is work, for of all the creatures that God created in the world, He granted work only to humankind." This text's author tells us that the fullest expression of soul or spirit or intelligence is to be found in one's work. It is work that distinguishes us as human beings, the way in which we express our essential nature and our reflection of the divine. These prophetic words capture the essence of process-centered work. By making them a reality, the twenty-first-century organization will truly be on the side of the angels.

—Michael Hammer, unpublished manuscript

Some will remember him for his brilliance, others for his wit, but we will remember him most of all for his unceasing love, and for teaching us always to ask why.

—Phyllis Hammer, Jessica, Alison, Dana, and David

To my husband, Brandt, who believes in me, at times more than I believe in myself, and who was a huge help in bringing this project to a successful conclusion.

To my mom, Dolores, whose zest for life is a constant encouragement to try new things and explore great possibilities. To my sister, Nadine, my brother, Greg, and my brother, Carl, his wife, Michele, and my nieces, Melissa and Katherine—thanks for cheering me on from the sidelines.

To my dad, Carl (CJ), whom I think about every day—I hope I'm still making you proud. I miss you.

And finally, I thank God every day for the many blessings—through opportunities, experiences, and people I meet—that He has granted me.

—Lisa W. Hershman

Contents

FASTER CHEAPER
BETTER

Foreword

M ichael Hammer was admired by people worldwide. What is most intriguing about his story is what you learn about him by talking to people who knew him or even met him just once in a class. They admired his commitment to his family, his enormous intellect, and his accomplishments. They also mention his passion for process and improving organizational performance. As the conversation continues, you find other facets that further describe Michael and why so many people found him intriguing.

He was one of the most remarkable presenters I had ever seen. His Socratic style, sharp wit, and uncanny recollection made him both entertaining and awe-inspiring. I remember my first class with him: four days of process reengineering. While I was looking forward to refreshing my skills, the thought of sitting for four days to review redesigning techniques sounded about as exciting as watching paint dry. Wow, was I wrong. He spoke so quickly, involved the class so widely, and delivered such wonderful insights that it was anything but dry. He used many quotes, both popular and obscure, to

make his points. He tiptoed on the edge of political correct-
ness (which he cared little about) with some of his favorite
Dorothy Parker quotes ("You can lead a whore to culture but
you can't make her think") and his definitions of training vs.
education (sex training vs. sex education: which one would
you go to and which one would you send your kid to?). Then
there were the slides that equated the process journey to bibli-
cal stories—a comparison that was fascinating, daring, memo-
rable, and accurate.

As he learned about my experiences implementing his
theories in manufacturing, service, and distribution industries,
he asked if he could study my work. I was immensely gratified that he would want to collaborate with me. I was able to
provide him with the problems and solutions I had encountered implementing process in many companies; he gave me
benchmark data, new approaches, and proven solutions from
others he had studied. And then there were the debates: challenging his theories, challenging my approaches. We learned a
lot from each other.

In the early 1990s Michael introduced the world to business
transformation with his work on reengineering, most notably
Reengineering the Corporation. People from a wide range of industries told him that they used it as their bible for transformation
efforts. This puzzled and perplexed him since it was not written
to be a handbook. It merely introduced the concept of transformation; it did not pretend to offer a comprehensive solution. In
the years following its publication Michael continued his work
on how to rethink the nuts and bolts of business. When executives from companies sought his counsel he offered no opinions on what they should do (i.e., what business they should
be in); his role was to tell them how to do it best. And that
meant how to do it differently by transforming how work actu-

ally gets done. His search for a comprehensive solution about why some companies succeed and others fail led to this book. He studied both the successes and the failures—what they had done and not done—to identify where they had run aground or what had made their efforts bear fruit. There are companies he studied for long periods of time, well over a decade in many cases. Some were first mentioned in *Reengineering the Corporation* and are reported on in depth in this book. Drawing on his extensive research, Michael formulated hypotheses, tested them, and refined them. He shared interim results with companies in the Phoenix Consortium, a group of Hammer & Co. clients committed to breakthrough performance. Finally, in 2005 Michael developed a framework that turned description into prescription. It was tested at several companies and many found it so valuable that they institutionalized it as a guide to their transformational efforts. This book builds on and expands these ideas into a structured approach to business transformation. That framework became the Process and Enterprise Maturity Model (PEMM), first published in the *Harvard Business Review* article "The Process Audit" in April 2007.

Michael believed, as do I, that the issue of how work gets done is central to success in a world undergoing a sea change. We are facing an unprecedented confluence of macroeconomic and business factors that are creating a new and unfamiliar business environment. The solutions to these issues are apparent and easy to state but hard to implement: wring out cost so that a company's direct labor differential with the competition is not an issue; do more for customers than the competition so that the value delivered is worth any additional cost; become more flexible and be the first to bring new products, excel at quality, and out-execute the competition in every way.

If there is no alternative—and there is not—then what is the problem? Why is it so difficult to accomplish the obvious?

It's simply that the way companies today are organized and operated makes it impossible for them to get the dramatic performance improvements they need, even if they were staffed by supermen and superwomen. The only option is deep and fundamental change to how they do their work. Providing the road map to doing so is the mission of this book.

One example told in depth in the book is that of Tetra Pak, the food packaging company that had been the juggernaut of its industry. By the early 2000s it showed symptoms of the kind of decline that too often dooms longtime industry leaders (think Sears and General Motors). Market share was starting to go down; customers were complaining about how hard it was to do business with the company; new competitors were creating a disturbing pattern of being the first with product innovations. It seemed as though Tetra Pak would be just another story of a corporate giant turned corporate dinosaur.

Instead, Tetra Pak used the idea of process-based transformation to create new ways of working. One of its first goals was to improve the accuracy of the dates it gave customers about when new products would hit the market. It had been late on almost nine out of ten new products. By rethinking the way it developed and announced products, it started hitting its promise dates nearly 90 percent of the time—a huge turnaround.

This improvement was no flash in the pan. First, it endured, as opposed to being a short-term blip that before long regressed to the unfortunate mean. More importantly, it was only the first in a series of breakthroughs. Tetra Pak subsequently turned its attention to how it installs equipment in customers' plants, and nearly doubled customer satisfaction with its installation experience. It examined how it schedules the engineers who maintain and upgrade the equipment in customer sites—and thereby saved money and further increased customer satisfaction. By rethinking how it manages its supply chain—ordering

raw materials, scheduling production, managing distribution—
it was able to cut inventory in half in some countries and
increase the number of "perfect orders" by 50 percent. The slide
in market share has been reversed and the list of achievements
continues to build.

Michael's research into how a company can transform its
enterprise processes focused on the relatively few (typically
five to ten) end-to-end sequences of activities that create all
the value a company delivers to its customers, such as order
fulfillment, product development, customer problem resolution, demand creation, and supply chain management. While
always present, these processes have largely been invisible in
the past. They represent a new way of looking at a company's
operations—not in terms of piecemeal fragments of work
performed in a slew of isolated functional departments but in
terms of large-scale holistic work units.

His research identified nine levers for action necessary to
achieve transformational results. They are broken into two sec-
tions. The first are called process enablers, and they are what a
company needs to address in order to achieve breakthrough performance improvements in an end-to-end process: the process
design; appropriate metrics; performers who do the work; a
process owner; and an effective infrastruture. Attending to these
five critical elements gives companies a road map for transforming a process and creating breakthrough performance. However,
merely having this road map, while necessary, is insufficient. He
discovered that, despite their best intentions, some companies
were simply incapable of making progress on these elements.
These companies seemed to know what to do but just couldn't
get it done. This led him to realize that companies able to follow
his road map did so because they had four enterprise capabilities in place—overarching characteristics that equipped them to
undertake fundamental transformation: leadership; culture; governance; and expertise. Without these capabilities, he found, a

company will simply not have the wherewithal to carry out the process changes needed to achieve its goals; with them, it is ready to embark on the journey and succeed.

Not only was Michael Hammer a serious scholar, researcher, and teacher, he was fun. His fondness for movies, musicals, Motown, and Monty Python always made it into the presentations and conversations. He found insightful elements in all of these and applied the lines, references, and characters to real-life business situations. He was a consummate entertainer, skilled in imitating voices and gestures.

He was also kind. I remember struggling with a problem at work that had to do with a particular executive. We had a chance to have dinner together and I said, "Michael, I need some help—" Before I could even finish, he responded with, "Name it." That was the last time I saw him. He passed away less than a month later.

He was a good citizen, an intellectual giant, and a great friend. He inspired us. He made us laugh. He made us think. And he encouraged us to be creative and to try new things. By continuing his work and building upon the foundation he created, I hope we make him proud.

—Lisa Wilkes Hershman
CEO, Hammer and Company

The Rise and Fall of Corporate Heroes

Everybody loves Bob. He's a corporate hero. Just last week Bob was watching television after dinner, but he wasn't really watching. Instead he was thinking about work, as he does most nights. Suddenly it hit Bob: he hadn't checked to make sure engineering had included the new wiring diagram in the customer's shipment that was due to go out first thing in the morning. Without the diagram the equipment would be useless.

"I don't know what time I'll be home," he shouted to his wife as he bolted out the door, jumped into his car, and sped to the plant.

Jerry was on guard duty at the gate and greeted Bob warmly. He was accustomed to Bob showing up at all hours of the day and night. Bob went straight to the shipping dock. Sure enough, the box was sitting there ready to go, and it didn't contain the wiring diagram. It took Bob an hour to track down a copy of the diagram, put it in the box, and reseal it for shipment. He got home at midnight.

That's the kind of thing Bob does all the time. And the

bosses recognize his devotion and applaud it often. He's gotten raises and been promoted, and he's been named Employee
of the Month five times in the past two years. Many of his
co-workers now emulate Bob and give an extra measure, too.

No doubt about it, Bob's a great guy. Trouble is, his company's approach to getting work done is a raging disaster.
Bob is forced to be a hero because he's a loyal and ambitious employee struggling to overcome his company's chaotic
processes for getting things done. He gets lots of credit for
making the fix to save the customer, but he's constantly creating dramatic work-arounds because the existing processes
create problems that shouldn't exist. Worse still, Bob's behavior
and the accolades he receives simply reinforce the notion that
everyone should work around the system. No one seems to
grasp that if the system were fixed, there would be no need for
heroes like Bob.

There are lots of companies like Bob's, fragmented and
inefficient. They survive despite themselves only because
people like Bob are constantly fixing things. It may take thirty
days to fill a customer order, but only three of those days
involve real work. The rest of the time people are arguing
about who's responsible for some part of the order or the order
is languishing in someone's in-box. It isn't because people are
dumb or lazy. Quite the contrary. Most people want to do a
good job. They are given goals and they strive to meet them.
They focus intently on doing their job correctly and well, and
they are rewarded for their efforts. But few understand how
their narrowly defined jobs fit into the overall picture of what
the company is trying to accomplish. As a result, what they
do in their own jobs may be at cross-purposes with someone
else's job.

Our favorite example of how people work at cross-purposes
is the sales rep of a large consumer goods company who
brought in a small order from a new customer. The customer

was very explicit: this was a trial, but if the company could fill this trial order well, there would be a lot more business to follow. The sales rep recognized the importance of performing well and slathered the order form with "urgent" and "expedite" stickers and submitted it for processing. The order passed from department to department until it arrived at shipping. Shipping took one look at the order and realized it wouldn't fill a single truck. Shipping less than a truckload is very costly, and the head of shipping knew his bonus depended on keeping shipping costs to a minimum. He ordered the material stacked on the loading dock until there was a full truck going to the same city.

Of course, we find this appalling, but the shipping department manager made an entirely rational decision. His responsibility was to minimize shipping costs, and that is what he was rewarded for doing. Delaying the shipment was neither wicked nor irresponsible. Indeed, to send it quickly would have violated the principles he was expected to use in managing his responsibilities. He was being relentlessly logical. It wasn't his fault the company lost the customer. The problem lay in the system, of which shipping was one small part. The shipping manager's job was so narrowly defined and so divorced from its larger context that doing it well hurt the company rather than helped it.

These problems aren't limited to companies. Our government, schools, and medical system all suffer from these chaotic conditions. If you've had a major medical problem in the past several years, you know what we mean: countless hours spent scheduling appointments, sitting idly in waiting rooms, and traveling from one specialist to another, all while besieged by innumerable bills and insurance forms. Chaos, indeed!

This state of affairs isn't accidental. For well over a century managers have achieved increasing productivity on ever larger scales by dividing and subdividing work into smaller and smaller units. The modern corporation that has evolved as a result consists of many specialized functional departments, such as sales, engineering, marketing, manufacturing, operations, and finance. The people who work in a given department all focus on the same departmental goal—advertising promotes sales, shipping moves the product, procurement buys the parts—and they report to the executive in charge of their department, who measures their performance and rewards or penalizes them according to the department's own metrics. The way we operate today is a legacy of the Industrial Revolution, but that revolution ended long ago and the ideas about how to organize work that grew out of it have outlived their usefulness in a world that has become smaller, faster, and much more competitive. To see that the old ways aren't working, you need only consider the havoc wrought in the last few years as the global finance system teetered on the brink, General Motors and Chrysler reorganized in bankruptcy proceedings, and millions of people—"our most valuable asset," as many companies like to say—lost their jobs, retirement savings, and houses.

Today the customer reigns supreme, crowned by the information age. You know how easy it is to comparison-shop these days. Need a new flat-screen television? You can get specs and prices on the Internet in just a few minutes. Hit a button and the television arrives two days later. Your customers can do the same thing. If a customer places an order with your company, he doesn't care that your product is designed in Texas, the parts are made in Spain and Brazil, and the whole thing is assembled in Turkey. Too often companies claim that they are global when they really are international. The difference is that an international company may have sales offices or manufacturing facilities in other countries but hasn't taken the extra step of seamlessly integrating those various operations. That forces customers to jump through the company's internal hoops:

pricing in different currencies, different delivery schedules from various sources, and language barriers in resolving problems. A truly global company has overcome national boundaries and makes life very easy and transparent for its customers. It knows that the customer just wants a quality product when and where he wants it and at a good price. If your company is like the chaotic place where Bob works, your customer probably doesn't realize and certainly doesn't care how heroic your people are in fulfilling his order. But one day you'll slip and lose a customer, either because Bob doesn't get the fix done in time or because a nimbler competitor undercuts your terms. It isn't a question of if, it's a question of when. The time has come to do our work faster, cheaper, and better.

Faster, cheaper, better. The elusive holy trinity of business. So desirable, yet so difficult. If we do it faster and cheaper, we can't do it better. If we do it cheaper and better, we can't do it faster. And if we do it better and faster, we can't do it cheaper. There always seem to be barriers to achieving all three.

No longer. If you believe a simple concept—that the way you organize your work makes all the difference in the world—there is an alternative to the fragmented work processes that grew out of the Industrial Revolution, and it allows us to be faster, cheaper, *and* better. It isn't easy and it won't happen overnight, but for those who master it the results are astounding. Rather than a series of discrete steps, work becomes an end-to-end continuum. People no longer focus entirely on their own jobs with no notion of how their work affects their colleagues' ability to do their jobs or even the customer. Instead, they are thinking about the whole and not the parts, about outcomes instead of activities, about the collective rather than the individual. What are now individual fiefdoms meld seamlessly into a unified structure with one goal: customer satisfaction. Michael Hammer first introduced this concept of end-to-end process in 1993 in *Reengineering the*

Corporation. Now, after seventeen years of preaching, teaching, and witnessing the immense potential of end-to-end work processes at a growing number of companies, we are convinced it is the way to organize work so that any organization can achieve its goals faster, cheaper, and better. Our intent with this book is to spread the gospel, making this new approach to how we do our work available to every organization that wants to compete and thrive in the global economy. *Reengineering the Corporation* explained *why* the end-to-end process is a better way. *Faster, Cheaper, Better* shows you *how* you can harness the amazing power of this simple concept to become more profitable and more competitive.

End-to-end process is a complete change in the way you and everyone who works for you do their work. It requires a revolution in the way you think about work and an evolution in the way you do your work. The most difficult part of implementing end-to-end process is sustaining the effort. There is a tendency to realize great benefits from the initial stages of implementing end-to-end process and then declare victory and move on, or worse, go back to the old ways. If that happens, an organization will fail to realize the even greater benefits that lie ahead.

If you think process is about flow charts and boxes on pieces of paper, you've got it all wrong. It's about running your business in a different way, achieving your goals in a different way, and pleasing the customer. It covers every aspect of your organization, from technology to the sales force, and it affects the way all your people do their jobs and are motivated and rewarded. Come with us for a moment to visit one of our clients—we'll call the company Andren Aerospace—to see the transformational power of end-to-end process.

In late 2004 Andren Aerospace, a large manufacturer of avionics components and systems, had a big problem. Its largest customer had just fired the company. The customer had been giving Andren descriptions of its needs and Andren would respond with a schematic—a description of the particular system to be built—together with a quote and a delivery date. If the customer approved, Andren would get an order, which it typically proceeded to mess up. Andren almost never met the delivery date it promised. And when the system did eventually arrive, all too often it suffered from quality problems—the assembly wasn't done correctly, some parts were damaged or missing, or the invoice was wrong. Periodically the customer would get riled up and hurl imprecations and threats at Andren. Andren would then promise that it would change its ways and do better. But it never really did. Eventually the customer simply told Andren that it had sixty days to move out, that their relationship was at an end.

As it happened, the customer fired Andren at about the same time Andren brought us in to review its operations with the goal of applying end-to-end thinking and techniques to Andren's business. The firing gave us a perfect opportunity to demonstrate how end-to-end thinking could make a huge difference. If we could redesign Andren's processes to save its business with that big customer, Andren would gain a lot of credibility because it was having the same problems with other customers.

This wasn't the first time Andren had tried to fix these problems. It had already tried applying vaunted Six Sigma techniques—statistical methods used for continuous improvement—to no avail. The fact that Six Sigma hadn't helped told us the problem wasn't an execution issue but endemic in the way Andren did its work. It had a bad process.

We started by convening a cross-functional team from the various groups involved in handling requests and filling orders—people from sales, customer service, engineering, manufacturing operations, and more. As a group, we walked through the entire process, from customer inquiry to delivered product, writing down all the steps in a flow chart on brown paper. The most remarkable part of this exercise was that until we did that no one at Andren actually had a mental picture of the whole process from beginning to end. Everyone knew his or her own job and what his or her department was supposed to be doing, but no one had the big picture. The brown paper diagram that we constructed eventually took up twelve feet of wall space. It began with the customer calling the sales rep with a description of what the customer needed. This went to the Engineering department, which created the design and specified what components should go into the system, and then created a technically valid specification. Customer service became involved to determine what the design would cost and to provide the customer with a quote and a delivery date. When the customer approved the quote, customer service would check to see if all the parts were in stock. If so, customer service would contact Inventory to have the parts sent to manufacturing, where they would be assembled into a system and then shipped. If not, the Materials group would be asked to purchase the missing parts or their equivalent.

It sounds nice and tidy. In reality the situation was uncoordinated chaos. The fundamental issue was that everyone was focused on his or her own piece and nobody knew nor much cared what anybody else was doing. They all meant well, but they kept getting in one another's way.

- Engineering might find an issue or a better design without bothering to let anyone else know; they would contact their counterparts at the customer company to negotiate a revised design, bypassing both the other Andren folks and the customer's purchasing agents, creating confusion all around.
- If the needed parts weren't in stock, materials might contact engineering to determine what parts it could

substitute, a negotiation that could drag out for weeks. The parts changes also created invoice inaccuracies, since the substituted parts might have different prices than the original parts.

- Customer service, accountable for order accuracy, would take weeks to verify the order, even if that meant missing the delivery date they themselves had given the customer.
- Materials might reallocate to another customer the parts that customer service had planned to use to fill the order.
- Or the sales rep, who was rewarded on gross margin, might put the entire order on hold to take advantage of cheaper parts that were on the way from a supplier.

These resulting delays had multiple ripple effects. By the time the order got to manufacturing, it would usually be extremely late, and the workers who had to do the assembly felt so pressured that they made mistakes and damaged the equipment. Andren also often felt compelled to ship late orders by premium freight, driving up costs. And products that arrived after the date the customer was expecting to receive them could end up on an overcrowded receiving dock without assigned space.

None of this was the result of incompetence, malice, or stupidity. Andren's workers were smart, well trained, and highly motivated. They were just all smart, well trained, and highly motivated to do different things without any coordination. Each did the best job he or she could and each felt empowered to do whatever they thought best—including dealing with the customer directly—to get the specific job done. They all had different concerns because each department had its own goals and its own metrics; some were measured on order accuracy, some on inventory turns, some on gross margin. But no one was measured on the same thing as anyone else, and no one was measured on anything that mattered to the customer. Nobody was in charge of the whole end-to-end process of turning a customer request into an on-time delivery. And since nobody was in charge of it, nobody paid attention to it.

Andren, like most companies, suffered from the effects of the division of labor. Its work and those who did that work were fragmented into many little pieces, each focused on a small part of the work and each with its own agenda and measures. The symptoms were classic: blindness to the larger picture, ignorance and indifference to what others in the company were doing, and a profound lack of responsibility for customer satisfaction and business results. Left untreated, the disease could be fatal.

As we worked our way through the documentation of how Andren's end-to-end process actually worked, the people on the team were astonished.

"I had no idea things worked this way," "Why in the world do we do that?" and "That makes no sense" were recurring phrases we heard. Looking at work in the context of process shines a very powerful new light on it. Our team found ninety-four steps in the end-to-end process and classified each of them as value-adding, non-value-adding, or waste. Value-adding work is work that the customer will pay for, work that directly contributes to creating the desired result. Non-value-adding (or business-enabling) work is overhead, work that the customer does not care about but which is needed for the proper functioning of the process: checking, tracking, prioritizing, scheduling, and so on. Non-value-adding work is meta-work, work that does not contribute to a result but just enables other work. Waste is what it sounds like: unnecessary and useless work, such as duplicate efforts, errors, and producing reports that no one ever reads. Of the ninety-four steps, only eleven were value-adding. Only eleven made any difference to the customer. All the rest were either pointless or overhead.

Andren's first response was to reorganize. That's very common. Many executives feel that every problem can be solved with a new organizational chart. One executive we know said that reorganization was a core competency at her company. Reorganization activities may provide the momentary assurance that comes from making a decision or taking action. *But the root cause of persistent performance problems is found not in who reports to whom but in how work itself is organized and performed.*

So we persisted, and after developing an understanding of Andren's dysfunctional process, we set about creating a new one. The root cause of the problems with the old process was fragmentation. The solution was integration. In this case we proposed creating two new roles with big-picture responsibilities, one to serve as the sole point person in contact with the customer and the other to identify and troubleshoot problems in operations. The two people assigned to those new roles were chosen because of their expertise, but also because they "got it"—they understood what an end-to-end process could accomplish and were imaginative and bold in helping design the new process.

Amal had been a top salesperson at Andren. He was given a job that combined the roles of sales rep, customer service rep, and gathering engineering data, and he became the customer's sole point of contact in the early stages of the process. He took the customer's request, devised a solution, checked inventory availability, quoted a price, and promised a delivery date. If he needed it, Amal could get technical support from engineering, but he was in charge and managed all contacts with the customer. He had the big picture.

Once the customer accepted the quote and responded with an order, Jane, an expert in operations, took over. She made sure that the parts needed for the system assembly were available to manufacturing. If they weren't in stock, Jane ordered them and made sure they arrived as needed. She also made sure that the people in manufacturing were expecting the relevant parts and were scheduled to do the needed assembly work. Like Amal, Jane might call on other people for help, but she was in charge of the order and managed all interactions with the customer once the order was placed. These two new broad roles meant that most of the non-value-adding work of the old process, things such as multiple credit checks of customers and repeated order verification by different departments, was no longer needed and all the waste work could be eliminated. The new process contained only twenty-eight steps, the original eleven value-adding ones and only seventeen non-value-adding overhead activities.

The new process replaced an uncoordinated free-for-all with a disciplined and integrated way of working. Two individuals with broad skills and personal accountability performed and managed the work from beginning to end. And to ensure that everyone stayed on the same page, Amal and Jane, as well as everyone else in what was called the "order-to-cash" process, were measured and rewarded on a common metric: on-time delivery.

It took us about three months to devise the new process and about six weeks to implement it with the first customer. The result was breathtaking. Under the old regime, Andren met the delivery date it promised the customer less than 15 percent of the time; with the new process, it hit the target more than 90 percent of the time. Under the old regime, it typically took Andren forty-eight hours to turn an inquiry into a quote; the new process cut that to less than six hours. The quality of the delivered systems almost doubled. With less confusion and less time pressure, there was less cause for error and damage, and with fewer hands involved, there was less opportunity for misunderstanding and mistakes. "Perfect orders"—orders filled correctly and on time, and delivered in good working condition with the right documentation— went from not much more than 10 percent to 85 percent. Andren's customer was shocked and amazed at what we had accomplished, and responded just as we'd hoped: it rescinded the divorce and increased its business with Andren by 34 percent the next year. This exceeded our own optimistic target of 25 percent. And the icing on the cake was that while such an increase in business normally would have required Andren to hire twelve more people to handle it, the new process made it necessary to hire just two more people. Overall, gross profit margins with this customer doubled. And the process was scalable to handle even more growth.

Faster, cheaper, better. All the result of looking at work from one end to the other, rethinking it, and getting everyone aligned toward a common goal.

End-to-end enterprise process is not a complex idea. Some companies explain it to their people with the phrase "look left, look right": that is, don't just pay attention to your own job, but think about the work that comes before you and the work that comes after you; think about the totality of work that is creating value for customers. And end-to-end process isn't just for such routine work as order fulfillment or procurement. It applies to creative work, too, including product development and demand generation. It applies to all of the three types of processes: core (e.g., product development, customer acquisition, order fulfillment), enabling (credit to collection, people development), and governing (strategic planning). It does not impose rules and bureaucracy, and it does not reduce opportunities for imagination and creativity. As one CEO told his engineers when they complained that end-to-end process would impede their creativity: "I want you to be creative, but I want you to be creative about the product, not the process." When we stroll through a potential client's facilities we can get a sense of how process-oriented the company is by the number of sticky notes on desks and computers. The more sticky notes, usually the less process-oriented the company is. Those sticky notes indicate that each person has a different and often ad hoc way of doing things. When end-to-end process is implemented, the sticky notes disappear.

While end-to-end process isn't a complex idea, we won't pretend you can fully implement it overnight. Remember, we're talking about a thoroughly different way of organizing work that affects everyone in your company. Change can be difficult for some people, and that is certainly true of the extent of change your business will undergo to become proficient at end-to-end process. Reward systems will change, reporting relationships will change, and authority and responsibility will flow much deeper into the organization. You will have to become an evangelist, preaching the transformative power of end-to-end process every chance you get. Still, there will be people who don't get it or don't like it. You may have to work overtime to convince them, but if they don't eventually get on board, they will have to leave. Those who remain will be challenged as never before, and most will rise to meet the challenge. Many will become evangelists of end-to-end process in their own right. Perhaps most amazing is that as you make progress in your efforts to become an end-to-end organization you will find that your company will continue to make progress as a high-performance process organization. People at companies that have been doing process work for years tell us that they are constantly finding new ways to apply process to improve how they do work and how they keep their customers happy. Adopting end-to-end process is a journey without end.

The successful implementation of end-to-end process will involve some intensive work at every level. While it is true that the focus of process work is to better serve the customer by discovering what it is the customer wants (voice of the customer), that focus must be balanced by what is good for your own business (voice of the business). That balance can be difficult to achieve at first. But our experience is that there are nine critical high-level organizing principles that guide process implementation. In the chapters that follow we will examine those principles and how they are interrelated. We will use many anecdotes about companies. Some of the companies you will recognize. Others will not be familiar, for good reasons: we've changed the names because we don't want to embarrass companies that have tried and failed to implement process, and others that have been extremely successful don't want that competitive secret to get out. To summarize and illustrate what each of the chapters is about, let's revisit for a moment Andren Aerospace's situation when we were invited in to analyze the company's problems and offer an end-to-end solution.

Chapter One is about designing a new end-to-end process. The design that will emerge must take into account your company's organization as well as your products, services, and customers. Andren's organization was a mess, to be blunt. It was characterized by extreme redundancy, a lack of understanding about what others in the company were doing, and almost no focus on customers and their needs. As you review your own company's organization through the lens of end-to-end process, some of the worst problems will be instantly obvious. As you design a new end-to-end process less severe problems will emerge, too. End-to-end process has the potential to solve them all.

Most companies get metrics all wrong. They allow each department to determine what it wants to measure. And because you get what you measure, each department gets a different and often uncoordinated result. That was certainly the case at Andren. In Chapter Two, we take a hard look at what should be measured, and how and why, in order to successfully implement end-to-end process. That will often require redefining what it is your company is really trying to do, which is almost always "get and keep customers." Measurements that accomplish that goal are the ones that matter.

One of the most profound changes that occurred when Andren adopted end-to-end process involved the role of managers. No longer were functional leaders managing their independent fiefdoms as they thought fit. Instead, there now were individuals—process owners—who had the sole authority to sanction changes to the process and the way the work was executed. These process owners are the subject of Chapter Three. Making sure that process owners and functional managers work together closely is an essential ingredient of successful end-to-end process implementation. That requires a change of mind-set for both the functional managers and the process owners.

The way people perform within a company involves not only how they're measured and rewarded but also how the company supports them. Chapter Four is all about people, the "performers" in your process, and the infrastructure that will be necessary to support their end-to-end efforts. As Andren learned, redesigning your work processes and resetting how you measure performance profoundly changes the way people perform their jobs. No longer encumbered by bureaucratic tasks and innumerable handoffs, Andren's employees became "professionals," doing what needed to be done rather than wasting time and energy. Not everyone will be happy with the new approach and some will leave, voluntarily or otherwise. But those who remain and buy in to end-to-end process will become far more energized, challenged, and productive than you could ever imagine. They really will become your most valuable asset.

But their new approach to work requires a new infrastructure to support them, too. To be successful, the professionals who emerged from Andren's change to end-to-end process needed new compensation plans, new training and development opportunities, a new reporting structure, and the necessary tools (many of which came from IT) to be successful.

No organization survives and thrives without the right leadership. Chapter Five explores the need for leaders who understand the strategic implications of end-to-end process, balancing what the customer wants and what the business needs. The initial impulse of Andren's leaders to reorganize is the classic mistake many leaders make. Fortunately, they were willing to listen, and they quickly understood that without a broader vision of the company and its customers, end-to-end process would almost surely fail to produce the results of which it is capable.

Chapter Five also addresses the corporate culture that successful leaders will create on the way to end-to-end process. Once leaders understand and embrace the potential of end-to-end process they must become evangelicals, convincing the entire organization that process will be the surest route to customer satisfaction and retention and, as a result, job security. As Andren discovered, the cultural shift will be embraced immediately by some and scorned by others. But the vast middle ground needs to be sold on the idea, and it is the leader's job to make that sales pitch if the change is going to be sustained.

Chapter Six examines governance and expertise. Governance is the overarching framework for implementing end-to-end process. It is the structure that takes care of such details as setting goals and allocating resources. In short, it is the process of managing end-to-end process. One of its primary functions is to ensure that the company develops a cadre of experts that know how to do and can teach the practice of process.

Chapter Seven opens Part II, which lays out how to bring together the nine components that make up a process-centric enterprise. Chapters Eight through Twelve comprise case studies of five companies that embraced end-to-end process with sharply different results. Two—Tetra Pak and Gamesa—have been extraordinarily successful. The other three, which will be presented under pseudonyms, failed despite valiant efforts. We hope their stories will illuminate the benefits of end-to-end process, show where to expect problems and how to solve them, and persuade you that the journey will indeed be worth the effort. Part III is made up of Chapter Thirteen, the Process and Enterprise Maturity Model (PEMM)—a framework to help you plan and assess your process-based transformation efforts.

PART I

CHAPTER I

Design: From the Worm's-Eye View to the Bird's-Eye View

THE PRINCIPLES OF DESIGNING PROCESSES

You've doubtless been at a party or some other social event where you're cast together with a bunch of people you don't know. At a loss for what to talk to these people about, most of us fall back on the standard inquiry: "So what do you do?"

Not surprisingly, we get the standard answer: "I'm a lawyer" or "I'm a dentist" or "I'm a writer."

Okay, so now we know what your job or occupation is, but we still don't know what you do. What kind of law do you practice? How do you find clients, decide which ones merit your attention, research their cases, file the necessary procedural documents, counter the other party's lawyer's assertions, prepare for trial, find expert and other witnesses, conduct the trial, research possible grounds for appeal if you don't succeed, and ultimately calculate and collect your fee? The answers to all those questions and many more are what you do. It's the way you run your job as a lawyer. It's your process.

Granted, the person who asked you that question probably doesn't want to hear all those details. In fact, you may not even know how to answer those questions very well. But if you think hard about it, we can almost guarantee you that you can find better ways of doing at least some of those things you've been doing for years. And if you actually change the way you do those things, the likely result will be that you are a better lawyer, your clients fare better, and you may find yourself earning more and growing your practice. You will have designed a better process for being a lawyer.

In a more formal setting we have often asked executives what their companies do. Typically the executive describes the products or services his company provides and why they are better than those offered by competitors. Pushed a little, the executive drags out an annual report, some product literature, and maybe even an organization chart. "That's what we do," he'll tell us.

Sorry, that's not right.

Now we know what his company makes, who reports to whom, and how well the company is doing financially, *but we still don't really know what the company does.*

These kinds of encounters suggest something that is very counterintuitive to most of us: we don't know what we are doing. Mostly we do the things we do because "that's how we've always done it." Few people have given much thought to the question "Is this the best way to do it?"

Before you can make your business or organization better, you have to understand with a great deal of clarity what it does. More importantly, all the people who work in your organization need to understand that, too. Most of them have single-mindedly focused on their jobs. They may do them well or not, but their jobs are what they are supposed to do and that's their main concern. They have a worm's-view of the world. They need a bird's-eye view, an understanding of what your company really does and the role they play in achieving its goals, or better yet, its results. That's why this first chapter is devoted to process design. Once you understand what it is your organization does, you can begin to design better ways to do it, ways that break you out of the old trap of "we've always done it this way." Designing the way your company works so that the processes fit together seamlessly from one end to the other is one of the most important assets your business possesses—perhaps *the* most important. It will permit you to get things done faster, cheaper, and better. And faster, cheaper, and better don't stand alone, without a context; they refer to somebody else. Faster, cheaper, and better *than your competitors*. That is a powerful weapon to differentiate your company from everybody else vying for your customers. Done right, process design will have an enormous impact on how both you and your business perform. You will have tremendous insights into how and why things are done, who does them, and where and what the outcomes should be. A process-oriented company, no matter how mundane its business, will be more innovative. And, believe it or not, process design—the art and science of figuring out how to do work more efficiently and effectively—is one of the most exciting and creative activities in the business world.

This entire book is all about how to utilize process to make your organization perform better, and there will be many more examples of how to do this. But let's take a moment here to see how one of the leading process companies, Progressive Insurance, used process design to change the rules of its industry and vault itself from a distant also-ran to an industry leader.

Progressive, based in Mayfield Village, Ohio, is now the third-largest auto insurer in the United States, with 2008 revenue of almost $13 billion, a huge leap from slightly more than $1 billion in 1991. That's a compound growth rate of nearly 17 percent. What makes it even more impressive is that the auto insurance industry is not exactly biotech; auto insurance is a mature century-old industry that grows at the same rate as

GDP. And Progressive's growth was entirely organic, not based on acquisitions, as are so many rapid-growth companies. How can a second-tier company in a moribund industry achieve this remarkable feat?

The answer is process design. By analyzing the who, what, when, where, and other aspects of how work is done, Progressive goes beyond concerning itself with individual task efficiency to look at how these tasks fit together into the whole.

Progressive began its redesign with its claims-handling process. Comparing the before and the after can help clarify what process design is all about.

Progressive's claims process used to be similar to that of most other companies in the industry. It started when a claimant—someone who has had an accident—reported the claim to the agent who sold the policy. The agent took the information, filled out a loss report, and sent it to a clerk in Progressive's claims department. The clerk logged the form, checked it for completeness and accuracy, and delivered it to a claims manager. The claims manager waited until she had collected a number of claims and then doled them out to adjusters. Typically, the manager assigned an adjuster a stack of claims in the same geographical area so that the adjuster could take care of them all in the same day. The adjuster contacted the claimant, scheduled a visit, and inspected the car to determine the amount of damage. The adjuster submitted his estimate back to the manager, who used it to determine how much to offer the claimant in payment.

In the standard industry model, everyone involved has a narrowly defined job: the agent interfaces with the customer, the clerk processes the form, the adjuster inspects the vehicle and estimates the damage, and the manager assigns the claim and calculates the offer. In fact, one of the key goals of this old process was that it optimizes the efficiency of the adjusters, just as traditional factories sought to optimize the efficiency

of their equipment by scheduling long runs. Combined with
the usual metrics (calls handled per day, number of claimants
visited per day), this process achieved the classical goal of task
efficiency, the minimization of the cost of direct labor. But
this narrow task efficiency was purchased at the cost of the
efficiency of the process as a whole. It typically took Progressive five days (and other companies often took even longer)
to get the adjuster out to see the vehicle because of the delays
caused by handoffs and by the need to batch claims on a geographical basis. This might make some sense for the insurance
company, but it certainly doesn't make sense for the customer.
Put yourself in the shoes of a claimant. You really don't care
about clerical efficiency; you want the claim settled. And the
longer it takes for the adjuster to see your car, the longer it
will take to get the claim settled and get your car (and your
normal life) back.

Progressive's new process, called Immediate Response, starts
by cutting out the agent, the customer service representative,
and the claims manager. People insured by Progressive are
given a card to carry in their wallet with an 800 number on it.
In the event of an accident, they call that number at any time
of day or night and are connected directly to a representative
who takes responsibility for their case. This individual checks
coverage, dispatches a tow truck, contacts the police if necessary, and helps in other ways. The representative has teammates
who are adjusters; they are not sitting in offices but are riding
around, three shifts a day, in Progressive claims vans. The Progressive representative contacts one of them while the claimant is on the phone and schedules a mutually convenient time
for the teammate to inspect the vehicle, preferably right away.
When the adjuster arrives to see the vehicle, he is equipped
and authorized to issue a check on the spot if possible.

The effects of this new process were nothing short of prodigious. Claimants got much faster service, typically in less

than one day rather than more than five, with less hassle, which means they're less likely to abandon Progressive because of an unsatisfactory claims experience. And the shortened cycle time reduced Progressive's own costs dramatically. The cost of storing a damaged vehicle or renting a replacement car for one day, around $28, is roughly equal to the expected underwriting profit on a six-month policy. It's not hard to calculate the savings this produces for a company that handles more than ten thousand claims each day. Other benefits for Progressive are an improved ability to detect fraud because it is easier to conduct an accident investigation before skid marks wash away and witnesses leave the scene; there are lower operating costs because fewer people are involved in handling the claim; and there is a reduction in claims payouts because claimants often accept less money if it's given sooner and with less travail.

It's easy to get lost in the details and the specifics, so let's step back and try to summarize how the new process differs from the old one. The key value-adding tasks in this process, old or new, are three: capturing the information from the claimant, inspecting the car, and determining how much to offer. Everything else is at best non-value-adding overhead, administrative work whose only purpose is to enable the real work to get done. What is striking is that the new process does not really change the ways in which these essential tasks are performed. It is not as though adjusters now have special X-ray devices that allow them to assess damage faster or more accurately. The tasks are still largely performed in the same ways. What has changed is how they fit together into a whole and the focus on a result that the customer cares about.

In the old process, it was the agent who captured information from the claimant. In the new process, it is the Progressive representative. This eliminates the agent and the clerk from the process, saving enormous amounts of time. In the old process, the adjuster visited the car when it was convenient for the adjuster to do so; in the new process, the adjuster does so at a time convenient for the customer and generally within nine hours of being notified of the accident. Progressive calls this "moving from our time to customer time." In the old process, the decision about how much to offer the claimant was made back at the office. In the new process, it is made at the point of customer contact, accelerating the resolution of the claim as a whole. These simple changes have stripped much of the complexity out of the claims process.

Faster, cheaper, better.

THE SEVEN PRINCIPLES OF DESIGN

Many businesspeople feel intimidated when they hear the phrase "process design" because they associate the word *design* with artistry or engineering. They seem to feel that to design something requires extraordinary amounts of artistic talent or inventive skills. Consciously or not, they may associate the creative endeavor with angst and pain, as in Edison's comment that genius is "1 percent inspiration and 99 percent perspiration" or Hemingway's description of writing as the act of staring at a blank sheet of paper until beads of blood form on your forehead. They can't imagine where they would start to create or reinvent a new process design. Indeed, some methodologies that claim to enable process design essentially have a step in the middle that amounts to "invent new design here," a step largely indistinguishable from waiting for lightning to strike.

But you needn't fear process design and you don't have to live in a Parisian garret to practice it. Process design, while not a routine activity, actually can be structured in an organized way and so differs from many other kinds of design. There are a limited number of choices available to a process designer, and process design amounts to choosing among them. We have identified seven principles that design should focus on: *what* tasks are performed; *whether* they should be performed and under what circumstances; *who* performs them; *when* they are performed; *where* they are performed; *how precisely* they are performed; and *what information* they employ. We saw three of these at work in the Progressive story. The company made changes to who did certain steps, when certain steps were performed, and where they were performed. That example highlights the real nature of process design: focusing on a relatively small number of aspects of the process and coming up with changes to them that produce powerful results. When you are trying to redesign a process, you should ask yourself a specific question: will changing any of the seven principles of design lead to better performances?

Simply asking the question doesn't automatically give you the answer. You will need to exercise your imagination to come up with different ways of doing things. You will also need to follow the traditional inventor's strategy of trying lots of different things until you find one or more that work. The Nobel Prize winner Linus Pauling said that the way to have good ideas is to have lots of ideas and throw away the bad ones. At least you won't be stumbling around in the dark. You have specific things to look at and specific questions to stimulate your thinking.

Let's take a look at each of the seven principles, exploring them not so much through theory as through examples. (We will save the first principle mentioned, *what*, for last.)

WHETHER. The first principle to consider is *whether and under what circumstances* something needs to be done. Recall from the introduction how Andren Aerospace, when redesigning its processes, identified each step in its processes as value-adding, non-value-adding, or waste? That's what this principle is all about. Many processes are performed the same way under all circumstances, come hell or high water: first this step, then the next, and then another. Here is a radical notion: let's do work only if its value or contribution to the result is greater than the cost of doing it in the particular situation we are facing.

Here's an illustration. If a company sends you a bill and you pay less than the full amount, most companies will invoke a collections activity that entails rebilling you for the balance, no matter what. What these companies forget is that issuing a bill is not free. It can literally cost hundreds of dollars. One computer services company has calculated the cost of billing for an underpayment and has changed its process as a result. If the amount of the underpayment is less than the cost of producing the bill, the company writes it off and saves money as a result. No, we won't tell you which company nor the threshold amount.

Another example involves auto insurers, which send adjusters to inspect cars for two reasons: to estimate the damage and to make sure the damage actually occurred. Yet the most common form of auto damage is windshield breakage, which does not need to be seen in order to be estimated. A windshield is either broken or not, and if it is, the cost of its replacement is standard. In other words, the only reason an insurer sends an adjuster in such cases is to verify the accident really happened and the claimant isn't lying. One insurer realized that long-term customers who pay premiums on time and have never filed a claim are unlikely to suddenly turn to a life of crime and begin with windshields. When such customers file a claim of windshield breakage, the company skips the step of sending an adjuster and just issues a check.

To take advantage of these insights, the process needs to include a new step that determines whether or not the step in question *should* be performed given the particular situation.

Then that step is performed or not, as appropriate. This technique makes particular sense when the step in question is costly or time consuming, and avoiding it can be very worthwhile.

HOW PRECISELY. *How precisely* to perform a step in a process is a close cousin to whether to perform it. Even if a step needs to be performed, it may not need to be performed as thoroughly or as precisely as it was in the past. As hard as it may be to believe, doing work less thoroughly or less precisely can save a great deal of time or money. On the other hand, it may be appropriate to do this step much more thoroughly and precisely, even if it costs more or takes more time, in order to have more exact results.

Most hospitals take it for granted that the bill they produce for a patient has to be as accurate as possible. A typical hospital bill will go on for pages and pages of line items. A few of these will be major, such as the room charge and doctor's fees, but the great majority are for small items such as a box of tissues or a pill. Pareto's law suggests that these minor items represent 80 percent of the line items on the bill and only 20 percent of the total charge, but Pareto was an optimist. His 80-20 rule is really more like 95-5 for a hospital. Putting all this detail into the bill makes it harder for the hospital to process and more difficult for the patient to understand. More to the point, the information on the bill does not appear there magically. It must first be collected, and that data collection is almost always done by nurses. Data collection, rather than providing health care, represents a significant fraction of nursing time. One hospital made the bold choice to be less precise. Specifically, administrators decided not to collect data on, or bill for, items costing less than $25, a large fraction of the items on the bill. To be reimbursed for these, the hospital calculated an average utilization of tissues and pills and factored them into the basic room rate. This made no material difference to patient behavior. No one overuses tissues because he is not being charged explicitly for them. On the other hand, it does save a great deal of nursing time. Nursing overtime was reduced by 37 percent, while the number of contact hours nurses spent with patients increased.

A home insurer serving upscale customers recognized that its quest for precise pricing imposed a burden on its time-starved customers: it forced them to provide lots of details about their homes so that the company could calculate the precise degree of risk associated with insuring it in order to calculate an exact premium. This insurer recognized that precision imposes costs, in this case on customers. Its response was to be less precise in pricing. It asked customers for far less data, which they appreciated. This meant that the company's calculation of risk was less exact, so the insurer compensated by estimating risk to be a bit higher than calculated. This meant that its prices were a bit higher, but customers were more than happy with this trade-off; upscale customers are often willing to pay for convenience and time. The insurer is now a dominant player in this market segment.

Amerin Guaranty (now a part of Radian) reinvented the mortgage insurance business by consciously deciding to be less precise. Mortgage insurance is paid for by the homeowner and covers the bank providing the mortgage in case of default. A traditional mortgage insurer would get the information about the homeowner and the mortgage from the bank that originated the mortgage, and then would undertake a detailed underwriting process to determine how much to charge for the insurance. Amerin realized that the bank had already done this work when deciding whether to issue the mortgage and that it was a waste of energy to do it again; it simply used the information from the bank to calculate the premium. In case of default, other insurers undertake complex analyses of the amount remaining on the loan in order to determine how much to pay. Amerin realized that on the average this came to a certain fraction of the original mortgage, and it told its bank customers that it would pay that percentage in every case, no matter how much was remaining on the loan, thereby avoiding complex analysis of the claim. To the banks, how much they received on an individual default did not matter. What mattered was that they received the right amount in the aggregate, which they did. By being less precise in both underwriting and claims, Amerin was able to do them both much more quickly and eliminate a lot of cost, which it turned into lower prices. In less than two years it went from a start-up to a $2 billion company with 6 percent of the market for mortgage insurance, and did so against such formidable competitors as GE and MGIC.

More precision, not less, can sometimes pay off. To see how, let's return to Progressive. Progressive had its roots in the high-risk auto insurance segment, covering people who had trouble getting insurance elsewhere because of their demographics, driving records, or other problems. Most insurers would simply lump all such drivers into a handful of categories, calculate average costs and an associated premium, and hope for the best. Progressive decided to be much more precise, using up to ten times as many categories as its competitors. For instance, instead of looking at all young men as accidents waiting to happen, Progressive would look carefully at an individual young man's education, credit history, occupation, and other factors, and come up with a precise price that reflected his specific characteristics. This meant that Progressive would sometimes charge less than its competitors for good risks and sometimes charge more for bad risks. Yes, this detailed evaluation meant that Progressive's analysis costs were much higher than those of its competitors, but it paid off. The bad risks often went to competitors, who were in effect undercharging, while Progressive got the better risks, who had fewer acci-

dents. Accident claims are where insurance companies experience their real costs. It is in the "combined ratio" (claims plus
expenses as a fraction of premiums) that Progressive shines.
Other companies often have combined ratios over 1, meaning they lose money on insurance, which they only recoup
on investment income realized from the premiums they are
holding until it is time to pay claims. Progressive, on the other
hand, has had combined ratios that range from .85 to .94. That
means Progressive makes money on the actual insurance and
treats investment income as gravy. This pricing accuracy was
key to Progressive's success in the high-risk market and gave
the company a significant leg up when it entered the "standard" and "preferred" markets for regular and good drivers.

WHAT INFORMATION. Most companies have lots of data, but
they don't always know *what information* is needed for their
processes to function well. They use historical rather than current data, projected rather than actual, and narrow rather than
broad. By employing better information, you can help ensure
that a process can perform better in many different ways. Take
a sales forecast, for example. Most companies make a host of
important and expensive decisions based on a sales forecast,
ranging from ordering materials to scheduling the workforce.
If the sales forecast is wrong—not surprisingly, it usually is—
then those other things are wrong, too. Fixing the sales forecast so that it is right fixes those other things, too.

General Mills, the maker of Cheerios and many other
consumer products, used to base its production plans on sales
forecasts even though everyone knew that a sales forecast is
usually a euphemism for a shot in the dark. General Mills'
distribution centers, which held inventory and handled orders
from customers, would project how much they expected to
sell, and General Mills would schedule production accordingly.
The distribution centers would then order what they needed

from manufacturing as orders from customers eventually came in. But projections are always wrong, and the result is Hammer's law of inventory: too much of what you don't need and not enough of what you do. This in turn leads to bizarre and sometimes quite expensive responses, such as emergency short production runs or trans-shipping goods from one distribution center to another. General Mills decided to use actual rather than projected data to drive production, what we call "pull" rather than "push." Real customer order data were provided directly to manufacturing instead of being filtered through and delayed by the distribution centers. As a result, the manufacturing group had a much broader and more up-to-date view of what customers were doing, as well as information about the actual state of inventories in the distribution centers. This expanded and more precise information allowed manufacturing to make more timely and more accurate production schedules and to ship the goods to the distribution centers directly without waiting for them to order. The result was that inventory levels went down some 25 percent while the number of out-of-stock situations (where a distribution center does not have the product a customer has ordered) declined 50 percent. At first blush, this seems to defy the laws of physics. Most managers take it for granted that lower inventory levels lead to more out-of-stocks and vice versa. But by redesigning its product deployment process to use better information, General Mills was able to achieve these seemingly incompatible goals as well as a dramatic increase in profitability.

Many consumer goods firms deliver their products to grocers' warehouses; others do what is called direct store delivery, delivering products directly to individual shops. One manufacturer with a large number of products used to load up the delivery vans with some of everything. Arriving at a specific store, the driver would check the shelves to see what was missing, pull what was needed out of the van, write up a form for the store manager to sign, and send the form to headquarters for billing. This process was full of delays and needed an enormous amount of inventory in the vans. It was based on the premise that the driver lacked information about what was needed in a given store until he arrived there. The company upended this premise by obtaining detailed sales information from the stores so that it knew what was still on the shelves. Using this information, the company preselected what each store would need, shrink-wrapped it as a bundle, stapled the bill to the shrink wrap, and loaded the bundles in the van in the order in which the stores would be visited. The driver now needs only to drop off the package with the bill and move on to the next store. Using fine-grained information in the process improved driver productivity and sharply reduced inventory.

WHEN. The story of claims handling at Progressive illustrates the principle of *when* to do certain work in a process, but that was just the tip of the iceberg. There are many ways to change the when of processes: by moving steps earlier or later, by moving activities previously in sequence into a parallel arrangement, or by changing the relative order of certain activities.

A New York City hospital wanted to increase its cardiovascular surgery practice, in which it had great expertise and significant capacity. However, it wasn't getting enough referrals because it took the hospital too long to respond to cardiologists who wanted to send patients to the hospital for surgery. It would take as much as nine hours to tell cardiologists that they could send a patient over, and by then the patient was often already at another hospital. On investigation, the hospital discovered that the reason for this delay was that the process first prepared a bed for the patient before returning the cardiologist's call. It was as if the hospital assumed the doctor might beam the patient to the hospital without a bed being ready. In

Manhattan traffic, however, patients do not show up instantaneously. The new process has the hospital immediately telling
the cardiologist to send the patient. While the patient is in
transit, the bed is being made ready. The result is a significant
increase in the number of cardiovascular patients treated.

The hospital also realized that it was keeping these patients
in the hospital for an average of two and a half days before the
actual surgery. This is very expensive for the hospital, since the
patient awaiting surgery was paying the base room rate while
other patients in need of more care could have been placed in
the bed at a higher daily rate. More importantly to the patients,
they were spending money and time and risking infection during a hospital stay that was longer than necessary. A close look
revealed that almost all of those two and a half days was taken
up by eating, sleeping, and waiting, all of which was, in terms
of the process, non-value-adding. The only important activities that took place during that period were tests and patient
education about the surgery and its aftermath. The hospital
realized that virtually all of this could be moved earlier in the
process and handled on an outpatient basis. Less than an hour's
worth of tests actually needed to be done after the patient
arrived in the hospital. This led to almost 40 percent of the
hospital's surgeries being done on a same-day basis, lowering
costs and improving patient health at the same time.

Even the hypercompetitive fashion industry, so dependent on capturing the seasonal attention of shoppers, can
change the timing. Zara is hip, Zara is cool, Zara is one of the
fastest-growing clothing companies in the world and one of
the most profitable. Their stores are everywhere in Europe and
are starting to appear in the United States and in Asia as well.
Zara's success is based on what seems to be a magical instinct
for having just the right fashions at the right price at the right
time.

But Zara's secret sauce isn't a roomful of brilliant fashion designers working in indentured servitude. The company doesn't have special access to Internet chat rooms where trendsetters talk about clothes. Rather, Zara's success is built on a process that is both prosaic and powerful. Most apparel makers do the bulk of their production in Asia today, for the obvious reason: it is much cheaper. Not Zara. It does most of its production in Europe, and in relatively small lots to boot. Not surprisingly, Zara's manufacturing costs are much higher than its rivals'. But Zara does not care. Manufacturing in Asia demands long lead times; apparel companies have to decide what they are going to make many months in advance of the season. The trouble with this is that the gods of fashion are fickle. By the time the season has begun, the clothes the company chose so many months ago may not be what the consumer actually wants. Zara, by contrast, makes more than 80 percent of its goods after the season has begun. At the beginning of the season it produces small numbers of various styles to see what sells. Then Zara goes all out to make lots of what does sell and none of what doesn't. Zara's manufacturing costs may be high, but it has the goods that consumers want and it sells more of them. When the season ends, it is forced to mark down fewer items, and the markdowns it does make are less steep. In our terms, Zara changed the *when* of its product development process, deferring the decision on what to produce until after it has tested small lots in the marketplace.

WHO. The most common change that results from process redesign is *who* does what work and how they work with others. One of the big mistakes made in answering the question of who does what work is to craft a process around a specific person rather than around what the job is. It's very easy to fall into that trap. Who should do inventory management?

Well, Harry has been doing it for years, he's the logical choice. Harry may have superlative skills in that position—or he may be parked there because he isn't good at anything else. Whatever the case, the job is built around Harry's abilities (or lack thereof), not around how the job relates to everything else in the process. Maybe the where part of that job should change, which in effect will also change the who part of the job. Don't be forced into building rework loops into the process just to accommodate a given individual. In process redesign there should be no sacred cows or favored individuals.

The most frequent change when we ask the question "Who should do the work?" is the designation of a "caseworker," an individual assigned and empowered to make sure that every step of a process gets done. In most companies managers are responsible for making sure that their chunk of some larger work gets done. But those managers seldom have direct and frequent contact with the managers of other departments that also must at some point handle part of the larger work. Each department does its work without knowing what the other departments are doing, have done, or will do at some point in the future to get the overall project done. It's the traditional silo organization. The caseworker cuts across those silos, taking what she needs from each and coordinating them all so that the work gets done faster, more efficiently, and with fewer delays and errors. By concentrating these tasks in one individual, we avoid the handoffs and attendant delays and errors that inevitably occur when work moves from one individual to another.

At a telephone company a trouble call from a customer usually involved three people: one to take the call, another to diagnose the problem, and a third to fix it. Now a single individual takes the call, determines the problem, and fixes it through a computer system. If the computer system can't handle it, the person dispatches a technician. "First-call resolution," the percentage of problems dealt with during the customer's first call, soared to 74 percent from 0.5 percent, an increase of nearly 150-fold.

Orders received by Shell Lubricants used to bounce back and forth among as many as seven different departments. Now one individual is responsible for the order from the time it is received until the production of the bill after the goods have been sent. As a result, the time consumed by this end-to-end process declined 60 percent, accuracy increased 60 percent, the cost of filling an order declined 40 percent, and customer satisfaction doubled.

The caseworker approach lends itself to processes in which all the steps are relatively simple and thus can be mastered, at least in the majority of situations, by a single individual. If necessary, the caseworker can be backed up by experts in specific areas who will provide assistance if a case of unusual complexity presents itself. However, if some or all of the steps are complex and require in-depth specialized training, then the caseworker technique will not work. It is implausible, for instance, to imagine one individual doing the design, engineering, market research, cost analysis, and manufacturing feasibility involved in new product development. But there is an alternative in complex situations: the case team.

A case team does the same thing a caseworker does but works as a coherent unit to apply the skills of its various members to solving a problem. Think of it as a multiheaded approximation to a caseworker. What distinguishes a case team from an assembly line? First, the members of a case team are working toward a common goal. While they perform different tasks, they are focused on the process as a whole and its outcomes, rather than just their individual bits. Second, their horizons extend beyond their narrow domains. They know the whole process and are aware of each other and how their work affects one another. They share information and have consistent views of the world. Finally, they may be physically located together. All of this means that they work together rather than at cross-purposes, and the resulting performance improvements can approach those realized by a caseworker.

Schneider National, a privately held trucking company based in Green Bay, Wisconsin, is the largest provider of full-load trucking services in the United States. One of Schneider's major end-to-end processes is called Acquire New Business. Essentially it is aimed at generating more sales, but it encompasses far more than just the sales department. A major aspect of this process is providing quotes in response to customers' descriptions of their shipping needs. In the past, any number of departments—pricing, contracts, billing, capacity management, and others—would be involved, and the request would languish in an interminable series of in-baskets and out-baskets. The complexity of these various areas made the process too complex for a single caseworker to handle. Instead, Schneider created customer response and development teams, consisting of people culled from these various departments, who would work together to respond to particular kinds of customers: one team for retailers, one team for manufacturers, and so on. In the past, it took Schneider thirty days or so to get back to customers with a quote. With the new process, the company can do it in less than two days. Being the first to get back to a customer gives Schneider the opportunity to shape the customer's thinking and avoid competitive "bake-offs." Schneider's win rate, the percentage of bids that it wins, increased by 70 percent.

At one of the units of Trane, the air-conditioning manufacturer, customer orders would drag their way from customer service to product design to industrial engineering to scheduling to production, with endless squabbling along the way because each department had its own agenda and concerns. Here, too, the company created a case team with representatives of each of these specialties to handle an order from beginning to end. The time to fill orders went down some 70 percent. The slogan "Speed kills" has been used both to prevent auto accidents and to reduce drug use. In the business world, however, speed is essential. By filling orders so much more quickly, Trane was able to reduce its inventory levels dramatically, saving precious cash. It was also able to help its customers reduce their inventory levels, since they had to keep less on hand waiting for Trane to deliver. And if you fill orders quickly, you can bill the customer sooner and get paid faster—maybe even before you have to pay your own suppliers.

There are situations, however, in which even a case team is not a realistic option. That is especially true when the same people don't work together on a regular basis. In health care, for instance, a patient in the hospital with a complex condition is likely to be treated by a host of different physicians with different specialties. But to call them a team would abuse the term. Each is focused on an individual specialty, and they may never even encounter each other, passing like the proverbial ships in the night. Because what one doctor knows may not get communicated to others, such uncoordinated treatment can lead to medical errors, problematic drug interactions, an inability to answer simple questions—"When can I go home?"—and poor use of resources. The solution that more and more hospitals are using is a hospitalist, a physician whose role it is to manage the overall provision of patient care, coordinating all the specialists involved in treating each patient. The hospitalist keeps track of such things as treatments, schedules, and drugs and is the patient's primary point of contact while in the hospital. The hospitalist is an example of what we call a case manager, who by coordinating the work of others streamlines the performance of the process as a whole. The case manager model applies to many situations characterized by loosely affiliated groups of experts performing complex tasks, from customer service to computer system installation.

There are other variations on the theme of "who." One is to ask whether the skill requirements for a particular task are what they need to be. Perhaps they can be lowered, or perhaps they should be raised. Some hospitals are replacing the triage nurse, who determines which patients need most urgent treatment, with a triage doctor. Even though putting a physician in this role is more costly, the physician can often make more precise assessments or may even deal with the patient directly, making the process as a whole more effective. At Duke Power, on the other hand, linemen in the field are now making decisions that engineers back in the office used to make. The company realized that the linemen had sufficient knowledge and expertise to make these decisions, and that doing so would speed things up and allow the engineers to concentrate on things only they could do.

WHERE. We can apply the old real estate saw that the three most important aspects of a property are location, location, and location to process as well. *Where* work is done is important in thinking about process design, but many organizations suffer an acute lack of imagination in deciding where work should be done. To be sure, outsourcing and offshoring have become popular of late, but one need not make such dramatic changes to get dramatic improvements.

An auto parts manufacturer used to have a simple policy: when making samples of new parts, the tool to be used in making the part should be made at the same plant where the part will be made. On the surface, this seems eminently reasonable, since it ensures that the tool does not have to travel from where it is being made to where it will be used. In reality, however, a plant that was able to schedule the making of a sample part was often able to do so only because it was in the process of retooling, which meant that its tooling facility would be busy. The company's policy was in effect dooming it to delay. The new process has the tooling work done at a nearby plant that has available capacity. Even with the truck ride between the two plants, the tool is available much faster and therefore so is the part. This was an important element in reducing the time to produce samples by 85 percent, which in turn led to an enormous increase in the rate at which the company won contracts for new products. This is an excellent illustration of the power of end-to-end thinking at work. Looking at the issue of where to make the tool in a narrow context leads to one conclusion; looking at it more broadly leads to another.

All the big automakers operate master parts warehouses, where they store vast numbers of parts that their dealers may order. As you can imagine, these are massive facilities. One of the challenges in picking parts in such a huge warehouse is the time it takes for a parts picker to get from the location where one part on the pick list is stored to the spot where the next one is stored. Many companies have tried various solutions to this, ranging from equipping pickers with bicycles to trying to have robots do the picking. The results of these attempts have generally ranged from modest to disastrous. One company had a very different idea: they moved the location of the picking. Instead of bringing the picker to the part, they bring parts to the picker. Most parts are stored in small bins located on moving conveyors (think of a dry-cleaning store). The picker keys into a computer the needed parts and the belts start moving. When they stop, the picker pulls out what is needed and moves on to the next item. The picker spends his or her time picking (value-adding work) rather than walking (non-value-adding).

And while the picker is waiting for the belts to bring him the parts for one order, he can be simultaneously picking parts off the conveyors for other orders.

Where work is done can encompass more than one place. In fact, centralization and decentralization are forms of rethinking the location of work. Do you want work done in one place and the results farmed out to regional facilities or shipped to customers, or do you want to do the work in multiple locations, perhaps because you can better serve customers in different regions that way? Those are excellent questions because each alternative offers both advantages and disadvantages. But most companies seem to have a hard time coming up with the right answer, so they wind up oscillating between the two, first centralizing a process and then deciding later that it makes more sense to decentralize it. A company might decide to centralize procurement to achieve better control and economies of scale. But then, in a classic "the grass is always greener" move, that decision will be reversed and procurement will be decentralized to achieve more flexibility and speed. They also use this decision as a blunt instrument, moving entire processes rather than just the parts of the process that it makes the most sense to move. Companies that do that harvest all the disadvantages of each process while forgoing the advantages.

Some companies, such as HP, have found a way out of this Hobson's choice. They have blended centralization and decentralization, taking advantage of the control and economies of scale that are inherent in centralized operations while at the same benefitting from the flexibility and speed of decentralized operations. A case in point is HP's global printer operations. Printers are pretty generic products and thus benefit from the economies of scale of centralized production. But, of course, printers need to plug into electrical outlets and the consumer needs to know how to operate the printer. Outlets aren't the same in different parts of the world, and neither are the languages consumers speak and read. So HP produces the printers, sans power cord and owner's manual, at central locations, then ships them to regional distribution points, where the appropriate power cords and owner's manuals are put in the package.

WHAT. Okay, we've covered six of the seven principles of process design: whether to do certain work and under what circumstances, how precisely it needs to be done, what information is necessary to do the work, when it should be done, and where it should be done. We saved the all-important question of *what* should be done until last because the answer to that question encompasses the first six principles of process design. What to do is the most fundamental aspect of process design. It poses the central question underlying all work: what do we need to do to deliver what the customer wants? Answering that question reveals what activities should be included in process design in the first place.

In most cases, a new process will contain the same value-adding steps as the old process. After all, you never want to eliminate something that adds value, something that the customer is willing to pay for. But it is possible that the new process will have additional value-adding steps beyond those in the original process. Recall, for example, how Progressive Insurance developed a process for identifying and categorizing potential customers using analytics to determine which customers are the most risky and which customers are the least risky. That process enables it to quote rates that vary a lot for people whom most insurance companies simply lump together, such as young men under twenty-five years of age. The aim was to price insurance according to the actual risk presented by the policyholder. But then Progressive went even further. Not only did it quote a rate for its own policies, but it told the prospective customer what its competitors would charge for a similar policy, even when a competitor's price was lower. That additional information had two effects. First, it created a sense of trust among people shopping for insurance. None of the other insurance companies did that, and people shopping for insurance appreciated the information. Trust is something that is very difficult for a company to create and has a value that can't necessarily be quantified, but it is a key differentiator among competitive companies. Second, because Progressive was able to identify high-risk individuals within broader categories and quote them a higher price, showing those individuals that they could get the same policy cheaper at another company persuaded many of them to apply elsewhere. Voilà! Progressive dissuaded risky people from buying its policies while drawing more careful drivers to buy Progressive policies. Talk about win-win.

But asking what should be done also permits a company to get rid of steps in the old process. Getting rid of wasteful steps that do nothing for either the company or the customers is a no-brainer. The real sweet spot, though, is non-value-adding work, the things that your company has to do but which the customer doesn't care about and won't pay for. Remember Andren Aerospace from the introduction? Before it redesigned its processes, it did no fewer than six credit checks on each customer at various stages from order to shipment. Needless to say, circumstances seldom changed between the first credit check and the sixth check. So why do five more credit checks after the first? Andren's new process calls for just one credit check, when the order is received.

The U.S. Air Force, like all organizations, needs to train its people in various skills on a continuing basis. But the registration process for some of its courses was very cumbersome. The person interested in a specific training class would go to his supervisor for approval. If the supervisor approved, a request for training would go to the base commander for approval. If it passed that hurdle, it would go the base commander's boss. Finally it would be submitted to the registrar. The problem? The process took forty days, which meant that people who needed training quickly could not get it. Analysis revealed that neither base commanders nor their superiors ever denied a request for this training. If the first-line supervisor approved, it was clear sailing thereafter. The base commander didn't need to approve, just needed to be informed. So the new process eliminated two approval steps and reduced the forty-day cycle time to one day.

MIT and Harvard, both located in Cambridge, Massachusetts, have long extended cross-registration privileges to each other's students. Originally each school would determine the credit hours being taken by students from the other school and send the other school an appropriate bill at the end of the semester. They did this until someone realized that the difference between the two bills was less than the cost of calculating, sending, and paying them. As a result, the entire billing activity was eliminated from the cross-registration process.

The widely adopted practice of vendor-managed inventory (VMI) can be viewed through the lens of "what." Under VMI, a supplier takes responsibility for managing the inventory of its products (or in some cases, even those of its competitors) in the customer's facility. It does so by tracking the level of that inventory and automatically replenishing it when it dips below agreed-upon levels. This certainly adds steps to the vendor's order fulfillment process. The vendor not only must fill the order but also must create it. But doing this work for the customer saves the customer much effort, which can translate into increased sales and even increased prices. Moreover, knowing the inventory levels at customer sites allows a manufacturer to streamline its own production, make better forecasts and reduce its own finished goods inventory levels, more than offsetting the added costs of adding steps to its process.

Most airlines have now installed airport kiosks at which travelers can check themselves in, instead of having an agent do it for them. From the viewpoint of process, a step has been *removed* from the airline's process and a step has been *added* to the customer's process, but both benefit. The customer can usually check in more quickly, with less time in line, and it is cheaper for the airline to boot.

Notice that each of these examples of *what* work is to be done encompass at least one other principle of process design. Too often people doing process design get hung up on drawing sharp distinctions between the seven principles. That's a mistake. The principles are not isolated but interrelated. You can get to the same destination through several different avenues. Air Force education registration involved changes in *who* approved applications and *whether* they were approved. Billing by MIT and Harvard posed the question *whether* to do that work or not. And a consumer products company adopting VMI has to change *what* work to do when it decides to manage inventory for retailers. But that direct store delivery process works only because the vendor has better information. It also represents a change in the *where* of the process (that is, the decision about what should be put on a store's shelves was made in the warehouse rather than at the store) as well as a change in the *when* of the process (that is, the decision being made before the van was loaded rather than after the driver arrived at the store). A new process design often includes changes to more than one of the principles of design, and that's fine. Precision and purity are not our goals. Stimulating your thinking is.

So there you have the seven principles for redesigning a process. Process redesign may not require artistic inspiration, but it does demand a certain degree of imagination and creativity, as well as some good business intuition and judgment.

You have to understand that redesigning a process may actually involve higher costs in some areas—Zara's cost of manufacturing, for example—in exchange for gains somewhere else. In Zara's case the company produces much less clothing that has to be heavily discounted or simply trashed and thus is more profitable than its competitors.

Let's be clear about something. The principles of process design we've just examined will not give you a complete process design. Rather, they will give you an *idea* for a process design. It takes lots of hard and detailed work to turn a breakthrough concept into a complete description of a new process. But that is not the work managers and businesspeople find so intimidating. The hardest and scariest part is coming up with the big idea in the first place, because implicit in the big idea is big change. If you can overcome your fear of change and decide to take the plunge, you now have the seven principles to guide you.

KNOW WHERE YOU ARE TO GET WHERE YOU'RE GOING

It is an axiom of ocean navigation that to get where you want to go you have to know where you are now. Using the principles of process design requires you to understand your existing process. But be warned: the most common error in process redesign is wallowing in the study of the existing process, what we call "as-is." There is a strong temptation to look for ways to improve that existing process, to isolate a flaw in the process or to tweak it to make it better. If you try to do that, then yes, details matter. But that kind of process *improvement* is a very bad idea. In process design the one thing we can be certain about is that the old process needs to be thrown out, not fixed or improved. The only things we want to keep from the old process are its value-adding steps. We will recombine them in different ways by changing one or more of the dimensions of the process, and then introduce the least amount of non-value-adding work we can get away with to make it work.

So forget the minute details of your as-is process. Instead, watch it in operation, walk through it from beginning to end, and note just the steps, especially the value-adding steps, that you see. If you insist, you can document what you find with one of the new software tools, such as Microsoft Visio, that are on the market. But, frankly, it's a lot more interesting just to plaster the wall with brown paper on which the steps are depicted. You can use the classic boxes to denote each department, but when you begin to diagram the process you should place those boxes in what we call swim lanes. You know how when you're swimming laps you stay in your own lane? Assign each department to its own lane. Then each time in the process that there's a handoff from one department to another you'll notice that you're crossing a lane divider. The more times that happens, the worse your process is. Those lane crossings represent delay and cost.

THE PROCESS OF PROCESS DESIGN

Process design takes place in steps. Over the years we've come to identify those steps as mobilization, diagnosis, redesign, and transition. More colloquially, we call the four steps Get Organized, Get Oriented, Get Crazy, and Get Real.

GET ORGANIZED. The first step, mobilization or Get Organized, is about bringing together the people you need to do the process design. Let's be clear: process design is not an individual sport. If you try to do it yourself with no help, chances are you will have a difficult time identifying all the steps in your current process. More importantly, you will have a hard time generating good ideas for the new design. You need a team to generate a wide range of ideas, evaluate and critique them, and combine the best of them into a winning whole. Your redesign team should contain both insiders and outsiders. Insiders are people who work in the existing process and are familiar with it. You need them for the credibility they will bring and for their intuition about customers and the realities of implementation. But a team of only insiders might merely create a slightly different version of what already exists. They are too close to the old process, and may have too much invested in it, to be able to come up with truly original ideas or to resist immediately discarding new ideas as unfeasible. The insiders need to be balanced by people working outside the process that is being redesigned. They may well know nothing at all about it, but if they're smart they will bring fresh perspectives, a willingness to ask the naive questions to which there may be no answer, and a decided lack of preconceived notions about how things "should" work. The size of the team may vary a little, depending on the size of the company and the complexity of the process, but for larger companies a design team of seven people, plus or minus two, is about right. Much larger is unwieldy, and much smaller won't have the energy.

There will also be a tendency to make participation in the redesign team a part-time assignment. That's a major mistake. Juggling schedules, balancing the design project with other responsibilities, coping with the inevitable emergencies in their day jobs, and being torn by divided loyalties are just a few of the reasons part-time design teams rarely succeed. It will take some diplomacy and persuasion on your part to tear these people away from their jobs and current bosses for months of full-time work on the redesign, but in the long run it will be worth it for everyone concerned.

Don't settle for just any warm bodies. The work requires talent and judgment. It also demands an analytic mind, the ability to focus on the big picture (the process) while managing the details, a real capacity for teamwork, and a willingness to "think different." The best design teams are characterized by true diversity: people with different educational backgrounds, different kinds of life experiences, different tenures in the company, different ranks and titles, and different functional specialties. One caution about different ranks and titles: someone who is too senior may unintentionally intimidate the team, just as when the boss pops in on the staff meeting and everyone suddenly goes quiet. The inevitable conflict that arises when such diverse individuals try to work as a unit is a wonderful thing. It can be harnessed and turned into the kind of imagination and energy that leads to the kind of new process design that has other people asking, "How did you ever come up with that?"

GET ORIENTED. The second step, diagnosis, or Get Oriented, as we call it, mostly involves understanding the existing process and how well it does or doesn't meet customer needs. We noted earlier that it can be most useful to simply display all the steps in the existing process on brown paper taped to the walls or in the form of a swim lane chart. Whatever approach works for you is fine. But the most critical step in diagnosis is discovering what your customers need and how your existing process is failing to meet those needs. This is the true meaning of the voice of the customer. And we can assure you right here that no matter how happy you think your customer is, he isn't that happy. Indeed, keep in mind that many efforts to adopt process are done in response to specific customer complaints or even customer crises. Remember Andren from the introduction? One of its biggest customers had essentially fired the company, and the turn to process was done to try to save that relationship.

The design team you have assembled will already know something about your customer relationships, but you don't know how much of that is accurate or how complete it is. So go to the horse's mouth. Have the design team either visit customers or bring the customers to your shop for a meeting. Find out what their beefs are. One effective way to do this is to ask one of your own people to go to the front of the room and write on the white board what he or she thinks the customer wants from your company. When the list is reasonably complete, ask the customer to go to the board and mark those that your person got right. You'll probably be shocked by the results.

Here's what typically happens in this exercise. Your salesman struts to the front of the room and writes something like "You want our product when you want it and you want good quality and you want the lowest price."

When the customer responds to that list, everyone is surprised to hear him say, "Yes, we want it when we want it, and we don't always get that. We'd be happy to pay you more if you could deliver consistently."

One company we worked with prided itself on always hitting the promised delivery date. But when the design team asked the customer what it needed, the customer said, "You give us delivery dates ranging from two days to three weeks and you always hit the date. But because there's so much variance we have a hard time forecasting and planning our own production. We would be a lot better off if you just gave us a predictable cycle time so that we always knew that we would get delivery two days or three weeks or whatever the cycle time is after we placed an order. We could plan our own work a lot better that way."

Many companies claim to have great customer relationships. But customer relationships are like any relationship. Over time we take it for granted, make assumptions without information, and quit listening to the other party. Instead of focusing on identifying and solving their problems, we just want to sell them something. To design a high-performance process you can't take your customers for granted. And don't make the mistake of thinking that writing down every word of your customers' complaints gets the job done. All that amounts is *recording* their beefs. What you really need to do is *understand* their complaints. That's a lot more complicated. As Mark Twain once commented, "I did not have time to write you a short letter, so I wrote you a long one." When you understand your customers' problems you should be able to state them briefly and cogently, not just regurgitate what they said.

GET CRAZY. We purposely call the redesign phase the Get Crazy phase. That's because the design team can now unleash all their creative energies and talents, truly thinking outside the box (or, more appropriately, the boxes that constitute work flow and the organizational chart). That's when they think hard about the seven principles of design, argue about them, and try different potential solutions on paper. Questions abound: If you do this here, how does that affect the results there? Who should do this, where should this be done, and why? The team members at this point should no longer be thinking in terms of departments or functions. That's the old way of doing things. Now it's a matter of who is the right person to do a job, keeping in mind all the time that we need to make huge changes in the way we serve our customer. And while the customer remains preeminent, the design team must also listen to the voice of the business to be sure that the resources and skills are available to make the new process work for the benefit of the enterprise.

Typically the Get Crazy phase ends with a simulation of the new process. This amounts to a rehearsal in which the team members, along with representatives of departments or functions that will be affected by the new process, walk through the steps, looking for glaring issues or omissions. The simulation *does not* affect the customers or your own company's continuing operations. You may not be able to use the necessary information technology at this point unless your IT department can create a demonstration mode that picks up information but does not transmit anywhere. The first simulation may be done by the team members themselves or with the actual performers who will be running the new process. Certainly if the team members do the first iteration, the people who will actually work in the process should be brought into the loop for the second and third simulations. And the simulations are designed to test not only the functioning of the new process but also those things that enable it, such as training and metrics. It's here that it will become painfully obvious to the team members that their first redesign has flaws, perhaps big ones. That's okay. If the leadership has done its work well, everyone will be expecting flaws and won't be discouraged. Instead, they'll see them as an opportunity to make the process better before it is unveiled. A cautionary note: There may be a powerful temptation to skip the simulation step, particularly if the design team is behind schedule or over budget. Don't succumb to that temptation. The result will be embarrassing for you, harmful to your customers, and perhaps fatal to the effort to become a process organization. Get as much right as you can before you go public.

GET REAL. The final step is the transition from the design work to the real-world implementation of the new process. We call it Get Real because now the process will affect both the company and its customers in very real terms. Much of this step is involved in pilot-testing the new process. Unlike the simulation, which was done in isolation, the pilot testing uses real inventory, real systems (assuming they're ready), real everything. You can approach the pilot test in a number of different ways: with one customer, with one product, or in one location. We guarantee you there are going to be some very nervous people when the pilot starts. The process owner will be like an expectant father. He wants to find out if he has an ugly baby. But since the pilot is on a small scale, that's okay. If he has an ugly baby, it can be fixed before the whole world has to look at it.

Before you begin the pilot test, be sure any customers that will be receiving the output of the new process are aware of what's happening. You might ease the way by inviting one or more of your customer representatives to sit in on part of the simulation so that they will be aware of what to expect. Still, there will be problems, no question about it. But they shouldn't be big problems; rather, they should be more akin to adjusting your mirrors and seat position instead of changing the tires on a moving automobile.

When you begin the pilot phase you will doubtless be oversupporting, overmeasuring, and overinspecting every aspect of the new process. That's okay; too much attention to detail is better than too little. The most important aspect of the pilot phase is that the metrics begin trending toward the new goals. It isn't necessary that you achieve those goals coming out of the starting blocks, but if the metrics aren't going the right way, it's time to call an immediate halt. Go back and look at both the design of the process and the way the performers are handling it. You must find the root cause of the problem and fix it. Chances are, though, that the numbers will be going your way from the outset if you run your tests correctly. As time goes by and your measurement shows the process is stable, capable of achieving the target (or trending that way), and repeatable, you can begin to relax and monitor everything less frequently and less intently. But be prepared for the unusual, such as an abnormally large order. If that happens, step up your monitoring to be sure the process can cope with the change of circumstances.

From this point it's all evolutionary. You'll be bringing more customers into the new process, expanding it to more locations, and generally adopting it as your new modus operandi. But don't relax! It's important to keep in mind that when you designed the new process you were receiving as input the output from a traditional process and providing input to a traditional process, either in your own company or in your customer's shop. Your redesign had to reflect those connections with old processes. The next step is to redesign those old processes, but when that is done it will affect the intersection with your initial process redesign. So it's back to the drawing board: your initial process design will have to be modified to accept output from a new high-performance process and to provide the input to another high-performance process. There truly is no rest for the weary!

Designing a process is the first step on a long journey toward better performance as an organization. Your design of a process will involve a lot of change for the people working the process. They will have to behave differently, and behavior is driven by measurement. In the next chapter we will examine metrics and the critical role they play in successful process work.

THE DOS AND DON'TS OF DESIGN

- Do take time to understand the process you are redesigning. One very good way to do that is to "attach" yourself to an order or to a facet of the process and follow it from beginning to end.

- Do document the existing process in a "swim lane" format, depicting a different horizontal row or vertical column for each department that has an effect on the process, so that you can see graphically how many times the process is handed off (and back) to various departments.
- Do prepare the design team and the organization for the inevitable mistakes that will occur in the redesign of a process. No one ever creates a perfect design the first time.
- Do use different design teams for each design and ensure that about two-thirds of the team consists of cross-functional representation from various departments that are involved in the process and one-third of the team consists of outsiders with no role in the process.
- Do let team members know in advance that they may move from the core of the team to an advisory capacity so that they will feel free to move and you will be in a position to move them without bad feelings.
- Do communicate openly and widely throughout the organization about what the design team is doing, to head off rumors and gossip and to ensure that team members feel comfortable being away from their usual jobs and applying all their efforts to the redesign.

- Don't overanalyze the process and become immersed in analysis paralysis that delays the redesign effort and the results it needs to achieve.
- Don't design the new process in the swim lane format that you used to depict the old process. That will put the focus on silo organizations rather than on the work that needs to be done and who the right person is to do it.
- Don't skip the simulation and pilot phase of the new design because that is the best time to uncover mistakes in a safe environment.
- Don't put more than nine people on the redesign team,

or fewer than five, to ensure that the design team doesn't become bogged down and that it benefits from a diversity of thoughts and viewpoints.

- Don't allow the new process to look like the old process it is replacing or you will wind up making only marginal improvements that will produce disappointing results and discourage further process work.
- Don't forget to have a reentry plan for the redesign team members so that they won't be fearful of devoting their entire effort to the redesign rather than trying to work part-time on it as well as their old job.

CHAPTER 2

Measure for Measure

GETTING PROCESS METRICS RIGHT

Every self-help and twelve-step program known to mankind begins with the same premise: you must admit you have a problem before you can begin to solve it. So take a deep breath, exhale, and fess up: "My company's measurement system is a complete mess."

There. Don't you feel better already?

You have in fact just confessed to one of the great dirty secrets of the modern enterprise: the tools most companies use to measure (and presumably improve) their performance are virtually worthless. It doesn't take much, at most a beer or two, for managers to start ranting about their terrible metrics, whether for manufacturing, customer service, marketing, procurement, or any other aspect of their business's operations. Among the hundreds of managers with whom we have discussed this topic, there is a near-universal consensus that their companies measure too much, too little, or the wrong thing.

Despite the nearly universal agreement among the people who have to live under most corporate measurement systems that the systems stink, it still comes as a big surprise to the people at the top. You would think that operational performance measurement is so fundamental to basic management that an efficient and effective system would have been devised long ago. But you would be wrong. Despite repeated efforts to make them better, the fact remains that performance metrics are terrible and companies seem incapable of doing much about it.

THE SEVEN DEADLY SINS OF MEASUREMENT

In the sixth century Pope Gregory the Great formulated his famous list of the seven deadly sins—gluttony, greed, wrath, lust, sloth, envy, and pride. There are also seven sins of corporate measurement. Gregory's list was meant to help an individual's quest for salvation. Ours is more mundane: saving companies from fatal flaws in performance measurement.

VANITY. One of the most widespread failings in performance measurement is to use measures whose sole purpose is to make the organization, its people, and especially its managers look good. As one executive said, "Nobody wants a metric that they don't score 95 on." This is especially true because bonuses and other rewards are usually tied to performance measures. For instance, in distribution logistics, it is common for companies to measure themselves against the promise date—that is, whether they ship by the date that they promised the customer. A moment's impartial reflection shows that this sets the bar absurdly low—a company need only promise delivery dates that it can easily make in order to look good on this metric. Even worse, companies often measure against what is called last promise date—the final date promised the customer, after changes may have been made to the delivery schedule. It takes real effort not to hit the last promise date. Moreover, achieving good results on the last promise date has no larger significance for company performance; it does not lead to customer satisfaction or any other desirable outcome. All you have to do is keep promising a later date. Even if you manage to hit that target 100 percent of the time, it's likely that your customer wanted the product days, weeks, or even months ago, so don't go patting yourself on the back.

A far better metric would be performance against customer request date. But achieving that goal would be far more difficult and might lead to managers not getting their bonuses. When executives at a semiconductor manufacturer proposed shifting from last promise date to customer request date, they encountered widespread resistance.

A metals refiner had been using yield—the percentage of raw material that was turned into saleable product—as a key performance metric, and everyone was very pleased that this figure was consistently over 95 percent. An executive new to the company made the observation that this figure glossed over the difference between high-grade and low-grade product. The refinery was supposed to produce only high-grade product, but poor processing sometimes led to low-grade product. The company then started to measure the yield of high-grade product and discovered that figure was closer to 70 percent. That was a much more meaningful representation of the refinery's real performance. Unsurprisingly, that insight did not generate a lot of enthusiasm.

PROVINCIALISM. This sin permits organizational boundaries and concerns to dictate performance metrics. On the surface, it would seem natural and appropriate for a functional department to be measured on its own performance. That is, after all, what its managers can control. In reality, however, measuring so narrowly inevitably leads to suboptimization and conflict. One insurance company CEO has complained that he spends half his time adjudicating disputes between sales and underwriting. The sales department is measured on sales volume. Not surprisingly, the sales force tries to sell any willing customer. Underwriting, on the other hand, is measured on quality of risk. Naturally, the underwriters want to reject all but the best prospects. The two departments clash constantly. If the salespeople win, the company will be paying out more in claims. If the underwriters win, revenue will be less than it would otherwise have been. Higher costs or lower revenue? The top brass has to choose between two evils.

NARCISSISM. This is the unpardonable offense of measuring from one's own point of view, rather than from the customer's perspective. One retailer measured its distribution organization on how well the goods in the stores matched the stock-on-hand levels specified in the merchandising plan. They had a satisfying 98 percent availability when measured in this way. But when they thought to measure to what extent the goods in the stores matched what customers actually wanted to buy, rather than what the merchandising plan called for, they found the figure was only 86 percent. Another retailer measured goods in stock by whether the goods had arrived in the store; eventually the company realized that simply being in the store did the customer no good if the product wasn't on the shelf—and on-shelf availability was considerably lower than in-store availability. These companies measured things that interested them, not their customers.

A consumer goods maker managed its distribution operations by focusing on the percentage of orders from retailers that it filled on time. Sounds sensible. By tracking, reporting, and relentlessly seeking to improve this number, the company got it up to 99.5 percent consistently. That's the good news. The bad news is that when the company happened to take a look at the reality of retailers' shelves—which is what consumers see—it found that many of its products were nonetheless out of stock as much as 14 percent of the time. Many companies measure the performance of order fulfillment in terms of whether the shipment left the dock on the date scheduled. This is of interest only to the company itself. Customers care about when they receive the shipment, not when it leaves the dock. Perhaps the most egregious instance of narcissism that we have encountered was at a major computer systems manufacturer. This company measured on-time shipping in terms of individual components; if it shipped, say, nine of ten components of a system on time, the company claimed a 90 percent score. The customer, of course, would give the company a 0 percent rating, since without all ten components the system is useless.

LAZINESS. This is a trap into which even those who avoid narcissism often fall: assuming you know what is important to measure without giving it adequate thought or effort. A semiconductor maker measured many aspects of its order processing operation, but not the critical (to customers) issue of how long it took from the time the customer gave the order to the time the company confirmed it and provided a delivery date—simply because the company never thought to ask customers what was really important to them.

An electric power utility assumed that customers cared about speed of installation and so measured and tried to improve it, only to discover later that customers cared more about the reliability of the installation date they were given than speed of installation. Companies often jump to conclusions, measure what is easy to measure, or measure what they have always measured, rather than go through the effort of ascertaining what is truly important to measure.

PETTINESS. Too many companies measure only a small component of what matters. Executives at a telecommunications systems vendor rejected a proposal to have customers perform their own repairs because that would require putting spare parts at customer premises, which would drive up spare parts inventory levels, a key metric for the company. It lost sight of the fact that the broader and more meaningful metric was total cost of maintenance, which is the sum of labor costs and inventory costs. The increase in parts inventory would be more than offset by a reduction in labor costs produced by the new approach.

INANITY. Metrics drive behavior, but too many companies implement metrics without giving any thought to the consequences of these metrics for human behavior and consequently for enterprise performance. People in an organization will seek to improve a metric they are told is important, especially if they are compensated on it and even if doing so is counterproductive. For instance, a regional fast-food chain specializing in chicken decided to improve financial performance by reducing waste, which was defined as chicken that had been cooked but unsold at the end of the day and then discarded. Restaurant managers throughout the chain obediently responded by driving out waste. They told their staff not to cook any chicken until it had been ordered. Thus did a fast-food chain become a slow-food chain. Yes, waste declined, but sales declined even more. Managers might keep in mind this variant of an old adage: "Be careful what you measure— you may get more of it than you want."

FRIVOLITY. Not taking measurement seriously is perhaps the most grievous sin of them all. The symptoms are easy to see: arguing about metrics instead of taking them to heart, finding excuses for poor performance instead of tracking root causes, and looking for ways to blame others rather than shouldering the responsibility for improving performance. If the

other errors are sins of the intellect, this is a sin of character and corporate culture. An oft-heard phrase at one financial services company is "The decision has been made; let the
debates begin." When self-interest, hierarchical position, and
voice volume carry more weight than objective data, even the
most carefully designed and implemented metrics are of little
value.

As with the seven deadly sins, the sins of measurement
often overlap and are related; a single metric may be evidence
of several sins. A company that commits these sins will find
itself unable to use its metrics to drive improvements in operating performance, which is the key to improved enterprise
performance. Bad measurement systems are at best useless and
at worst positively harmful. And don't be fooled by the old
adage "That which is measured improves." If you are measuring the wrong thing, making it better will do little or no
good. Remarkably, these seven deadly sins are not committed
only by poorly managed or unsuccessful organizations; they
are rampant even in well-managed companies in the forefront
of their industries. Such companies manage to succeed *despite*
their measurement systems, rather than because of them.

GETTING MEASUREMENT RIGHT: OUTCOMES
AND DRIVERS

If you have been reading carefully to this point, you may be
saying, "The problem with these sinners is that they aren't measuring their processes." You would be correct, but only par-
tially. It is true that measuring the performance of end-to-end
processes, rather than of functional silos, helps inoculate against
the sin of provincialism. But just deciding to measure processes
doesn't guarantee that you will measure the right things about
these processes, or that these metrics won't get you into as

much hot water as bad functional metrics can. It's not enough to have process metrics; you need to have the *right* process metrics. But how do we know what those are? If we are looking at order fulfillment, product development, or customer support, how do we know exactly what metrics we should construct for them? There are any number of things we could measure, but how do we choose the right ones?

The answer is to connect processes to overall business performance. The experience of a large fashion retailer shows both why this is important and how to do it. This company was seeking revenue growth. Since most of the management team had backgrounds in merchandising, executives immediately assumed that the key to this would be improving the company's advertising program to attract more shoppers into the stores. However, the chief operating officer had recently joined the company from a different industry and was unwilling to jump to this conclusion. Instead, he led an exercise to determine what factors were most critical to the company's success and to identify metrics that expressed them. A simplified version of this analysis goes as follows: increasing sales requires attracting shoppers into the stores and selling things to those shoppers; thus traffic (number of customers coming into the store) and what is called the conversion ratio (the percentage of customers who actually make a purchase) are important metrics. These, however, are outcome metrics—desirable goals, but not ones that can be achieved directly.

The next step was to determine the drivers of these outcomes, the factors under the company's control that increase traffic and the conversion ratio. Advertising effectiveness and product quality were identified as the key drivers of increasing traffic and therefore as important phenomena to measure as well. The factors needed to increase the conversion ratio were ensuring that products were on the shelf (since customers can't buy what isn't there) and having enough salespeople available to help customers decide what to buy; thus on-shelf availability and customer coverage (the ratio of customers to salespeople) were recognized as important metrics as well. It is interesting to note that in the past, the company had paid little explicit attention to conversion ratio or on-shelf availability, neither measuring them with regularity nor doing much to improve them.

Using these metrics, it became apparent that the assumption that the key to improving revenues lay through improved advertising was false. When measured, customer traffic, advertising effectiveness, and product quality were at levels that ranged from acceptable to high. The problem lay in the conversion ratio—not enough shoppers were becoming buyers. The root of this problem was twofold: neither on-shelf availability nor customer coverage was as high as it should have been. These, not advertising, were the areas that needed attention. But how could on-shelf availability and customer coverage be improved? This is where the connection to the processes is made. For each of the factors that is measured, the processes that affect that factor must be identified. The factor becomes a key metric for that process, whose achievement is to be accomplished through having a high-performance design and executing it correctly.

In this case, on-shelf availability was recognized as the result of the supply chain process and so became a key overarching metric for that process. Customer coverage was determined by the employee scheduling process. Changes were made to both of these processes to improve the identified measures, which in turn increased the conversion ratio, which in turn led to the desired improvement in revenues. In particular, this analysis led to the recognition of a very deep-seated problem with the employee scheduling process. In the past, it had been driven by when employees found it convenient to work, rather than when customers were coming into the stores. Consequently, there were too many people working on weekday afternoons, and not enough on weekends. The new metrics and the process redesign effort they spawned soon changed that.

This story illustrates two key ideas in the metrics arena: outcomes and drivers. Outcomes are things that you want to achieve but can only do so indirectly, through other things. Increased revenue is one such outcome. You can't increase revenue directly, merely by waving a magic wand, but only indirectly, by getting more customers into the store and selling more to them once they are there. These are drivers, controllable factors that lead to achieving your desired outcomes. However, one person's driver is another person's outcome. Getting customers to buy more is an outcome that can only be achieved through other drivers, such as having the products that customers want on the shelves. And how do we achieve that? Through processes. By making them perform better in terms of the right metrics, we influence intermediate outcomes and eventually the overall enterprise outcomes that are the point of the whole endeavor. Identifying desired enterprise outcomes, connecting them to process drivers, and creating metrics for both outcomes and drivers is the basis of an effective measurement system.

DETERMINING WHAT MATTERS

The very first thing you need to determine in order to improve the performance of a process is the specific metrics on which you need to focus your efforts. Recognizing how your process affects desired enterprise outcomes is the key to doing this, as Deborah Whatley discovered.

In 2005, the leadership of Michelin, the giant tire manufacturer, was getting nervous. It seemed as if the company had settled into a rut and had lost its competitive edge. The company didn't really know how its customers regarded it, and internally Michelin didn't really have a readily identifiable corporate culture, just a hodgepodge of different cultures in its multiple facilities around the world. That had to change, the leaders decided. To jump-start the change the company decided to focus on the demand-to-cash process, the process that most affected customers. Demand-to-cash extended from the customer's order through payment to Michelin after receipt of the shipment, including any after-sale service.

Deborah Whatley was a natural to become the North American process owner of the demand-to-cash process in North America. She had both engineering and MBA degrees and had worked as an industrial engineer at Michelin for several years, rising through the ranks and doing sales and operations planning and supply chain management. As the North American demand-to-cash process owner, she would work closely with her counterparts in Europe reporting to the global demand-to-cash process owner.

Some three hundred people are involved in the demand-to-cash process in North America, principally in South Carolina and Mexico. Deborah focused on creating a new process for them to use. She commissioned a design team to rethink the entire process from beginning to end. But first she needed to give her team some marching orders, in terms of what they were to achieve, and that meant telling them what the process metrics would be.

Deborah and her team first made a very simple observation: the real point of transforming a process is to improve the company's performance. At Michelin at that time the company was looking to reduce working capital, increase operating margin, improve return on capital employed, increase free cash flow, and enhance overall customer satisfaction with Michelin. To accomplish those objectives Michelin would have to simultaneously reduce its operating costs, lower its inventory, accelerate payment from customers, and improve the quality of service it provided to customers.

Deborah's team members asked themselves what outcomes their process could achieve that would in turn affect the overall enterprise goals. After some research and debate, they identified six key performance metrics for the demand-to-cash process.

Customer perception of the performance of the demand-to-cash process. When customers feel good about how their orders are being filled, they are likely to be more happy with the company as a whole.

Right the first time. These are orders that are filled exactly as the customer wants them to be. This would contribute to customer satisfaction as well as help lower the company's costs, since correcting errors is a very expensive proposition.

Operating cost of the demand-to-cash process as a percentage of the company's sales. Reducing the cost of filling an order would directly affect Michelin's operating margin.

The amount of receivables more than sixty days old. This is simply the extent to which customers were late in paying their bills, a significant impediment to cash flow.

The number of order lines per employee in demand-to-cash. This measures how efficiently performers executed the demand-to-cash process, which also has a significant effect on costs.

Incremental revenue. A well-designed order fulfillment process should lead to opportunities for upselling and cross-selling, leading to more revenue.

Each of these factors could be directly measured, and they became the primary results metrics for the demand-to-cash process, that is, the metrics the company would use to manage the process, assess its performance, and determine whether the redesign project was a success.

In theory, Deborah could have stopped then, with just those six metrics for the demand-to-cash process. But she realized that for a process as large and complex as demand-to-cash, those high-level metrics, while necessary, were not sufficient. The six were outcomes driven by finer-grained issues such as order handling, delivery, and billing. So she began identifying subprocesses within the demand-to-cash process and determining how to measure performance of those subprocesses in terms of time, quality, and cost. In the delivery subprocess, for example, she identified key metrics for time, quality, and cost that would contribute to one or more of the overall desired process outcomes: time (complaint cycle time, or how long it took Michelin to resolve customer problems with the delivery), transportation cost (the cost of getting the product to the customer), and quality (percentage of shipments that were over, short, or damaged, known collectively as OSD).

Amazingly, Deborah discovered that up to that point Michelin had not been measuring the percentage of shipments that were over, short, or damaged. That didn't mean there hadn't been any such shipments. There were, and customers regularly filed claims about them. But the only metric the company used for delivery, and therefore the only metric its people cared about, was cost. So claims were logged and stuffed in a drawer. Deborah discovered to her horror a two-and-a-half-year backlog on these claims. Lord Kelvin, the nineteenth-century British physicist who invented the absolute temperature scale, is credited with having said, "If you cannot measure it, you cannot improve it." Shining the bright light of a new metric on your operations will uncover the most remarkable things.

Another new demand-to-cash metric Deborah introduced was the percentage of orders processed after the official daily cutoff of noon for next-day shipment. Orders processed after noon would throw off the distribution center's planning for the next day's picking and trucking, which would in turn drive up costs. Such rushed orders could also lead to incorrect invoices and/or OSD shipments. Until this aspect of demand-to-cash started to be measured, people vaguely knew it was an issue but didn't really take it seriously. Introducing that metric focused attention on, among other things, "Five o'Clock Susie," who was regularly processing orders at the very end of the day, creating all kinds of problems downstream. Susie got coaching and counseling to help her understand the consequences of her behavior and to get her to change it. This new metric, by the way, illustrates another important theme: problems in one area (in this case, late order processing) create problems that show up elsewhere (as high costs in the distribution center). The disciplined tracking of outcomes back to drivers helps to isolate the real reason that problems occur and gives you metrics to identify where the fault really lies.

But this still was not the end of the line for the demand-to-cash metrics. Deborah took many of them down a level further, to create process-related performance metrics for the individual process performer. These were used to track the performance of individuals and identify situations where individual behaviors, such as that of Five o'Clock Susie, were creating process performance problems. For instance, one possible source for an OSD shipment could be a picker who had trouble reading the picking slip. Tracking individual picker error rates would highlight such situations and allow them to be addressed.

Everyone involved in the demand-to-cash process was accountable for the process metrics. Managers were accountable for the five top-level measures and the subprocess measures; frontline performers and their supervisors were accountable for subprocess measures and personal measures. For people on bonus plans, parts of their bonus were tied directly to achieving these metrics; for people without variable pay, the metrics were used in performance reviews.

While demand-to-cash metrics are obviously important in assessing individual performance, their central use was guiding the process redesign effort. As Deborah's team gained an understanding of what was important about the process, they were able to focus their redesign ideas on these issues. A central aspect of the new demand-to-cash design was its use of the case team concept, the "who" part of the seven design principles (see pages 43–48). Teams of people from customer service, accounts receivable, and logistics were formed and dedicated to particular customer groups. It was a simple change, but one with dramatic consequences. For one, the accounts receivable person is no longer sitting in an isolated department, disconnected from customers, and merely processing payments. The accounts receivable specialist now is customer focused, understands the customer's ordering and payment patterns, and has a relationship with people in the customer's payables unit. In many, if not most, instances, a delayed payment is not a sign the customer is going bankrupt or is trying to cheat; rather, a delayed payment is usually a sign that there was a problem with the delivery or the invoice. A customer-focused accounts receivable person can recognize a payment that is late but not yet overdue and work with the customer service representative on his team to identify and resolve the underlying problem before it escalates. The customer service rep on the team now also has broader skills and responsibilities. Customer service reps are trained to be able to answer the most frequent questions a customer asks (such as what kind of tire should go on a particular kind of vehicle) rather than handing them off to someone else, saving time and money and making life easier for the customers. The customer service rep's role has also been expanded to include the responsibility for managing transportation (previously done by the distribution center). Because the customer service rep has better knowledge of the customer's ordering patterns, she can plan loads better, thereby getting more onto an individual truck; this both saves money for Michelin and means that customers have to unload fewer shipments each month. The customer service rep also has become the point of contact for OSD claims, which no longer languish endlessly in a drawer.

The outcomes were nothing short of breathtaking. Billing errors decreased nearly 60 percent; past due accounts went down by more than 80 percent; the cost of filling orders went down more than 10 percent; and, perhaps most importantly, the percentage of customer inquiries resolved on first contact went to more than 98 percent from an unknown base (it had never been measured). And just as the outcomes/drivers analysis predicted, the demand-to-cash improvements turned into improved customer satisfaction and financial performance for Michelin as a whole.

All told, the demand-to-cash process owners have access to more than one hundred metrics of the process. Don't be shocked by the number. They were not randomly chosen. Each and every one of them was selected because of its impact on the critical Michelin outcomes. The most critical of these (the key demand-to-cash metrics) are presented on a regular basis to the process owners and Michelin executives. Many of the others, however, are automatically tracked by computer and brought to someone's attention only if they are out of an acceptable range. Some of the demand-to-cash metrics are computed and tracked daily (such as number of orders being handled per person, so that teams experiencing an excess of orders can be supplemented with additional resources), while others (such as the percentage of orders that are filled correctly the first time) are measured monthly since more frequent measurement would have little point and could in fact be misleading.

The Michelin story illustrates three important principles of effective process metrics:

- You need a balanced set of metrics. For some years now, the "balanced scorecard" has been part of the standard management lexicon. In the strict meaning of the term, it refers to the need for diverse enterprise key performance indicators, or KPIs, including customer-focused measurements as well as financially oriented ones. At the process level, you need to consider a range of metrics (as Michelin did in the areas of cost, speed, and quality), or you run the risk of improving the elements of the process you are measuring at the expense of having the ones you aren't measuring go to hell in a handbasket.

- Metrics are not ends in themselves but tools for improving process performance. If you don't know how you will use a metric, you don't need it.

- The best metrics are those that predict performance rather than just track it. Customer satisfaction, for instance, is what is often referred to as a lagging indicator; by the time you have measured it and realize you have a problem, it is too late to do much about it. On the other hand, recognizing that a customer's payment is later than expected can help forestall difficulties.

HOW THE RIGHT METRICS SHAPE BEHAVIOR

The right measurement metric not only focuses process redesign correctly but also shapes behavior to an extraordinary degree, as D. W. Morgan learned. Morgan, a privately held company with sales in the $50–$100 million range, provides transportation management services to its customers, primarily high-tech manufacturers. Morgan's job is to make sure that its customers have what they need (whether parts or finished goods) in the right place at the right time, so they can make products and fill customer orders. Morgan uses both its own resources and third parties to get this done.

On the surface, Morgan was extremely successful—fast-growing, profitable, winning industry accolades, and being named supplier of the year by such customers as Cisco. Yet Grant Opperman, the company's president, had a gnawing feeling that problems were looming. He noted that while revenue was growing rapidly, margins were declining. He was concerned that what had helped the company achieve success thus far—an obsession with doing whatever necessary to get the job done for the customer—would not be able to keep pace as the company continued to grow. And he found himself spending more and more time adjudicating disputes between different functional groups that were measured and rewarded on different functional metrics. Operations, for instance, cared exclusively about on-time delivery, while the sales department was interested in top-line growth. Unfortunately, that meant that salespeople were not averse to closing deals that operations would be hard-pressed to deliver on. Worse, neither of them cared much about whether the company was profitable.

So Grant decided to knit the company together by using end-to-end processes and process metrics. The first process he focused on was order-to-cash—another name for what at Michelin is called the demand-to-cash process—and the key metric he devised for it was "perfect shipment." He developed a precise definition of perfect shipment:

- The order is in Morgan's computer system within thirty minutes of receiving it.
- It is picked up at the time promised to the customer.
- The customer is informed about the status of the shipment at four specific key times.
- There are no damage claims on the shipment.
- Morgan can give proof of delivery (POD) within an hour.

- Morgan bills the customer within twenty-four hours of delivery.
- Morgan makes an acceptable profit on the shipment.

These components of the definition may sound obvious and simple but were anything but. It took Grant and his team months to come up with this metric. The components were not chosen carelessly; it is not hard to see how they all help drive customer satisfaction, growth, or profitability. Some drive several. For instance, not only did billing quickly improve Morgan's financial performance, but customers preferred it as well, since they did not like getting invoices after they had closed their books at the end of a reporting period.

Once they had defined the metric, Grant and his team estimated that a successful company like theirs must have at least 40 percent perfect shipments. But when they actually calculated it, they were astounded that Morgan's perfect shipment rate stood at a mere 6 percent.

"I wanted to hang myself," Grant said.

To be sure, performance was not so bad in all of these factors, but some were bad indeed. Grant was insistent that these not be eight different metrics, but a single integrated measure for which every department and every individual in the company would be accountable. Otherwise he ran the risk of encouraging finger-pointing and conflict, as people optimized their own metric with no regard for the others.

Grant was determined that everyone in the company pay attention to perfect shipment. The first step was to tell people about it and to publicize it; every week, everyone in the company got an email or a printout showing where things stood on perfect order and its components. It was also discussed in a weekly cross-functional management conference call. This was a major departure for Morgan, as it would be for many other companies. Sharing profitability information with every employee is not common practice. Yet Grant recognized that if he wanted people to buy in to what he was trying to achieve, he had to involve them and be open with them.

He also had to make it worth their while to care about perfect shipment. To that end, he established a quarterly bonus pool, based on the perfect shipment metric, that would be shared equally by all employees irrespective of their base pay. The prospect of earning thousands of dollars in extra pay by helping to boost the perfect shipment rate was a real motivator for those on the front lines.

Rewarding people on a performance metric such as perfect shipment is much more effective than rewarding them on a corporate financial measure such as profitability. The reason is line of sight: everyone in the company can see how her actions affect one or more of the components of perfect shipment. Being rewarded for something you don't know how to influence can easily lead to despair or cynicism.

It didn't take long for the metric to start shaping behavior. For instance, Morgan can't bill a customer until it has a lot of data about the shipment (size, weight, pickup and delivery information, and more). In the past, Morgan people would focus on getting the shipment delivered, but not necessarily on collecting and entering the data with dispatch. A measurement system is a communication system: it tells people what is important. When people recognized that prompt billing was key to perfect shipment and that prompt billing required prompt data capture, they responded. Similarly, sales reps stopped making promises that could not be met (well, mostly), started bringing issues to the attention of other areas, and stayed involved with the customer after the deal was closed rather than running off to the next opportunity.

Whenever you create a new metric, you will inevitably have people who tell you that it is unreasonable, incalculable, or impossible to improve. Grant encountered all of these. Some people squealed that he was violating a law of physics (or at least of management) by holding people accountable for an outcome they do not fully control. He replied that customers and shareholders are not interested in people's narrow responsibilities but want results, and it's everyone's responsibility to deliver them. Others argued that they couldn't calculate the perfect shipment metric since they didn't have all the data; he said to do the best they could in the short term while they got it right in the longer run, but that he wasn't compromising. Others said that third parties (such as trucking companies) had a major impact on perfect shipment and that they were beyond Morgan's control. Grant responded by taking the metric to these third parties as well, showing them how they affected it, and replacing those who did not comply. You need to emulate Grant's commitment. Introducing new metrics is a very scary thing for many people, and you can't let their objections deter you.

Grant commissioned a process design team to make more systemic changes that would boost and institutionalize higher performance. One of the team's key ideas was to install a "customer service advocate" who would be the customer's key point of contact and would interface with everyone involved in a shipment to make sure it got done perfectly.

The best part is that it worked! In slightly more than a year, perfect shipments zoomed from 6 percent to 85 percent, and business results improved along with them. Revenue grew by more than 40 percent, margins increased by 10 percent, and both customer and employee satisfaction increased. Now Grant is taking the process approach to work and measurement to Morgan's other processes.

IMAGINATION AND INSIGHT

The basic rationale for developing metrics—push desired business outcomes into process performance requirements—is fairly straightforward. But selecting the specific metrics requires some imagination and precision, as Don Cimorelli learned at Fidelity's Human Resources Services (HRS) business unit. This unit of the financial services giant provides human resources services to companies that wish to outsource HR administration.

Don is the senior vice president of HR services process ownership and the focal point for the business unit's end-to-end process efforts. In developing process metrics, he started with enterprise key performance indicators (KPIs) and translated them into process terms.

For the request-to-fulfillment process, through which HRS responds to inquiries and requests for service from employees of its customers, HRS developed the metric of first-call resolution (FCR): the customer's problem is solved with a single call to HRS. This process metric was a driver of several enterprise KPIs, such as customer satisfaction and operating margin.

HRS was very stringent in defining FCR. A customer call would be graded as having met FCR only if the customer did not call back on the same issue within the following six weeks. Otherwise it would be too easy for a CSR to mark an issue as resolved when it was not.

Real insight into the business is needed to translate enterprise KPIs into process performance metrics. Sometimes the drivers of business success have not been sufficiently thought through. For instance, in developing metrics for the grow-the-business process (essentially the sales process), HRS identified estimation cycle time as a key metric. This captures how long it takes to respond to customers who want to change their employee benefit plans and want to know how much Fidelity would charge them to implement the change. The sooner HRS gets back to the customer with the estimate, the more likely they are to close the deal and book the revenue. Remarkably, this factor had not been measured at HRS in the past, and as a result, nobody paid much attention to it. Once you have identified a process metric, you have to think creatively of ways in which the process might be changed to improve that metric. One obvious way to increase FCR is to give call center reps additional skills and training so that they can deal with more complex issues instead of handing them off to someone else. Another is to post information on a website so customers can deal with issues themselves instead of calling. A somewhat less obvious way is to ensure that customers have no need to call in the first place. By using all of these, Don and his colleagues have dramatically improved both process metrics and business performance.

DEFINING MEASUREMENT

The examples we've discussed have given us real insight into what aspects of a process you should measure and how you can use those measurements. However, you also need to find the right way to measure. Deciding what needs to be measured, by connecting desired outcomes to process drivers, is something of a science. Deciding how to measure, however, remains an art, since as a rule there are many different ways of putting a number on a phenomenon that has been determined to be worthy of measurement. For instance, how should customer satisfaction be measured? One common approach is through customer surveys. However, this is costly and slow, and it isn't clear how well customer responses on surveys correlate with desired behaviors. Measuring complaint volumes may not capture the full spectrum of customer attitudes and is subject to manipulation. Not answering the complaint line guarantees a higher reading of customer satisfaction. Measuring attrition and repeat buying comes too late to do anything about it. The point is not that these or any other specific measures of customer satisfaction are good or bad, but that virtually every metric has some advantages and drawbacks. You have to design metrics with these considerations in mind.

PRECISION. A metric must be defined carefully and exactly so that there can be no doubt or dispute about it. Thus, "on-time delivery" can be interpreted in numerous ways, depending on what the target is (first promise date, last promise date, request date, etc.) and what it means to be "on time" (on the date, within twenty-four hours, within forty-eight hours, etc.). It should come as no surprise that when a metric is not unambiguously defined, people will interpret it in ways that work well for them. The manufacturing organization at a consumer goods company used an imprecise definition of productivity as an opportunity to take downtime and turnover time out of the equation. The definition of a metric should also include the units being employed and the range and scale of the measurement.

ACCURACY. In many situations, a company needs to measure what amounts to a platonic ideal (customer satisfaction, advertising effectiveness, product quality, etc). Any actual metric will inevitably represent only an approximation to this ideal. It is necessary to keep in mind the distinction between reality and what is being measured and to close the gap between the two, subject to the limitations imposed by these other considerations.

OVERHEAD. Organizations often fall prey to the temptation to construct a complex mechanism for calculating a metric when a far simpler one would suffice. The fashion retailer discussed above needed a way to determine the conversion ratio at its stores (the percentage of shoppers who bought something). Complex schemes were bruited about, involving the use of RFID tags and various types of sensors. In the end, the company decided on the low-tech approach of hiring high school students to sit outside stores and count the number of people who went into the store and the number coming out carrying shopping bags. The more inexpensive and convenient it is to calculate a metric, the better. The periodicity of the metric—how often it needs to be calculated—must also be taken into account here.

ROBUSTNESS. The designer of a metric must be conscious of the extent to which the metric can be manipulated or gamed by people with something at stake, or the extent to which the metric can encourage undesired behaviors. At a telecommunications company, for instance, using call duration to measure the performance of customer service representatives led CSRs to rush through calls.

PUSHING THE ENVELOPE WITH MEASUREMENT

There is one more issue that we need to explore before we leave our discussion of metrics: setting performance targets. It is very well to say that you need to be faster, cheaper, and better, but *how much* faster, cheaper, and better? It is tempting to say "as much as possible" and to instruct your design team to do the absolute best they can, that the sky's the limit, that you want to them to make the process as cheap, fast, and good as they can. This would be a terrible mistake. Given such a vague charter, it is a virtual certainty that your design team will come back to you with very minor improvements. Why? Because making fundamental changes to a process is a very frightening thing to do. It demands that people take a clean-sheet view of the process, question lots of assumptions, and to use a shop-worn phrase, "think out of the box." Many in the organization will find this deeply threatening, including many of the people on the design team itself. It is human nature to shrink from such an onerous duty. Giving open-ended performance targets invites your design team to make only minor changes, shrug, and insist that it was the best they could do. The only way to avoid this is by giving them hard, specific performance targets that will make them gasp. Setting stretch goals is the way to get people to stretch their minds and consider ideas that they would otherwise dismiss out of hand. There have been countless occasions in which a design team assured the process owner (see pages 97–100 for the definition of "process owner") that they could not possibly meet the target they were given. When the process owner holds firm, they will resign themselves to the effort and, much to their own amazement, come up with a design that actually exceeds the targets they were given.

But how do you derive these targets? You don't want to make them arbitrary and unachievable, because that will dispirit your team and make them cynical. They need to understand the logic of your targets so that they buy into them. There are six important approaches to developing meaningful stretch performance goals.

CUSTOMER REQUIREMENTS. If customers tell you that they require a certain level of performance, then the conversation about targets is over. A major credit card company, for instance, conducted a survey of customers to determine what they wanted in order to stay with the company and not defect to an aggressive competitor. The answer was clear: the replacement of lost cards within twenty-four hours. The problem was that the fastest the company could replace cards, under the best of circumstances, was seventy-two hours. They could not see any possible way to do it in twenty-four hours. Then an executive had a brainstorm. The company took out large ads in newspapers, announcing that lost cards would henceforth be returned in twenty-four hours. They then turned to the newly convened design team and said, "Guess you're stuck now." The design team was panic-stricken. They also were highly motivated to come up with a design for the lost card replacement process that could be executed in less than twenty-four hours—and they did.

CUSTOMER INSIGHT. It is a mistake, however, merely to poll customers and set a target based on their explicit request. In some cases, customers will ask for less than they really want or need, either because they think achieving their real requirements is impossible or because they do not know what they want until they see it. Your job is to understand customers even better than they understand themselves and to identify what would make a real difference to them, whether or not they explicitly request it. When Progressive began the redesign of its claim process, the company was not responding to a formally stated customer need for faster claims handling. Rather, the CEO, Peter Lewis, had a deep intuition for insurance customers. He understood that having an accident was a traumatic experience and that customers would respond very positively to seeing an adjuster quickly. Despite endless arguments that his goal was neither desirable nor achievable, he stuck to his guns and demanded that the seven-day period for claims initiation be reduced to nine hours. It was, and the rest, as they say, is history.

COMPETITOR CAPABILITIES. The widespread practice of benchmarking is also an important input to setting stretch goals. If a competitor is capable of a certain performance level, you should be, too. There are two mistakes that companies often make in this regard, however. The first is defining the range of competitors too narrowly. Comparing yourself against the companies with which you compete every day is of only marginal value; you are all familiar with each other's operations and are probably all working under the same limiting assumptions. Real breakthrough thinking will be stimulated by seeing how nontraditional competitors (new entrants into the market, companies coming from adjacent industries) handle things. And you should look more broadly than that, too. See what companies in other industries are capable of achieving in their analogous processes. Shell, for instance, took lessons from the airline industry in designing its preventative maintenance process.

The second mistake to avoid is treating competitor capabilities as ceilings when you should treat them as floors. Merely attaining what others are already doing will gain you little, because by the time you have caught up to them, they are likely to have moved on, leaving you to play catch-up once again.

FINANCIAL VIABILITY. Just as you need to listen to the voice of the customer, you also have to listen to the voice of the business. Companies need a certain financial performance to remain viable and competitive, and this can be translated into very specific process performance goals. Senior executives at Michelin, for instance, set a goal of a 16 percent reduction in working capital in order to achieve needed financial results; this cascaded down to more detailed demand-to-cash process performance targets for such things as aged receivables.

EXTRAORDINARY CIRCUMSTANCES. Many companies find themselves able to rise to the occasion when circumstances demand it. At a nuclear power plant the managers complained how slow and bureaucratic the process was, and how it took weeks to make even the simplest repair. But when asked if it would take weeks to make a repair if there were a true emergency threatening the safety and health of workers or even nearby residents, the answer was, "Of course not. Those repairs would be done in a matter of minutes."

So why doesn't that happen for any repair?

It wasn't long before they had redesigned their process so that routine maintenance was done as quickly and as well as emergency repairs.

INSPIRATIONAL VISION. A key process at an auto parts manufacturer had a cycle time of twenty weeks; the president announced that the target was twenty days. How did he choose that particular goal?

He replied: "Sounds great, doesn't it?"

Actually, there was a bit of method to this madness. A key competitor could do the process in six weeks (forty-two days), so exceeding that was a requirement. Given that, the symmetry of twenty weeks to twenty days had great appeal: it was easy to communicate and easy to remember. The design team protested that the goal was completely unachievable, and then proceeded to come up with a design that got it done in eighteen days.

Once you have set these goals, you need to communicate them broadly in the company. Formally announced goals have a power that private ones never do.

You may still fall prey to the temptations of gluttony, lust, or another of the seven deadly sins, but you are now equipped to avoid the deadly sins of performance measurement. You know how to derive end-to-end process metrics from enterprise goals, and you are sensitive to what's involved in doing it right.

METRICS DOS AND DON'TS

- Do examine the behaviors that your current metrics are driving to determine if they are counter to the results you are trying to achieve.
- Do balance voice-of-the-customer and voice-of-the-business metrics to ensure that the process meets the needs of both the customer and the enterprise.
- Do review your metrics regularly and adjust them when necessary to reflect changing conditions in the economy, your customer base, and your business outlook.
- Do create alignment between your enterprise's key performance indicators and your process metrics.
- Do keep appropriate functional measures but ensure that process metrics take priority over departmental metrics.

- Don't settle for using only metrics that your IT system can capture instead of the metrics that really matter, even if you have to capture them manually.
- Don't have so many metrics that you are data rich and information poor. Instead, focus only on those metrics that truly drive the voice-of-the-customer and voice-of-the-business results you seek.
- Don't allow people to keep metrics and targets that they were comfortable achieving but that are the wrong measures.
- Don't align your metrics to departments. Align them to the process, and ensure that all the departments that support the process have the right metrics.

CHAPTER 3

Taking Ownership

CREATING A NEW ROLE FOR A PROCESS ORGANIZATION

The purpose of end-to-end process is to create a more logical and efficient framework for getting work done. But that work gets done by people, and those people have been accustomed to working in a certain way. That's especially true of managers. The people heading up functions such as marketing, engineering, and research have played important roles in their respective departments and have accumulated a certain amount of status and authority. Now along comes a process redesign that crosses departmental boundaries. None of the managers whose departments the process encompasses have natural responsibility for that process from beginning to end. And you can be sure that without ultimate responsibility, no one will take the responsibility of ensuring that the process performs as well as possible. That is why any effective process organization needs process owners.

A process owner's role is unfamiliar territory not only for the people doing the job but also for the organization. We know what a general manager is, what a CEO is, what a vice president of manufacturing is, and what a treasurer is, but nobody has ever heard of a process owner. And you can be sure that those managers whose departments are involved in the new process will be wary and skeptical. Here they were enjoying their authority and scheming how to get their boss's job, and along comes this person called a process owner who looks like competition. "What the hell is that all about?" is likely to be their first reaction.

What the role of process owner is all about centers on the design of work rather than the traditional management job of supervising people. It depends on exercising influence more than on having control; it demands advocacy rather than authority, and it focuses on fire prevention rather than fire-fighting. A process owner is not a firefighter but an architect who makes sure the fire doesn't start in the first place. Process owners are diplomats who use their intellect and imagination to break new ground. They have to have a tough hide, but most importantly, they must have the support of the top leadership. If the leaders don't sanction the position, it will die on the vine. The role of process owner is much less glamorous, much less sexy, but much more important than that of functional managers because it ties together the formerly separate silos that characterize the traditional organization. It's likely nobody has ever tried to do that before in your organization.

Of course, it's important that every person with a role in performing the process has to feel ownership and responsibility for the process and its results, as do their managers. Otherwise there is no escape from the world of "it's not my job" and passing the buck, of infighting and arguing and misalignment. So what does a process owner own? The design, nurturing, and evolution of the process.

In the simplest form a process owner has responsibility and authority for an end-to-end process across an organization. The process owner owns the design of the process, but not all the resources that comprise the process.

Let's take one important function in every business—the supply chain—and see how it plays out. The head of materials may be the process owner for the supply chain process that includes purchasing and inventory, but the heads of purchasing and inventory have their own people and budgets. The process owner has to work with them to make sure the process runs smoothly and efficiently. That's a very different job from the one held by the general manager of the supply chain, who traditionally had the heads of purchasing, materials, and inventory reporting to him. They still do for things such as resource allocation and performance evaluations, and they still have people reporting to them, but it's the process owner who makes sure the supply process is running smoothly and who, if it isn't, authorizes changes or a wholesale redesign of the process.

The role of process owner is very flexible. One can have the formal title of "process owner," but that isn't necessary. The process owner's job can be full-time, but it doesn't have to be. The process owner can have expertise in some aspect of the process, but that isn't necessary. Often someone from another area altogether makes a good process owner, as do general managers. The process owner can be a senior person in the organization, but doesn't have to be. It is necessary, however, that the process owner have some clout in the organization, if not by virtue of seniority then by virtue of outstanding performance and recognition.

The first and most important responsibility for a process owner is the design of the process. Without a design, there is no process; without a process owner to create and enforce it, there is no design. The process owner doesn't single-handedly design the process. Indeed, if the process owner is a senior person in the organization, it's best that she stay out of the design team's regular deliberations so that the team members will feel free to come up with lots of ideas, argue about them, and make their own decisions without the fear of appearing silly in front of a senior person or, worse, offending that person. The process owner should comment on the team's efforts periodically and will approve the final design. And once the process design is in place, only the process owner has authority to implement or change the design of the process. People throughout the organization, especially those performing it, can and should provide the process owner with input and ideas, but they can only act on those ideas if the process owner approves.

Even the finest design will not deliver the desired results if it is not properly executed. The process owner has the responsibility to ensure that the process is actually followed and to address execution problems that arise. Execution problems can come in many forms and flavors. They may be traceable to inadequately trained personnel, to malfunctioning systems or tools, to insufficient resources, or to a host of other causes. The process owner needs to determine if a performance problem is the result of a design flaw or an execution issue. If it is a design problem, the process is redesigned to fix it. A problem in execution might for example be solved through the use of such techniques as Six Sigma.

Because the role of process owner is new to you and your organization and changes the traditional ways that work is done and that people relate to one another, it might be helpful to watch a process owner in action before we move on to discuss some of the challenges surrounding the role of process owner and the methods and tools for solving them.

TRIMMING TREES

Benny McPeak is the quintessential "good ole boy," born and raised in Mt. Airy, North Carolina, the home of Andy Griffith and the prototype of the hamlet of Mayberry. Benny exudes easy southern charm, but his drawl masks a smart, disciplined manager with a graduate degree in electrical engineering. Until his recent retirement Benny worked at Duke Energy Company, one of the largest electric power producers in the country, for thirty-four years in roles of increasing responsibility. For the last ten years of his career, Benny was a process owner, one of the first people at any company to play this new role.

Benny owned the reliability and integrity process at Duke, and his authority extended across all five states in which Duke does business. In simple terms, the process was designed to make sure that the wires delivering power to Duke's customers stayed where they were put and did their job. The company measured its performance as "average outages per year per customer"—that is, how often a customer lost electric power. When Duke began working on this process, this figure stood very close to two outages per customer per year, and the company was committed to reduce those outages by 50 percent. At first blush, there does not seem to be much that can be done to reduce outages, since most are caused by storms and even the best process owner can't manage storms. But while storms may be the root cause of outages, trees falling on power lines are the immediate cause, and something can be done about that: the trees around power lines can be cut back so that if they do fall in a storm they won't bring the power lines down with them. When Duke began working on the reliability and integrity process and before it named a process owner, the company found that there was no process for tree trimming. Sure, trees were trimmed occasionally, but it was an ad hoc and reactive move, not a disciplined and repeatable process. The first step was to establish which steps were to be performed, by whom, with what tools, and on what schedule. Just that simple outline of what amounted to a rudimentary process brought outages down to 1.1 in just two years.

By the time Benny was formally named the process owner, the tree-trimming process was encountering problems. The original approach called for clear-cutting a thirty-foot path on either side of a power line. While customers appreciated not losing power, they did not appreciate having their trees butchered. Duke wasn't so happy, either. The clear-cutting process was costly, and a fixed budget for tree trimming limited the number of lines that could be maintained annually.

With his experience and self-confidence, Benny wasted no time tackling the challenge of redesigning the tree-trimming process. He didn't do the redesign himself. Instead, he put together a design team and gave them their charge: to improve customer satisfaction and reduce cost while maintaining the low level of outages. And they rose to the challenge. The redesigned process recognized that not all trees grow at the same rate—dogwoods grow a lot faster than poplars or oaks, for instance—and that only the trees that would grow into the lines before the next tree trimming needed to be dealt with. In the new process, a trained planner would walk the lines, decide which trees needed to be cut and by how much, and produce an engineered drawing of what needed to be done. This drawing could then be put out to competitive bid, which could not be done under the old process because crews didn't know what they would have to do until they arrived on the scene. As a result, public acceptance—always an important consideration to a public utility—increased because of the more natural look, and the cost per mile of tree trimming declined by more than 10 percent. This meant that for the same budget, the company was able to increase by 10 percent the number of lines that were cleared of trees each year, which further improved reliability. Note, by the way, that by selecting which trees to cut and having explicit directions that allowed competitive bidding, Duke was applying two important principles of process design: *whether* to cut some trees and *when* to cut them.

But over time conditions change and Benny began to notice that the costs of the tree-trimming program, which had been declining, were beginning to plateau. To find out why, he took to the field and discovered that although all the field units were following the process, they were executing it in different ways. This by itself is neither surprising nor unusual. A process design specifies what people are to do but gives them some latitude in how to do it; a process design is an outline of the work, not a procedure for executing it. However, as Benny found it, some Duke units were doing the process a lot better (i.e., less expensively) than others. Much of the work of this process was performed by contractors. Some units took care to ensure that contractors did not work near other utility lines because they would charge more given the need to exercise greater caution, while others did not; some units made sure that a site was ready before the contractor arrived to do work, and others did not, and some units were very diligent in checking contractor bills, while others were not. Rather than punish the poorly performing units, Benny created methods and incentives for them to improve. He paired high-performing groups with lower-performing ones and offered a bonus for groups that were able to improve their performance by learning and adopting the practices of their higher-performing counterparts. The tactic worked and costs resumed their decline. The lesson is that process owners cannot sit in an office and study performance scorecards; sometimes, as Benny puts it, you have to "put on your muddy shoes and go out and chase rabbits."

On another occasion Benny noticed that despite his terrific process, the average number of outages was creeping up. That wasn't supposed to happen! Again, he investigated and found that most of the increased outages were occurring in one specific geographical region that had a higher than average number of power lines and a lot more trees than other regions. Despite its best efforts and despite the fact that it was assiduously following the process, this region just could not keep up with the amount of tree trimming it should have been doing and the outages reflected that. The region did not have the financial resources it needed to do the amount of tree trimming that was needed. So Benny took an unusual step: he decided to increase the region's funding at the expense of another region.

Duke Energy was unusual, although not unique, in giving budget authority to its process owners. The company gave Benny the money needed to perform his process, and he doled it out, along with his process design, to the operating managers who headed the company's various regions. This is a very powerful, but not the only, solution to the problem of how to give process owners the clout they need to discharge the role.

Benny's research revealed that while the region with increasing outages didn't have enough money to implement needed tree trimming, another region had more than it needed and was using the extra funds in another area of operations. Benny ordered some money reallocated from the overfunded region to the underfunded region, which used the money to step up tree trimming and thus reduce outages. Average outages across the system once again declined. As you might expect, Benny's take-from-the-rich, give-to-the-poor tactic didn't sit well with the general manager of the overfunded region. He railed against it and against Benny but was ultimately powerless to do anything about it.

Benny's experience as a process owner contains some important lessons about process owners and process ownership. First is that the process owner must be savvy in the ways of the organization and must have some clout. Benny, like the head of the region who objected to his decision, reported to the head of the business. Benny also had been with Duke Energy for many years before becoming a process owner and had extensive experience in managing field operations. You couldn't fool Benny; he knew his way around the organization and the games that regional managers played. A junior person would not have been able to enforce a sensitive budget decision and would have become a sacrificial lamb.

The second lesson is that the process owner must have the full support of the most senior executive. In exercising authority, even on issues less sensitive than budget, a process owner inevitably intrudes on what other managers feel is their private domain. It is only a matter of time before one of those other managers decides to go to the mat or make an end run to the boss to get a process owner's decision overturned. If the top leaders of the organization won't back the process owner, the role becomes an empty shell.

MEETING THE CHALLENGES

It has probably already occurred to you that establishing effective working relationships between process owners and operating managers is one of the central challenges in making process ownership work. It requires an extraordinary degree of collaboration and teamwork. Most managers are all in favor of teamwork as long as it doesn't involve them. But they become a lot more enthusiastic about teamwork when they are rewarded based on shared goals and metrics. If you and I are both accountable for the results of process performance, even if we are nominally responsible for different things, we will find a way to make things work.

Teamwork is vital in implementing process ownership, but clarity about roles helps, too. Every company should establish ground rules about authority and decision making so that it is clear whose writ runs how far. Such ground rules are often framed in terms of what is called a decision rights matrix. One axis lists various managerial roles in the company, the other key decisions; the entries indicate who gets to make which decisions, who must be consulted or merely informed, who must approve, and so on.

The Decision Rights Matrix

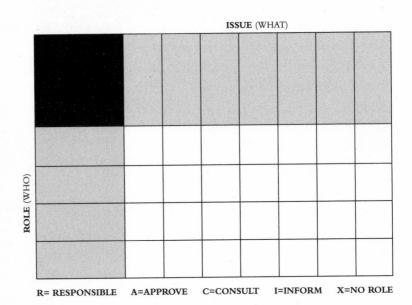

ISSUE (WHAT)

ROLE (WHO)

R= RESPONSIBLE   A=APPROVE   C=CONSULT   I=INFORM   X=NO ROLE

At Duke Energy, the issues included personnel assignments, work scheduling, resource allocation, process changes, and budgeting. Getting closure on these issues once and for all, though stressful, saves a lot of argument down the road.

Benny wielded the very big stick of budgetary control, but there are less dramatic ways, albeit somewhat less effective, of giving the process owner clout in the organization. One is to give process owners exclusive control of IT expenditures. That means only a process owner has an IT budget and can request system development or system modifications from the IT organization. This puts real handcuffs on operating managers who are considering defying the process owner and his or her process. The rebels have no means of obtaining a system to support the way they want work to be done.

Another is giving the process owner authority to specify the performance metrics that operating organizations must use when reporting results of their performance. Inadequate performance in terms of these metrics will draw the process owners' attention. If the organization is adhering to the process and reporting subpar metrics, the process owner may need to change some aspect of the process or even resort to a redesign of the process. But poor performance may also indicate and penalize those who don't follow the process. Indeed, organizations that aren't following the process probably won't even be able to express their performance in terms of the specified metrics, which can be tightly linked to the specifics of the process design. For example, a metric for a sales process might be the percentage of deals getting to stage two of the process, which is a performance descriptor only meaningful to those following it. Taking steps like these amount to giving the process owner control over more columns in the decision rights matrix.

Dialog is a simple way for smoothing the relationship between those who design processes and those who carry them out. Rather than setting targets and approving a design alone, a process owner should invite functional managers to critique and comment on a process design before it is approved. This assumes, of course, that everyone is acting in good faith and not trying to sabotage the process. That's where backing from the organization's senior leadership is critical. Functional managers have to know that they will be working in the process and that their future depends on working in it willingly.

Some companies are creating advisory groups, consisting of managers and/or people from the front lines who carry out the process, to provide input to the process owner. They are the process owner's eyes and ears, alerting her to difficulties and issues even before they show up in formal metrics. The advisory groups also provide a sanity check, giving process owners frank assessments of envisioned design changes or other initiatives before the process owner becomes committed to them. Perhaps most importantly, these groups represent a mechanism for ensuring that operating managers and personnel feel their voices are heard by the process owners and that they are not merely the process owner's victims.

ENVISIONING THE PROCESS

Fully implementing a process takes time measured not just in weeks but in months and sometimes even in years. To stay on track, a process owner must have a vision for the process and a plan for realizing that vision. When in 2001 Rick Magoun became the first process owner at Clorox he created a three-year journey map for the order-to-cash process that he owned. The order-to-cash process essentially captures an entire transaction from the time the customer places an order to the time the company is paid for delivering the goods. Rick's journey map specified the level of performance for the metrics that the order-to-cash process was to achieve in each of the coming three years, including on-time delivery, error-free order receipt, and forecast accuracy. The map became the basis for an annual action plan and a monthly scorecard of process performance. Using these tools, Rick knew where he wanted to go, how he was going to get there, and the progress he was making. As process owner, Rick had to orchestrate and oversee the various teams making either step changes to the process design or making fixes to its performance. His monthly scorecard told him whether things were on track, and his annual action plan gave him a framework for managing the projects as a whole. Under Rick's leadership, the order-to-cash process achieved true breakthrough results: the percentage of perfect orders (orders filled completely and on time, and for which the customer paid on time) went up more than 300 percent even as costs went down.

Every process owner should have a plan like Rick's. But the plan is useless without the resources to carry it out. Getting those resources is a real test of the process owner's persuasive powers. The process owner has to speak for the process in order to get it the attention and resources it needs. A process owner will, at best, have a small staff. Most of the people working on process initiatives will have to be supplied by others, and such people are in short supply and highly valued where they are. Thus the process owner is an unusual blend of an engineer and a salesperson, adept at analysis and planning but also a forceful spokesperson.

Many companies find the role of process owner too much for one person to fill, especially when the process extends across the company and the owner is a senior executive. A common solution is to divide the role into two parts: an executive process owner, sometimes called a process leader, and an operational process owner, sometimes called a process manager. At Rich Products, the executive process owner role is filled by people such as the president of the consumer brands division and the senior vice president of operations. While their day jobs keep them more than busy running each process, they also have bottom line accountability for processes. They advocate for it, make the annual plan for achieving their goals, obtain the resources needed to execute the plan, and take ownership of the outcomes. In other words, they are on the hook for these processes. The operational process owner is a step lower in the organization and acts as the field general, closer to the action, who carries out the plans for redesign and improvement.

PROCESS OWNERSHIP IN LARGE
OR COMPLEX COMPANIES

Process ownership at its heart is a very simple idea: have someone manage work on an end-to-end basis across organizational boundaries. It can appear complex, as you will see momentarily, because larger organizations must create layers of process owners. Merck, for example, has three major end-to-end business processes that capture the essence of what a pharmaceutical company must do: create new drugs (the Discover and Develop process), deal with customers (the Manage Customer Demand process), and distribute the product (the Supply Product process).

Each of these processes has its own process owner. And since these processes are so large and extensive they are broken down into subprocesses. One subprocess for Discover and Develop is called Conduct Trials and Regulatory Activities to Support Product Lifecycle. For simplicity we'll just call it "Conduct Trials."

Conduct Trials is part of Merck's effort to develop new drugs and conduct the studies that gather the data to prove to the FDA and to physicians that the drug should be approved and used. Conduct Trials is an end-to-end process that is comprised of tasks performed in different parts of the Merck organization.

The process owner of Conduct Trials is Janet Keyser, a veteran of many years of service at Merck. She started as a toxicology biologist, processed data from clinical trials, wrote protocols for trials, and headed the organization that supplies the materials to investigators who conduct trials of Merck's compounds. She has lived much of the Conduct Trials process, and her responsibility as process owner is to make sure that the process performs as well as possible.

The four thousand people involved in the process don't

work "for" Janet in the traditional sense of reporting to her, but they must follow her process. She owns none of the resources, so she is only able to get things done through influence and the use of process metrics. The meetings she holds with the functional managers who perform the work of her process, in which they review process metrics, are in her words "tense and not fun." She works hard to get these functional managers to see past their own silos to focus on the process as a whole and get outcomes—that is, getting new approved drugs faster, cheaper, and better.

One of the biggest challenges she has faced is getting people accustomed to the fact that only she, as process owner, can make changes to the process. The functional heads who are executing the process cannot change it. The functional areas must learn to move from being decision makers to being stakeholders. While they all have an interest—career, financial, ego—in how the process works, they cannot control it, and that isn't always easy for a manager or even for the people within the manager's department to swallow. As Mark Twain observed, "Habit is habit, and not to be flung out the window but coaxed downstairs one step at a time."

Conduct Trials, while a subprocess of the Discover and Develop process, has nine of its own subprocesses, including Planning, Delivery, and Destruction of Clinical and Ancillary Supplies (Planning and Delivery). Each of those nine subprocesses is a cross-functional, end-to-end process with a process owner.

Thus Janet is a ringmaster of a nine-ring circus. She has to make sure that the right work is going on in each ring and that the acts don't bump into each other. Each subprocess owner comes up with projects; Janet's job is to decide which have the greatest priority, get funding and figure out how to fit it into other projects of Conduct Trials.

The Planning and Delivery process gets the necessary

supplies to the doctors in the field doing trials of Merck drugs. In addition to the drugs, the physicians may need other supplies as well, such as cookbooks and bathroom scales for testing a drug to combat obesity. In the past, the scientists designing the trials would purchase and ship these supplies. It wasn't a good use of their time, nor were they good at it. Now this process is done by a group of procurement experts. And instead of shipping the supplies to fifty-two subsidiaries around the world, which would then reship them to the physicians, Merck mostly ships directly to the doctors. They may be obvious changes, but the results have included millions of dollars in savings, better use of people's time, and more consistent availability of needed supplies. Until Planning and Delivery was recognized as a process and provided with a process owner, there was no one with the perspective, authority, or incentive to make it perform better. It was just a nagging problem that everyone knew about but no one did anything about.

Janet is in effect a program manager, orchestrating a large number of projects, and, as you might expect, she is structured and disciplined. She employs a scoring system to assess the project ideas that come to her, since the number of ideas always exceeds the amount of resources available. Projects that are needed to achieve regulatory compliance go to the top of the list, as do small-scale projects that can be done quickly and require no IT resources. Other assessment criteria include the impact on the process's strategic objectives, the cost and risk associated with the project, and the ability of the affected business areas to absorb the change the project will require. Every process owner needs such mechanisms for deciding how to allocate resources to achieve the process performance objectives. There are real similarities between the work of a process owner and how modern product development is carried out, including portfolio management (deciding which products to work on, monitoring their progress, and making adjustments as needed) and project execution (doing the actual work of creating the product).

Just to be sure you understand the complexity that a process owner like Janet oversees, let's list her major responsibilities:

1. Create and implement a design for the process
2. Ensure compliance with the process
3. Measure process performance in terms of designated metrics
4. Decide the level of performance required by customers and the strategy of the enterprise
5. Formulate a plan for realizing the required level of performance through redesign and improvement projects
6. Commission teams to conduct these projects, track their progress, and intervene as necessary
7. Review results of the projects against performance goals and make appropriate changes to the process

Doing all those things through a process structure is far more effective—faster, cheaper, better—than the traditional way most other companies would do them.

THE LOCAL PROCESS OWNER

As a process owner at Merck, Janet oversaw thousands of people working in many different locations. But processes take place within specific locations, too, and because of that there is yet another variant of the process owner role: the local process owner. Think of a large company with many different locations, all over the country or even all over the world. Now pick one of these facilities and think about one of the processes being performed there. Certainly that process can have an owner like Janet, working hundreds or even thousands of miles away. But who looks after the process, measuring its performance, ensuring it is being followed, answering questions about the process and recognizing problems with the process and bringing them to the attention of the distant process owner? The local process owner, or LPO.

The local process owner is the overall process owner's deputy, representing her at a particular location. By and large, the LPO is not going to design the process. Letting every local process owner design a local version of the process is a good definition of chaos. Rather, the LPO focuses on helping the performers at the site perform the process as it should be done.

Here are some of the specific responsibilities of a local process owner:

- Ensuring that appropriate resources are allocated to the process
- Ensuring that the process is followed and delivers the needed results
- Measuring local performance
- Identifying and solving local performance problems
- Making sure that process documentation and training materials are kept up to date and available
- Learning best practices from other locations and bringing them into this one
- Coaching the people who perform the process and answering their questions
- Suggesting improvements to the overall process owner

Let's take a look now at how a local process owner executes those responsibilities. Shell Oil's Downstream business has some $100 billion in annual sales, with thirty-four refineries and six chemical plants around the world, and some 70,000 employees. Shell is aggressively using end-to-end business processes to transform its performance. It has identified six top-level processes, each of which has a global process owner. These processes are then implemented at each refinery and plant by local process owners.

One of Shell's top-level processes is Manufacture. It is implemented at local levels by a process called Ensure Safe Production (ESP). Ensure Safe Production covers the work done by refinery operating people from the time they arrive until they leave at the end of their shift. ESP includes shift handover, shift orientation (recognizing how things are running), and alarm management (understanding and responding to the alarms that are raised when something goes awry). Shell found that this work was being done in many different ways in different refineries, and often differently by different shifts in the same refinery. With highly combustible materials being processed under very high pressure, a refinery is not a place where you want to see a lot of variations in how work is performed. So Shell's Ensure Safe Production process owner created a standardized design that is now implemented in all of Shell's refineries and plants.

Brett Woltjen is the local process owner for ESP at the Deer Park refinery, some twenty miles east of Houston. Deer Park is a huge facility that spreads over many acres; it employs more than a thousand people and turns some 350,000 barrels of oil into refined products such as gasoline every day. A little arithmetic shows that this is a substantial business indeed. Brett is a member of Deer Park's nine-person leadership team and is officially the site's production manager. That means the people involved in running Deer Park's machinery, and their managers, ultimately report to him. He is also the site process owner for ESP. While the people who perform ESP do report to Brett, the people who do the other processes do not.

Brett's role as a local process owner involves wielding influence, not power, and is not so much devoting a specific amount of time to a specific activity as being sure that the process design works at Deer Park—that the people who perform it and who report to their own functional managers understand it and buy into it. He also measures and assesses the performance of the process and looks for ways to make it better. Implementing a process includes, but is not limited to, installing the systems and tools and training the performers. At Deer Park it involved physically moving people around so that people from different departments who work on the process together are in the same place. Brett also ensures that people are complying with the process and demonstrating the right behaviors. For example, in a lot of manufacturing plants, when a shift changes, the people on the old shift run for the exits. The ESP process design requires that they do an explicit review of the status of operations with the incoming shift before they leave. Otherwise a problem might not be handled correctly. This is a change from "now it's their problem" to "it's our problem," and one that not every operator at Deer Park was able to make very easily. Brett had to describe in very clear terms what behaviors he expected, check to see if these behaviors were being exhibited, and coach and counsel and reward to get them. If there is some lack of clarity as to what the process requires, or when there are differences or disputes between process performers, Brett steps into the breach.

Brett has also had to deal with the inevitable discomfort of front-line people being asked to change their work patterns and their behaviors. For example, the new ESP process required that operators in the refinery control room actively monitor a list of performance variables and track their trends. A senior foreman, a thirty-five-year veteran of the plant, didn't seem enthusiastic about this new process until Brett helped him see that the new process really would help operators recapture the ability to have an intuitive overview of refinery performance, something that they used to have in the old days of pneumatic instruments and that had largely been lost when computer systems were introduced.

Another tactic that Brett has used is spending less time talking about the process in abstract terms and more discussing the concrete goals that following the process will achieve, such as improved safety, something everyone favors. Yet Brett has had to reassign or let go some people who could not or would not adopt the behaviors the new process demanded.

Perhaps the most important aspect of becoming a local process owner required Brett to change his own point of view and management style. "It was a shift to leading the organization using processes and metrics, leveraging the metrics and using them to coach the organization instead of fighting the fire or the issue of the day and then running over to fight the next fire," he said. He also had to become a teacher, learning the process well enough that he could teach it to others. Along the way he found the wisdom of the Japanese proverb "To teach is to learn." Teaching the process allowed him to develop a better insight into how it works.

Okay, we've hit you with quite a few new terms: process owners, subprocess owners, executive process owners, operational process owners, local process owners. You may be excused for thinking this process owner stuff is complicated. Actually, it is as only as complicated as it needs to be. Remember that you are essentially breaking down large processes into smaller processes. If you have a smaller organization operating mostly in one location, you may be able to get by combining all these roles into a single job. However, if you are a large, complex company with many locations, such as Merck or Shell Downstream, you are going to need all these roles. But whether the job is filled by many people or just one, the value that the process owner brings to the organization is the same: designing a process, implementing it, teaching it, enforcing it, measuring it, fixing its problems, replacing it when necessary, and above all, making sure that the process delivers the results the enterprise needs.

THE PRINCIPLES OF PROCESS OWNERSHIP

As this chapter has explained in some detail, the definition of a process owner is flexible, but it always involves an end-to-end process that crosses two or more functional areas of management responsibility. In the broadest sense, the process owner does process design or redesign, handles operational planning for the process, leads improvement initiatives, and solves problems with the process while the operational manager manages performers and leads the performance of process. How the intersection of process and function is handled goes a long way toward determining how much benefit the organization derives from a process approach to work. With that in mind, the following list lays out some of the responsibilities and obligations of process owners and functional managers.

The Process Owner's Responsibilities and Authority
- To be accountable for the design of the process, for ensuring its successful execution, and for its continuous improvement
- To design, document, publish, and develop training content, supporting tools, and/or templates for the process
- To identify and monitor metrics against which process performance can be measured
- To use metrics and audit results to evaluate compliance and continuously improve the process
- To understand relevant internal and external benchmarks and use them to identify and drive process improvements
- To ensure that all process participants understand their role and how they fit into the end-to-end design

- To identify, prioritize, and govern changes to the process
- To establish and evaluate metrics to monitor the health of the process
- To evaluate external benchmarks
- To ensure adherence of the organization to the process
- To resolve issues within the process to help ensure that the process executes as designed

The Operating Manager's Responsibilities and Authority

- To know the process and its upstream and downstream effects
- To ensure training of staff in understanding and executing relative to the process
- To ensure consistent execution of the process
- To dedicate appropriate resources to execution
- To provide local support evaluation of process or execution problems

Senior Management's Obligations

- To position process ownership as a senior role in the organization
- To fill the process owner position with a powerful and respected individual
- To provide process owners with the full support of top management
- To help the process owner adapt to a new style of managing
- To be absolutely clear about the relationships and divisions of responsibilities and authority between process owners and operating managers
- To give process owners real power and tools for wielding their authority

PROCESS OWNERSHIP DOS AND DON'TS

- Do have the leadership sanction, legitimize, and announce the creation of the process owner role and the authority it will have.
- Do select leaders for the role of process owner who are influential in the organization, with not only a span of control but also a span of influence.
- Do give the process owner full authority over the design, including choosing the design team and setting the performance targets.
- Do ensure that the metrics used to evaluate the process owner's performance are aligned with the corporate key performance indicators and are balanced between the voice of the customer and voice of the business.

- Don't allow the process owner to delegate the role to subprocess owners or direct reports.
- Don't assume that the process owner role has to be full-time and be reflected as a new position on the organizational chart, although that is an option.
- Don't forget that the functional managers own the resources and therefore are critical to the implementation of the process owner's design and should not be neglected.
- Don't forget to align the functional managers' metrics with the process owner's metrics to ensure they are closely integrated for optimal performance.
- Don't simply keep the same structure and call functional managers process owners.

CHAPTER 4

Performers and Infrastructure

GETTING END-TO-END WORK DONE

R emember Bob, the corporate hero profiled in the introduction? Nice guy, but in a company where processes
are structured correctly, there is no room for heroes like Bob.
Instead, the company overflows with professionals. Now, there
are lots of definitions of the word *professional*, some of which
require academic qualifications or even licenses. But the definition of *professional* that applies most aptly to the world of
process comes from the unlikely venue of Hollywood. You
may never have seen the 1984 movie *Body Heat*, starring Kath-
leen Turner, William Hurt, and Richard Crenna, and even if
you have, you probably wouldn't call it a classic. Yet in the
movie William Hurt and Richard Crenna become embroiled
in a debate about what it means to be a professional. Ultimately they conclude that a professional is someone who does
what it takes, as opposed to an ordinary worker, who does
what he's told.

Perfect! A worker worries most about what the boss thinks,
focuses on limited tasks, and has little authority to change what
is done or the way it is done. His job security and income

121

depend upon the boss's approval. A professional, in contrast, focuses on outcomes and customers and has broad latitude to do what needs to be done to ensure that the company gets and keeps happy customers. A professional understands the concept that the company's health and the individual's job security is in the hands of the customers, not the bosses.

Creating a cadre of professionals at every level in the company is what this chapter is about. Much depends, of course, on the selection of the right people. But it is equally important that those people be given the tools to do process work and have their performance measured in ways that ensure the process is working. Process work is very different from how most people have done their jobs. You will be taking people out of an environment in which they merely performed tasks. When you perform a task you don't need to know much—you don't care about outcomes, the business climate, or how the guy working next door is measured. Sure, lots of companies talk about teamwork, but they're usually confusing real teamwork with having lots of meetings and working well with others. In real teamwork the intersections of activities and responsibilities tend to overlap because everyone is aligned with the same goal: making the customer happy. In process work it isn't the least bit unusual for self-directed teams to pop up seemingly out of the blue to get something done. But for that to happen the people doing process work need the right design for the process, a design that automatically bridges barriers. Probably the single most forbidding barrier is budgetary. Budgets can make people do crazy things because it is a key metric of performance.

Consider a utility with a planning department that figures out how to connect new businesses or homes to the grid and a rights-of-way department that negotiates with other businesses or homeowners to get access for the necessary cables to run to the new customers. In a traditional organization each department works separately and has a separate budget. Managers are rewarded or punished in part by whether they come in under or over their budget and they do all sorts of things to get on the right side of the budget ledger. But in a process organization, as we will see momentarily, there will be one person, a caseworker, handling both the planning and the rights-of-way negotiations. Who pays for that person? The answer usually is both departments, but someone in leadership of the organization, a senior executive, has to make the decision of how much of the case worker's salary and benefits comes from each department. One department is almost certain to feel that it is bearing too much of the cost, but in a process environment everyone recognizes that some departments must carry more of a burden than others for the good of the enterprise. And, by the way, managers are rewarded or punished not so much by whether they come in or over their own budget (although that may be a factor, too) as by how well the overall enterprise performs. That's what we mean by infrastructure. It is the sum total of the various mechanisms—budget, training and development tools, evaluation, compensation, and information technology, among others—that are necessary to make process work move along smoothly. And yes, the changes in your organization's infrastructure that you will be making to implement process work are enormous. But anything less will fall short of the optimal benefits that process can bestow.

POWER TO THE PEOPLE

Before we get into the details of a business composed entirely of professionals and show how to develop the environment to support them, let's take a look at the difference it can make in a company's performance on behalf of its customers. We'll use an electric utility in Great Britain that was having a hard time getting new houses in suburban developments hooked up to the electric grid in a timely manner. The old process began when a developer or builder called the utility and was directed to customer service. The customer service rep filled out the request for electrical service, specifying the location and other details. That form then went to the manager of the planning department, who assigned a staffer to draw up a plan for getting power lines from the nearest substation to the new construction location. That plan then went to the manager of the rights-of-way department, who assigned one of his staff members to go out and negotiate with the landowners between the substation and the construction site to get permission to drag cables across their property. When the necessary permissions had been granted, the plan was sent along to the manager of the construction department, who assigned a crew chief to put together a construction team with the right mix of skills to do the job. The crew chief also was responsible for overseeing the execution of the project, from the purchase of the necessary cables to the installation of the distributed wires to the new houses. Only then was the plan sent to the metering department, which assigned a crew to go to the site and connect cables to each individual house and install a meter to measure electrical consumption. A typical installation took about six months.

Was six months a reasonable amount of time for such a project? The builders who had to wait that long to get power to their projects certainly didn't think so. But were they right? A very simple equation—value time (VT) divided by elapsed time (ET)—answers the question. If in a typical installation the total time that elapsed (ET) was 180 days and 178 of those days were spent on hard labor contributing to the end result (VT), the equation would yield a quotient close to 1, which is the ideal. The builders would have no cause for complaint. But that wasn't the case with our electric utility. The value time typically amounted to about 20 days. In other words, it took the utility 180 days to do 20 days of work. The rest of the time was consumed as requests sat on some manager's desks before they were assigned to people who had other projects going on and let the request sit some more. After each department finally did its part of the job, the request was sent back to sit again until the relevant manager signed off on it and sent it along the way. And what if someone should make a mistake! Then the process had to start all over again. It's easy to see how the VT/ET equation produced a quotient of just .11, abysmal by any measure and rightly the target of the builders' anger and complaints.

Of course, the utility was well aware it had a problem. It did what most companies do under those circumstances: throw more people at it. Great. Now we have even more people looking over other people's shoulders, reviewing plans and generally bogging down the connection process even further. As things got worse instead of better, the top brass laid down the law to each department head: fix it or else! A few months later all the department heads claimed they had fixed their part of the process. But it was still taking six months to hook up new houses!

Finally the utility executives realized something was deeply wrong and decided to essentially start from scratch and review the entire connection process, from developer contact with the company to power on. When a design team mapped the utility's process for making new connections it became obvious that the process was way too complicated. There was a screamingly obvious lack of coordination. There were multiple rework loops, redundant activities and days upon days of simply waiting for approvals from each of the bosses of various functional silos. It became very clear why customers were complaining. Each customer was passed off to so many people that there was no continuity and therefore no one who fully understood what the customer needed. Here's what the faulty process looked like:

The Old Process Design

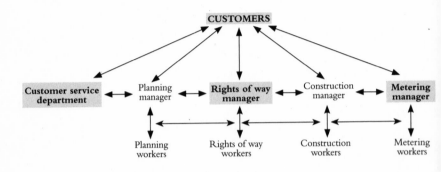

Now that the utility had a clear picture of what was wrong, it set about fixing the problem by redesigning the process from top to bottom. Out of that redesign emerged a new position, that of "caseworker." The caseworker job grew out of customers' demands for a single point person and the utility's simple recognition that all the tasks in the process were deeply interconnected. Unlike a process owner, who serves as an executive with strategic oversight of a large-scale process, a caseworker position is a tactical, hands-on job that focuses on a relatively small process or subprocess. In the utility the caseworker is a single person responsible for shepherding a customer's request for new electric service through the entire process until the power goes on. The caseworker develops the plan, negotiates the right of way, assembles the team, and ensures that the work is done. The result is much less dead time because the request is not sitting on a variety of desks awaiting action or approval. More importantly, though, the caseworker understands the needs of the construction crew as well as what is needed for negotiation. In other words, the caseworker has a better end-to-end view. As a result, the plan that is developed is more accurate from the first draft. The caseworker, with the backing of senior executives and the process owner, also has the authority to call in subject matter experts, such as lawyers, to assist in complex situations. Augmenting the caseworker is a new position, field technician, that combines the tasks of constructing the system and installing the meters. Focusing on value time and giving the workers more authority and responsibility reduced the 180-day cycle time to approximately 23 days. The number of people required to do a typical installation dropped by two-thirds, providing the company the flexibility and scalability to take on additional work without hiring new people. They instead retrained and repurposed those who were previously dedicated to single tasks.

Clearly the caseworker's job description is no longer that of a mere cog in the earlier process. The caseworker has more autonomy and responsibility as well as accountability. The work is more complex, involving planning, crew selection, and crew management. The goal is straightforward: customer satisfaction. The caseworker doesn't wear different hats one at a time, but instead wears multiple hats simultaneously. Handoffs are far fewer. The field technicians, who were deemed construction workers under the old structure and performed one or two tasks repetitively, now perform a variety of tasks in jobs that are broader, more complex, more challenging, and far more interesting. In the old scheme there were so many handoffs and people involved that if someone made a mistake, it might not have been noticeable. Now a mistake is almost instantly visible and the responsible party easy to identify. But rather than playing a fruitless blame game, the mistake gets fixed, a lesson is learned, and future results will improve.

That isn't to say that the redesign was smooth. Candidates for the new caseworker positions were largely identified by their bosses based on what customers had to say about the people they enjoyed working with. Much of the selection was based on who had showed the aptitude to learn different elements of the business in the past. Most worked out. But there were some who didn't like working directly with customers, preferring to work behind the scenes.

Because this was a new position, the training of caseworkers was ad hoc at first, a combination of classroom and on-the-job training. But as caseworkers matured in their jobs and the company began to really understand their value in expediting the process, the caseworkers themselves began to nominate colleagues for positions and helped train them. It wasn't long before human resources, eager not to be left behind, jumped in and began developing profiles of what made a successful caseworker and creating formal training courses in the various aspects of the connection process, including engineering design and negotiation.

One of the most fundamental changes for the caseworkers was the measurement and reward system. They were no longer measured and compensated based on just their tasks. The largest percentage of their compensation came from the timeliness of completion and customer satisfaction. And it wasn't just the direct boss who evaluated the caseworker, but others in the organization who had both direct and indirect interaction with the caseworker.

Managers had to deal with a new world, too. Some of the more traditional, authoritarian ones couldn't adapt to the more collegial interdepartmental teamwork or to the idea that the caseworkers were now performing work that the managers believed was their purview. In fact, though, the managers hadn't actually been *doing* the work; they had merely told others to do it. Now the caseworker had all the necessary information to pull together everyone needed to accomplish the goal. Rather than managers telling people what to do, there was a team of professionals just getting the job done.

The managers were no longer needed in their old role. Some left voluntarily, and others were fired. The managers who did adapt emerged with a new role, that of coaching the professional teams. They removed roadblocks, helped the professionals develop the right skill sets and attitudes, set metrics, and ensured that the company held fast to the implementation of the design. The managers who saw and understood the results of the changes became enthusiastic supporters. Some became caseworkers themselves and, in recognition of their seniority and previous accomplishments under the old system, were assigned to bigger, higher-value customers. A few opted to return to such specialties as accounting or engineering and provide expertise to the caseworkers.

Here is what the new process looks like:

The New Process Design

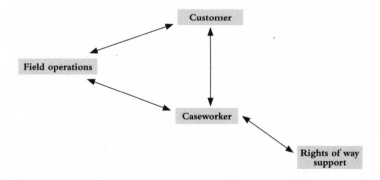

This is what we mean when we talk about converting mere workers into professionals, a hybrid breed of employee who not only does the work but manages the work as well, with all the requisite decision-making authority, responsibility, and accountability that implies.

Faster, cheaper, better.

A NEW KIND OF PERSON

It should be obvious now that staffing a process designed for high performance with conventional task workers won't be very effective. It isn't because employees are unable or unwilling to do a good job. Rather, the way most systems are designed and the way most workers are measured prevent them from doing anything but the most simplistic and focused tasks. A company redesigning its processes for high performance needs a new kind of person, with new capabilities to carry out the most complex tasks of a process-centric organization. The right kind of people will be focused not on the boss but on the customer; not on individual performance but on team performance; not on the task but on the outcome. Most of us won't have the luxury of creating a workforce from scratch by choosing only those people who will easily understand and adapt to the demands of a high-performance process organization. But it does happen occasionally, and the results illustrate the immense potential of hiring or creating professionals.

The traditional approach to hiring is to identify a need and hire someone with the skills and experience to do that job, preferably at the lowest cost possible. A process-centric organization doesn't worry a lot about skills and experience. Instead, it takes the approach "draft the athlete, teach the game." In other words, hiring for *attitude* and *aptitude* becomes the strategic approach to finding the right individuals for an organization. The mechanics of the various jobs can be taught easily enough to someone with the right attitude and aptitude.

Finding people with the right attitude is the most difficult of the two criteria to fill. Attitude isn't usually a factor in traditional job interviews. As long as a candidate is polite, prepared, and professional, there isn't much more evaluation for attitude. It's also hard to test for attitude, and most companies don't know the truth about new hires for perhaps the first six months or year of their employment.

But discovering attitude is an important part of hiring for a process organization. It helps that process organizations usually put a candidate through interviews with several people involved in a specific process. The ideal candidate would have two outstanding qualities, known colloquially as "plays well with others" and "runs with scissors." Teamwork and the ability to think outside the box are critical but often scarce attitudes. Employees in traditional silo organizations are conditioned to want to stand out, perform, and get noticed as individuals. They seek ego gratification and advancement, most often to their boss's job. Rarely do such employees cross over into other departments where they might not be able to excel. But those who do cross over may be just the kind of people you need. They often see the big picture and are adept at working across functional boundaries. They acquire a reputation within the organization for accomplishments, vision, and implementation. They are ideal process owners.

Most companies preach the gospel of teamwork to their employees. But companies that adopt a process orientation often are shocked to find that many of their employees are *not* team players. That doesn't mean that they don't work well with others, but it is hard to convince people to put aside individual recognition and advancement because they will be working as a team and measured and rewarded as a team. If we had to name the characteristics of these people the list would include working with others, helping others, focusing on results, being hardworking, working for the greater good, desiring to learn and excel, eager to work out issues, able to handle constructive criticism, to be good listeners and communicators, a willingness to be an "unsung hero," ambitious but not to the detriment of others, and assertive but not aggressive. How's that for the dream employee?

Aptitude is more about the ability to learn and tends to differ among organizations. A financially focused job requires an aptitude for understanding math, accounting, financial statements, and financial relationships, while a utility or science-based position requires relevant technical skills. But aptitude also includes an ability to understand what others in the organization do. An employee might not need to be able to parse a financial statement, but she has to understand how financial people work and the role they play in the organization's success.

Hills Pet Nutrition, the maker of Science Diet pet food, is a process-centric company with the bottom-line results to prove the value of process. When the company built a new plant in Richmond, Indiana, it took the aptitude/attitude approach to hiring to fill three hundred jobs. The advertising for the new jobs probably seemed a little confusing to the people of Richmond because it emphasized teamwork and explicitly stated that no factory experience was necessary. With more than a thousand resumes, the plant manager and human resources staff sifted through the stack looking for people with the kinds of backgrounds that indicated they were highly motivated and had the ability to learn new ways of doing things. Among the new hires were teachers, who are, after all, accustomed to being in a learning environment and helping their classroom charges work well together. Police officers were hired, too. They know all about following rules (which is what process is all about), think fast, and are skilled at working together to protect one another in dangerous situations. But perhaps the most unusual background among the new hires were people with military experience, and not just any military experience. Several new employees had served in the U.S. Navy on submarines and turned out to be great employees. After all, if you work on a submarine you have been deeply immersed (pun intended) in process, cross-trained to do other jobs should a

fellow crewman become sick or injured, highly aware of the
need and benefits of teamwork, and well versed in rapid and
effective problem solving. After all, if a disagreement arises on
a submarine, nobody is going to step outside to work out their
differences.

We don't mean to imply that every company that adopts a
process-centric structure should go out and hire teachers, cops,
and submariners. The only point is that when you look for
attitude and aptitude, there's no telling where you will find it.

THE 20-60-20 RULE

Most companies on the journey to becoming a process-centric
organization won't have the luxury of hiring an entirely new
workforce. Don't worry, that isn't really a problem. As you
move toward process work you will be amazed at the number
of diamonds in the rough among your employees. It is true
that many people resist change and that redesigning a company's process represents huge change. Reporting structures
change, job descriptions and titles change, responsibilities and
accountability change, and compensation and reward systems
are different. Nevertheless, the right kind of people among
your employees will, once they realize the immense benefits
to be derived from redesigning processes, find exciting opportunities for themselves. They will realize that performing a job
that is more complex, broader, adaptable, and capable of adding tremendous value not only will be stimulating but will do
more than anything else to guarantee their jobs. No longer
will they be a mere cog in a wheel; rather, they're the wheel
itself. They will find themselves making a material difference
both at their company and for their customers.

Over the years we have found that when a company initially undertakes the transformation to a high-performance,

process-based central structure, it discovers the 20–60–20 rule. About 20 percent of your employees will love the process approach. They're the ones who enjoy change and thrive in an innovative environment. They typically are volunteers for new initiatives and are promoted or considered for new assignments often, and do each one well. They get excited about change and often are frustrated with the status quo, aren't afraid to speak up in meetings, and have a constant stream of new and creative ideas, even when their past ideas have been shot down. They usually make it a point to know many people outside of their organization because they want to appeal to as many as possible for their ideas or change. Those with many contacts in the organization and whose ideas and opinions are respected can become leaders of the transformation if they are in senior positions, or caseworkers if they are lower in the hierarchy. Not everyone in the company is going to be on board, and a person who can influence others to get excited and join the team is invaluable. Grab them. They usually make excellent designers on the design teams or great internal consultants. But be warned: if you don't use their enthusiasm and skills, and reward and acknowledge them appropriately, they will be discouraged. And if your company for some reason abandons the process initiative, they will start looking for greener pastures elsewhere. Economic circumstances will dictate how many leave. Obviously, if the economy is mired in the doldrums it will be more difficult to find other opportunities, but we know from experience that in a growing economy or in a healthy industry these idealistic activists can and do get jobs in organizations better equipped to make use of their talent and enthusiasm.

At the outset another 20 percent will hate it no matter how logically you explain its benefits or how clearly you demonstrate the results. Either they simply don't get it and fear the effect it will have on their jobs, or they just hate the idea of change. Many will endure and, over time, become effective workers in a process environment. Some of those with a negative attitude will leave the organization voluntarily over time because of their own discomfort, lack of skills, or lack of interest in working in a process environment that demands teamwork, responsibility, and accountability. That's fine. You can replace them with people more likely to thrive in a process environment.

The ones who you really need to worry about are the tiny portion among the unwilling who become saboteurs. Some saboteurs are obvious. They're constantly complaining or pointing out how things were better the old way. But some remain in disguise. They'll say the right things in the meetings, in front of the boss, or in public, but in reality they are working to derail the effort. Surprisingly, you will sometimes find these "onboard terrorists" among people who have been identified in the traditional environment as high potentials and wield some measure of influence. To them teamwork means they might have to share the limelight. They fear getting lost in the crowd and not being recognized, rewarded, or promoted based on their performance. They've also become comfortable with the current methods and measures and they've mastered them, part of what makes them successful in the traditional environment. Changing disrupts what they feel they've worked so hard for. A case in point is Gary, the vice president of manufacturing at a electronics maker. Gary was a genuinely pleasant person, quiet and thoughtful. He had been brought into the company to turn around a failing factory and had succeeded, which earned him the post he held. When the company decided to move toward process work as a way to reinvigorate growth, Gary seemed to be on the bandwagon. At meetings he would make mostly positive comments, but he would usually also voice a "concern" about some facet of process work. It took many months, but it eventually became apparent that Gary was protecting employees loyal to him who weren't good performers.

Instead of becoming part of the process team, they wanted to do things their own way, and Gary's "concerns" provided cover for that quiet rebellion. Only when the CEO began to notice that manufacturing was becoming a roadblock to the process transformation did the company take a closer look at Gary's performance in the context of process. He was soon gone, and an engineer who had become an outstanding advocate of process became the vice president of manufacturing.

As this example illustrates, onboard terrorists can be very subtle in their efforts to sabotage the change to process. You have to be alert to see the clues. Beware of someone who frequently brings up an opposing view under the guise of "I'm hearing this from the troops." What they are really doing is gauging the reaction to their own view. Other tactics include delaying the design or implementation by coming up with a thousand what-ifs and trying to find and address every exception; finding others to agree with their issues and to speak out so they don't have to; and focusing on mistakes and creating a sense of fear and risk as a result of any mistakes that are made. All of these things are usually hidden behind their efforts to "protect the company" or "protect the customer." When you find one of these people, throw them off the island. Now. They can only harm your efforts.

Your real challenge is the 60 percent who are on the fence. They will have an open mind, but are undecided and will look to both 20 percent groups to decide which "side" to take. You will need to explain over and over again how and why process redesign will improve the company's prospects and their own job security. You do that through consistent and frequent training, casual interactions, and, most importantly, involving them in the process. And don't mistake someone with questions for a saboteur. You don't want robots; you want people who are thinking about things, who can highlight or uncover some great what-ifs that the others may not have

seen. One-on-ones with these questing minds can be powerful, especially if you ask them questions such as "What are you
hearing others say about this initiative?" You can give them the
cover they need to air their own issues. Then you can solicit
their further ideas. "How do you suggest we address their concerns?" is a good way to co-opt them and make them part of
the solution. They are also great for anticipating issues in the
plan, so involve them in the review. Finally, they should be
part of the test group for testing the communication and mes-
saging. Obviously, you should also recognize them for their
involvement and valuable input. If they are influential, others
will see them getting more deeply involved, and that sends a
strong message. You might also send them to other companies
to review what they are doing for process and report back.
That way they can take what they want, make it their idea,
and be "heroes."

You're likely to be surprised at the result of those efforts,
particularly as you watch quiet employees who aren't known
for their participation experience the aha moment, come out
of their shells, and turn into significant contributors. That
happened at Michelin. In the old system these people never
would have piped up, but now they have specific metrics and
authority. The company was having lots of problems at the
end of each month as salespeople rushed to meet their targets,
often quoting customers prices that weren't on Michelin's
specifications sheets. The result was chaos. Invoices reflected
Michelin's prices, not the prices the salespeople had quoted.
Angry customers complained and refused to pay. Accounts
receivable grew at alarming rates. When the company shifted
to a demand-to-cash process, the executive in charge of order
processing authorized his people to reject any order from the
sales department that didn't reflect Michelin's stated prices. At
first the order entry people were very tentative about telling
a forceful salesperson that his order was being rejected. But

as the process began to smooth order flow and billing, the order entry people realized their value and grew more confident about just saying no. Eventually even the sales force, often one of the hardest nuts to crack when it comes to process, came to respect their judgment and authority, and end-of-the-month billing problems largely disappeared.

MEASURE, REWARD

Despite the fact that companies have hundreds or even thousands of measurements of how they are performing, many of them don't perform very well. Ironically, all those measurements are part of the reason for the poor performance. Companies that don't perform well often are measuring the wrong things and, therefore, driving the wrong behavior. It is very typical for a company to measure individual activities and find that each activity is being performed very well. "But if that's the case, why aren't we doing better?" they ask. Think of it as if the company is a person on a diet. If the dieter measures the amount of vegetables she eats every day, the picture might be very encouraging: at least six servings of vegetables every day. That's pretty good. But if the dieter is measuring only vegetable intake and not paying any attention to desserts, alcoholic drinks, or red meat, is it any wonder she isn't losing weight?

The measurement and reward system is designed to drive new behaviors, the right behaviors. In short, it measures collaboration and end-to-end results, the total performance of the organization rather than the sum total of all the piecemeal performances that take place in a traditional organization. The difference can be astounding, as the following example shows.

Argent, Inc., had a typical measure-and-reward system in place that it had used for years. Order takers were measured on order accuracy. After all, an inaccurate order causes all sorts of headaches: returns, billing problems, and dissatisfied customers. Trouble was, the order takers, who were rewarded for accurate orders, kept checking and rechecking the order. That took time and multiple phone calls, and it resulted in significant delays in getting each order into the production system. As a result, the orders were very accurate, but the customers were really unhappy about receiving their orders late. When Argent became a process-centric company it changed the way the order takers were rewarded. In addition to order accuracy, they, along with others in the order fulfillment process, were also rewarded for on-time delivery. The order takers retained their concern about getting things right; they just didn't take so long to do it.

As Argent's example shows, most individual departments in a traditional organization have their own set of metrics, and people within that department are measured in a way that often does not link to or align with other departments. A process organization, in contrast, measures those things that encourage alignment and collaboration among departments. These performance measures usually strike a balance between the voice of the business (what the business needs to operate efficiently) and the voice of the customer (what the customer wants and will pay to get). That doesn't mean individual departments can't keep their own metrics, only that in the hierarchy of measurement, the process metrics take precedence over the department metrics. The right measurement policy can create huge changes in behavior if the metrics are right, as we can see in a U.S.-based high-tech company, Helseth Industries.

Helseth had three core processes: Customer Acquisition, Supply Chain, and Order Fulfillment. The sales and marketing departments were part of the Customer Acquisition process, the materials and inventory departments were part of the Supply Chain process, and the operations and logistics departments were part of the Order Fulfillment processes. While each retained its own department measures, all the performers within the three processes also were given a voice-of-the-customer metric (on-time delivery) and a voice-of-the-business metric (total cost to get the product to the customer) as part of their compensation plan. The policy dictated that the process metrics always took precedence over the functional measure. As a result of implementing end-to-end metrics coupled with a policy for setting priorities, this company was able to improve on-time delivery alone by 84.6 percent.

Before becoming a process organization, Helseth had a traditional departmental structure, and each department had its own measure-and-reward metrics. Salespeople, like salespeople at most other companies, were measured on revenues, gross margins, and profits, the standard financial metrics. The supply chain folks were measured on inventory levels and cost of inbound freight. The order fulfillment employees were measured on quality, on-time delivery, and labor costs.

In his pitch to a customer, a salesperson would typically quote a delivery date sixty days out. He knew that the longest lead time to source the various components for Helseth's product was twenty-five days and that it took the manufacturing department twenty-five days to build the system. That provided Helseth with ten extra days for cushion, plenty under most circumstances. But because the salespeople were measured partly on gross margin, they stayed abreast of the pricing of the components that went into Helseth's products. If the salesforce got wind of a coming price reduction in a component two weeks from now, they did what their incentives told them to do: they held the order fifteen days, so that when purchasing ordered the necessary materials the cost would reflect the price reduction on the component and the gross margin by which the sales force was measured would grow. That was great for the sales force, not so great for the supply chain people. "Oh no, we gotta get this done fast if we're gonna ship on time" was the typical reaction. The parts were ordered with expedited (and much more costly) delivery. Even then, the manufacturing department didn't have the full twenty-five days it needed to build the system, and they panicked. In a hurry, the manufacturing people worked overtime, the assembly would go poorly or parts would be damaged, and the order would sit until replacement components arrived. Sometimes Helseth managed to make the delivery on time, but just as often it didn't. In any case, incoming freight costs and labor costs went through the roof. The supply chain people earned smaller bonuses, as did the manufacturing people, while the salespeople collected extra money because they increased the gross margins.

Finally Helseth decided to redesign the entire order process and to apply end-to-end metrics. One was a voice-of-the-customer metric: on-time delivery. The other was a voice-of-the-business metric: total cost to build and deliver an order. Nobody had done the total cost measurement before, and at first it had to be done manually because the Helseth IT system didn't have the software to capture that data. It wasn't precise, but it was accurate enough to give the company a sense of where the costs were. The results were astounding. For the first time the sales force realized the adverse implications of trying to boost their own income by holding back an order. Like the supply chain and the manufacturing operations, the sales force now had skin in the game of delivering on time, and it changed their behavior. Orders were submitted as soon as they were received. Parts shipped at regular rates arrived in plenty of time, and manufacturing could do the careful assembly work necessary to ensure that the customer was happy. And nearly 90 percent of orders were filled on or before the promised date.

The process metrics didn't mean the end of the various departmental metrics at Helseth. The departmental metrics revealed what kinds of deals the salespeople were making, pre-

vented the inventory people from overordering and building
expensive inventory just to be sure they would have the right
part when it was needed, and still allowed manufacturing to
schedule overtime if things got really busy. But the process metrics aligned everyone to think in terms of serving the customer
while running Helseth's operations as efficiently as possible. To
sustain the change, the Helseth employees' compensation was
changed to align with the measures.

Making changes to compensation systems can be traumatic,
so the changes are usually made gradually over time, often
months and sometimes years. A great place to start is when
implementing a process design. During simulations and pilot
runs, the new job descriptions and compensation scheme can
also be tested. In the earlier stages of transformation the new job
descriptions and compensation plan is used for the new process
even while the rest of the company is using traditional measures and rewards. The goal is to evolve the compensation plan
into one with a specified base rate supplemented by additional
compensation reflecting results from the process, a performer's
own personal contribution, the overall enterprise results, and
some amount to reward a person for taking steps toward professional development. Here is a simple model, not drawn to
scale, of the reward structure in a process organization:

PROCESS RESULTS	PERSONAL CONTRIBUTION/ FUNCTIONAL PERFORMANCE	ENTERPRISE	PROFESSIONAL DEVELOPMENT
A	B	C	D

BASE
E

Process results covers the process within which the performer is working or to which his duties directly contribute. For example, if someone is working in the Supplier Management subprocess of the Supply Chain process, the process performance might be just how the subprocess performs or also might include a portion of how the overall Supply Chain process performed.

Personal contribution (functional performance) should not be mistaken for each individual's results; rather, it is their contribution to the end result of the process. This would include how the individual contributed to the results of the Supplier Management process.

Enterprise results are not the typical items such as a bonus based partly on how well the company did. That's because traditional bonuses are usually so far removed from the employees' control that employees cannot have any direct effect, and this results in either frustration or coasting (letting others carry them along). Rather, enterprise results measure how the various processes connect to one another and the result of those connected processes. For example, how well did the Supplier Management process connect with the Materials Procurement process, and how did it affect the Supply Chain process? Additionally, it might include how the Supply Chain process connected to the Order Fulfillment process.

Finally, *professional development* is important for taking the enterprise toward continued improvement and increased maturity levels. For example, this metric might measure understanding of the Materials Procurement process, of how the Supply Chain Process affects the Order Fulfillment process, or of how the two together are affecting the business in terms of cost and revenue. It might also measure communication or negotiation skills (needed to effectively manage suppliers) or even how to effectively write supplier contracts. Finally, it might also include how well the performer solves problems with other teammates or other process performers.

There are some built-in challenges in administering this approach. For example, a person who is conscious of being measured on personal contribution may be unwilling to take time away from the process to develop new skills and abilities. It's a legitimate concern, especially if the connections among various processes are very tight and any slack in one process has upstream and downstream ripple effects on other processes. The key is balance. Just as chief executive officers are constantly trying to balance present and future performance of their companies, a process organization has to develop both balance and alignment to achieve the business strategy. Therefore, as measures and rewards change for the process performer, the measures for the process owners and resource managers must change, too, to stay aligned. Remember, the process owner is responsible for the design, the resource manager and the performers that work for her are responsible for the implementation, and everyone is responsible for the results. Seemingly trivial reward systems also need to be reevaluated, especially the traditional Employee of the Month and similar motivational awards. Perhaps you remember your school days when students were rewarded for perfect attendance. Believe it or not, some companies have a similar program. What kind of behavior does that drive? People stagger to work sick with the flu when, for their own sake and that of colleagues, they should be home in bed rather than infecting everyone else. Such incentive programs should be completely overhauled and redesigned to drive the right behaviors and aligned with what is trying to be accomplished through process. Measurement drives behavior. Reward systems are honorable but too often drive behavior counter to what we want. In a traditional functional organization such motivational tools encourage heroism, and we know that there is no place for heroes in our new process environment. Heroes are merely symptoms that the process isn't working.

EVALUATE, DEVELOP

New compensation schemes naturally lead to a different approach to performance evaluations. In a real teamwork environment, which is what process is, an individual should be evaluated not just by the functional manager to whom she reports but by her team members as well. They're the ones who have deep and personal knowledge about her contribution to the team's performance, and they can be both tougher and more lenient than functional managers depending upon their more detailed knowledge of the person's situation. The process owners will also have input into evaluations, especially with regard to compliance with the process. Nevertheless, functional managers still provide a great deal of input and will usually continue to administer the review.

Development plans also look different in a process-centric organization. Traditional organizations have a strict hierarchy of rankings, reflected in the phrase "moving up the ladder." The aim in such an organization is to win promotion to the next higher level, which brings with it more responsibility and more compensation. But in a process organization career goals aren't so much directed "up the ladder" as they are at widening one's scope of influence and taking on increasingly important roles in process work. Think about the airline pilot who starts as a co-pilot and then moves into the pilot's seat of a small plane, usually a nineteen-seater. Her career goal typically isn't to become senior group vice president in charge of pilots! Rather, she hopes to move from the nineteen-seat plane flying short commuter hops to flying transcontinental and then transoceanic flights, each with increasing size, complexity, and responsibility. She flies because she wants to fly and is good at it. She doesn't need the personnel management or financial management skills that come with being an administrator, and trying to force her into a management track not suited to her experience or aptitude is a recipe for managerial disaster. Apply that same thinking to a process-centric insurance company and an entry-level adjustor starts by evaluating accidents with small amounts of damage to low-cost vehicles. As the adjuster learns and his performance improves, he can become the process owner for adjudicating issues for luxury vehicles with more significant damage. The performer progresses to having bigger and broader responsibilities that have a greater effect on his company's financial performance and thus creates increasing value. The performer is having an impact on the company without being in the executive suite. That's the empowerment that process can provide.

SKILLS, KNOWLEDGE, AND TRAINING

Process professionals need different skills and knowledge than the average worker in a traditional functional organization. Skills are those things a worker can do. They are not limited to hands-on skills, such as calibrating a machine. Rather, they can be defined more expansively to include decision making, problem solving, team dynamics, communication, process activities, and self-management. Knowledge is the key ingredient for these "heads-on" skills, including knowledge about the business, company, customers, suppliers, and what is happening in the industry.

You almost certainly already have a training and education program in your organization that provides these elements, usually in the form of a management development curriculum. A process curriculum is very similar to what you have, but goes beyond to include an overview of the compensation changes, a focus on process, an understanding of the company processes and the enterprise process model, the voice of the customer and voice of the business, how process owners work, what it means to own a process as opposed to owning the resources, and the concept of redesign. These programs are wonderful and tend to yield great results, but they also require significant investment. Our research indicates that companies truly serious about investing in process increase their training and education budgets 400 percent or more. That money is directed to various targets, including where necessary new facilities and equipment, but mostly for bringing in external trainers and reaching out to the entire population of the organization rather than just a targeted few. The cost of devising a new process design and determining metrics is cheap by comparison, but without the investment in training people and providing the infrastructure for them to do their jobs, the process simply won't work.

We've all heard—any maybe repeated—the old bromide "Our employees are our most valuable asset." The recession of 2008 proved that isn't true, as several million "assets" were shown the door. But an investment made in developing employees who perform with a focus on results is how you truly can turn people into assets. A results-oriented employee is a business development and retention tool bringing true value to a company

TECHNOLOGY: ENABLER OR DETERRENT?

Too often the technology side of infrastructure in a process-centric organization is misunderstood as the need to automate. Certainly there is terrific synergy between process and automation. But too many organizations don't get it right. You can have high-performance processes without technology, but combining technology with high-performance process can be a game changer. It's critical, though, that you get the order right. Technology *follows* process, not the other way around.

If these two steps are performed out of order, or if the process step is overlooked or bypassed, it leads to costly problems. Automating a bad process simply produces bad results faster.

This is the fault not of the IT organization but of the way the infrastructure supports IT. In functional organizations, the head of a function contacts IT to build them a new system to solve a problem within a given budget. This imposes a burden on IT, which winds up creating islands of automation that are difficult to integrate. So many IT leaders are frustrated because their internal customers press to get their own projects done quickly, then rail at IT because "this isn't what I wanted, you're late, and you're over budget."

There is a way to end this frustration: focus on the end-to-end process first, then enhance it through technology. The high-tech distribution company we talked about earlier in this chapter wanted to reduce quote turnaround time from forty-eight hours to ten minutes. The benchmark performance at the company's competitors was four hours. The budget allowed for some automation, but at first the design team wisely redesigned the process for a turnaround time of thirty minutes without automation. Only then was automation brought to bear to carve out the additional twenty minutes of cycle time.

IT must be tightly integrated with process to support and turbocharge the design for the execution of activities within that design, but it also must supply data aligned with new metrics that performers, managers, and process owners need for decision making. Too often there is an urge to perform according to the way the technology is designed, rather than focusing on the design for achieving goals and the technology to support. This is common when implementing an enterprise resource planning (ERP) system such as SAP or Oracle. They are great systems that can take performance to the next level.

But you must determine your design first, then configure your IT system as closely as possible to enhance performance of the process design.

THE SHIFTING ROLE OF THE MANAGER

Think back to the example of the electric utility installation process described in the first part of this chapter. Imagine what it would be like if the caseworker was one of your direct reports. It would be difficult to keep close tabs on what the caseworker was doing each day because every day would be different, often seeming complex, ambiguous, and even chaotic. In high-performance organizations, people are more autonomous, can make decisions, and have a greater degree of ownership. They don't need a lot of close supervision, especially not the kind of micromanagement to which many traditional managers are wed. Instead, they need their managers to assume new roles such as process owners and coaches. We covered the process owner role in a previous chapter, but let's spend some time now reviewing the role of the coach, also known as the resource manager.

In our electric utility example the caseworker position is a critical part of the process. People who fill critical roles are assets, worthy of investment in training, education, and development. That investment, in turn, reduces the need for hands-on management since workers are more autonomous and don't need as much direction. This opens an opportunity for the traditional manager to focus less on task management and more on new or different roles. Some of them go back to "real work" by taking a direct value-adding contributor role. Too often, traditional organizations take fantastic engineers or salespeople and reward them by making them managers of

engineering or sales teams, removing them from the work that
they did well and enjoyed. We assume that because they excel
in one job, they should be able to (or want to) lead a team of
engineers or a sales force. While this doesn't make sense in
terms of outcomes, it is how the internal system is designed to
acknowledge contribution and performance. Without many
other options within the company, they eagerly accept the
opportunity. But in a high-performance process organization
with the right systems in place to enable results and recognize
different means of contribution, there are new opportunities
for recognition and reward beyond the traditional "fight for
the only VP slot" that exists today.

PERFORMERS AND INFRASTRUCTURE
DOS AND DON'TS

- Do include the input of those who will be performing the
  process by including some of them on the design team.
- Do create new training and development plans for the
  new roles in the process to alleviate fears among people
  whose performance measures will change.
- Do redesign the process first and then evaluate how
  technology can further enhance the process performance.
- Do ensure that new metrics are aligned with compensation
  and reward to prevent confusion among the performers.

- Don't allow the boundaries of departments and budgets
  to prevent you from creating the right combination of
  activities or from having the right people perform the
  tasks in the new process.
- Don't run the simulation or the pilot test of the new

process without also testing the new performer roles, compensation, reporting structure, and other changes.

- Don't allow the technology to dictate the process.
- Don't evaluate performance without asking performers, the process owner, and the functional managers to provide input.

CHAPTER 5

Leadership and Culture

CREATING CHANGE AND MAKING IT STICK

D oing a keyword search for "leadership" in the catalog of the Harvard Business School's Baker Library turns up more than twelve-thousand items. Amazon offers more than two-thousand books for sale on the topic of leadership. Googling "leadership" yields 188 million hits in a fraction of a second. And the day's mail invariably contains at least one announcement of a new seminar or conference or video series on the subject of leadership.

The topic does not lack for attention.

So why does this book need a chapter on leadership? Hasn't everything that could be said on this subject already been said?

Actually, it hasn't. Besides the fact that most of what is written about anything is often useless, our concern is not with leadership in general or in the abstract but with a very particular kind of leadership, the leadership of business transformation that is centered on end-to-end business processes. On one hand, this limits the range of our concerns; on the other, and even more importantly, it dramatically raises the stakes for leadership and increases the demands on leaders,

153

since process-based transformation is the most comprehensive and extensive change that most companies will ever experience. Much of the conventional wisdom about leadership is either insufficiently on point or inadequately powerful for the challenges that process transformation presents its leaders. So we will step into the breach.

Why is leadership so critical and so demanding for process-based transformation? Let's make it simple. Process transformation changes the entire culture of an organization. It changes the structure of the work done in the organization (the design of the processes); it changes people's jobs; it changes how people and their work are measured and how they are rewarded; it changes managerial roles and relationships; and it changes the systems that people use and through which they are managed. In short, process transformation changes everything about an organization, and not by just a little. These are massive changes, a fundamental reordering of the culture that has existed for years. And if that isn't enough, all those changes happen simultaneously!

This kind of broad, deep, and dramatic cultural change does not happen organically or by itself in an organization. It does not bubble up from the bottom. It is not spontaneous, like the musical numbers in a Judy Garland–Mickey Rooney movie. Process-based transformation usually starts with the people below top management, but the top has to eventually support it. Only a senior manager has the authority to demand such change, to ordain it, to direct it, to fund it. Nor is it enough for such a leader to launch process transformation and then retire from the fray. Change on the scale that process transformation entails inevitably provokes anxiety, fear, and resistance, and that resistance comes in many more forms and guises than you can imagine. Only a senior leader has the clout and leverage to deal with this resistance, especially since it is often most pronounced among other senior executives.

Put simply, the role of the leader is to make transformation happen, whatever that entails. The leader is the individual
who formulates a vision for the transformation effort; decides
on goals, priorities, and time frames; provides the needed
resources; appoints the process owners and other key figures;
persuades everyone that transformation is vital to the company; demands and ensures the participation of people at all
levels of the organization; removes barriers and roadblocks;
administers consequences to those who stand in the way and
rewards those who contribute; and keeps the effort going
through the inevitable dark hours of the transition. And by the
way, in his or her spare time, the leader also keeps the business
running.

Unsurprisingly, rising to this challenge is not easy, but there
is no choice. Without committed, engaged, strong leadership,
process transformation will not get off the ground; if by some
accident it does, it will crash and burn. We have seen far too
many companies start down the road to end-to-end transformation and even achieve some results before going off the rails
because of weak and inadequate leadership. A brief sampler:

- A supplier to the automotive industry found itself, after
  five years of discussion, still in the planning phase, because
  the leadership group was indecisive and afraid to act.
- A heavy manufacturer backed away from a successful
  process transformation effort because the incoming CEO
  did not understand it and was committed to techniques of
  incremental improvement that had served him well in his
  previous company.
- A financial services firm saw its program lose all
  credibility, despite a strong start, when responsibility for
  it was delegated to an incompetent manager who made
  extravagant promises but failed to deliver on them.
- A supermarket chain's transformation plans went awry

when the CEO backed down in the face of protests by divisional managers who feared that process would infringe on their autonomy.

- A consumer durables maker abandoned its process efforts to focus on e-business during the Internet bubble, then outsourcing, then ERP implementation, and then supply chain integration, because the company's leaders did not understand that all these issues could best be seen and addressed through a process lens.

The "leaders" of these organizations were not leaders at all. They didn't understand what end-to-end process meant and what it entailed, they lacked a bias toward action and results, lacked the independence of mind and strength of spirit needed to commit to a new approach, lacked the follow-through and personal engagement to ensure the effort stayed on track, lacked the backbone to face down resistance, and lacked either convictions or confidence in them. Unfortunately, these lacks are all too prevalent.

One of the most wrenching laments we have ever encountered came in the form of a memorandum written by a group of middle managers at a major manufacturing company, whose name you would recognize immediately. We cite it often to our clients, and each time we and they learn from it. It is sort of a corporate samizdat, one of those underground dissident publications from the darkest days of the Soviet Union that were passed from hand to hand by members of the underground. Read it and weep.

We have been a classical functional organization. We are moving toward a process organization, but we lack any systematic program of organizational change. Each function is trying to make the minimum possible change, to preserve the function and business as usual. Departments say, "We control that data," or "We don't do it that way," or "There's no place on the org chart for that." Ad hoc groups are creating new workarounds. We seem to be replacing one set of complex procedures with another. Management fears the advent of processes and is trying to protect their turf. The new processes are being compromised in the face of organizational resistance.

There is reticence on the part of senior management to take decisive action. They are not insisting on real progress and seem not to care. They approve the familiar parts, but the least familiar parts are the most important. We devoutly wish for company leadership to change this functional orientation and control the resistance to change.

We grieve for the success of this program.

There is no more eloquent statement of why process transformation demands leadership nor a more eloquent description of what is required of that leadership. Process transformation inevitably provokes pushback from people, especially functional and business unit heads, who are more comfortable with the old ways of doing things. Without leadership intervention, this pushback will doom the effort.

What is perhaps most discouraging about this statement is that at the time it was written, there were undoubtedly very senior executives of this company who thought they were doing a fine job at leading the organization and its transformation program. To understand why they were wrong, let's unpack some of the phraseology, to see what transformational leadership truly requires.

- *"Lack any program."* Leadership is not just about personal charisma. It is about creating a disciplined program for getting from here to there.
- *"Reticence to take decisive action."* *Decisive* is the key word

here. So-called leaders who temporize, who compromise, or who hope that problems will resolve themselves are not leaders at all.

- *"Not insisting on real progress."* Massive change cannot be an optional exercise or a voluntary activity. Real leaders don't ask for results; they demand them.
- *"Seem not to care."* This may be the most damning indictment of all. To drive major change across an organization, a leader must care deeply. You cannot infect others with an enthusiasm you do not feel yourself. *Passion* is the most important requirement of a transformational leader.
- *"They approve the familiar parts."* To be effective, a leader must be prepared to follow the logic of a major change wherever it goes. A leader who declares certain areas off-limits or who does not appreciate the full implications of what is happening is no leader at all.

Given the high demands of transformation and the failure evidenced by these dispiriting stories, you might despair of the possibility of leadership. Don't. Companies that succeed with process transformation—and there are many—do so because they are blessed with leaders who rise to the occasion. These leaders come in more shapes and sizes than you might imagine and it will be instructive for you to meet them. From their experiences and stories we can learn what it takes to fill the leadership role and discharge its duties.

RUNNING THE REVOLUTION

You don't have to be the top person to make things happen, but you do need at least tacit approval from the top. "The top" does not necessarily mean the top of the corporation; it can be the top of a part of the business, so long as that part contains real end-to-end processes. Tom Purves was far removed from the CEO of Shell Oil, but he began a revolution that is transforming the third-largest company in the world.

Tom Purves does not fit the Hollywood stereotype of a business leader. He is a big, friendly, low-key midwesterner with a master's in chemical engineering from Iowa State. He started at Shell as a plant engineer, troubleshooting problems in refineries. He rose through the ranks, overseeing various aspects of operations and maintenance in a number of different refineries, until in the early 1990s he found himself as the head of production for one of Shell's U.S. refineries and very frustrated.

To appreciate the dilemma Tom faced, you have to know a little bit about how an oil refinery works. A refinery is a vast chemistry set spread out over hundreds or even thousands of acres. Crude oil comes in and is fed through all kinds of processing units that distill it, crack it into various products, clean the products of nitrogen and sulfur, blend them in different ways, and so on. These units are huge machines that operate at high temperatures and under high pressure; they are connected with each other and with storage tanks by miles and miles of pipes, fitted with countless valves, pumps, monitors, and gauges.

There is an old joke that in the factory of the future, there will be only two living creatures: a man and a dog. The man's job will be to feed the dog, and the dog's job will be to make sure the man doesn't touch the equipment. An oil refinery isn't quite there, but it's moving in that direction. The equipment in the refinery does the work; the job of the people is to make sure the equipment is working right. Most of the people who work in a refinery fall into three categories. Control room operators sit in a facility that looks like NASA's Mission Control and monitor hundreds of instruments that tell them the condition of all the equipment and what is flowing through the system; they make adjustments to the flow and take action when there seems to be a problem. Often that action entails calling on outside operators, who perform basic maintenance on the equipment, such as changing filters. Finally, there are professional maintenance personnel, machinists and welders and electricians, who get called in for complex tasks such as removing and repairing a failed pump.

Making sure the equipment is working is the lifeblood of a refinery. And because a refinery has so many pieces of equipment that are working under extreme conditions, maintenance is not an occasional concern but a daily one. Refineries are regularly shut down for major maintenance—called turnarounds—but the rest of the time they are supposed to be working, with maintenance quickly fixing problems as they occur. Tom's refinery had an unplanned downtime of more than 10 percent, an embarrassingly high number. Tom says he spent a lot of time "beating up on the maintenance guys," trying to get them to do better, until he realized it was not their fault. They were individually working and doing their jobs, but they just didn't fit together well. For instance, suppose a control room operator notices that a pump needs to be replaced and takes a unit down until that happens; an outside operator needs to be notified to block the flow into that pump, drain the oil from it, and flush it out, so that a machinist can remove and repair it. But the work of these three individuals was so poorly coordinated that it could take a long time for the outside operator to be informed of the problem, or the machinist might show up before the operator's work was done. The result is that the unit would be down far longer than it should have been.

Tom intuitively realized that the real issue was a lack of coordination between people in different functional silos, so when he encountered the concept of end-to-end process, the lightbulb went on. He decided to apply an approach to maintenance that originated in the airline industry, called reliability-centered maintenance, and so he created a new end-to-end process called RCM. The concept was to be more proactive and more disciplined with regard to maintenance, rather than just rushing from crisis to crisis. A key aspect of this new process is that every day, outside operators sit down with engineers to assess what the data say about how the equipment is doing, and they construct an activity list of what is to be done that day, by whom, and when, that is distributed to everyone involved.

Tom also applied process thinking to a process he called Ensure Safe Production (ESP) that introduced teamwork and discipline to the control room operators. In the past, every operator had a different opinion of what constituted a situation that warranted attention. When an alarm went off, different operators would respond in different ways, with the result that critical alarms might go unattended. The mantra of ESP was "We know our limits and everything runs within those limits, all the time." There was clarity about what the data coming from the machines meant and what exactly needed to be done under what circumstances. The new process also formalized the transition from one shift to another. Now the outgoing shift has the responsibility to review specific aspects of the equipment's performance with the incoming one. The process also included a formal daily control room meeting among operators and engineers, supervisors, maintenance personnel, and others that afforded a structured review of equipment performance. In other words, what had previously been ad hoc became disciplined. The new process also vested more responsibility in the operators, to follow the process and to be accountable for its performance; the other functional disciplines were positioned as supporting the operators, on whose shoulders responsibility lay.

Implementing RCM and ESP had dramatic consequences:

unplanned downtime at the refinery dropped precipitously from 10 percent to 3 percent. Tom was not the CEO of Shell Oil when he made this happen; he was not even the head of the refinery. But he was determined to do something about refinery performance, had a vision of what could be achieved, and was passionate about making it happen. He did have enough authority over the various departments involved in the process to get them to follow the new process. People were willing to take Tom's ideas seriously, radical though they were, because his experience and down-to-earth manner had earned their respect. He also had the backing of his boss, the refinery head, and the early results that he got from implementing RCM and ESP bought him and the processes a lot of credibility in the organization.

The results that Tom achieved got noticed by other refineries, which started to adopt RCM and ESP as well. We define the leader of transformation as the person who makes it happen. Tom definitely qualifies under that definition. At first he made it happen not through force and authority but through influence and the power of an idea. Tom is the Johnny Appleseed of transformation at Shell, spreading the power of end-to-end process across the company. He used the power of irrefutable facts to help the leaders of other refineries swallow the process medicine; he organized meetings of people representing different refineries, so that people could hear firsthand what was being accomplished at other sites and become equipped to preach the gospel themselves. Tom was undeterred, despite the lukewarm (at best) response he got from some peers and superiors. He was a man on a mission.

There is a wise but cynical saying that "no good deed goes unpunished." Before long, Tom found himself promoted to the position of site manager, the top executive, of Shell's Port Arthur refinery, one of the largest oil refineries in the United States. This was his opportunity to apply process-based transformation on a big and broad scale, but it came with new challenges. Shell had acquired Port Arthur from another company, and both the management team and the front lines were skeptical about all this process stuff. On top of that, Port Arthur was much larger than the previous facilities where he had made process work. Tom's challenge was to get all twelve hundred people in the refinery to understand what this process stuff was about and to buy into it.

One of his first steps was to clean house of some recalcitrant managers. Citing a well-known saying in the process transformation world, Tom told his managers, "We are going on a journey. On this journey we will carry the wounded and shoot the stragglers." In other words: *If you need help, you will get it, but if you try to slow us down, we will throw you off the bus.* And he did.

But this would not work with the one thousand frontline performers. Tom had to convince them to join him on the journey. Tom's approach was to relentlessly beat on the process drum until they realized that he was serious about it. Tom left his office and went out into the refinery, into the control rooms and out in the field, to talk personally with the operators and the maintenance personnel. He explained to them endlessly not just what he was trying to accomplish but why—that the purpose of process transformation was not just to make more money for Shell's shareholders but to enable Port Arthur to remain a viable plant that had jobs for its people and to be a safe place to work. It is a cliché that a leader has to communicate, communicate, communicate. Based on Tom's experience, that's an understatement. He calculates that in five years he repeated "fifty million times" his basic mantra of the five goals of process transformation:

- Nobody gets hurt
- 100 percent compliance with all rules and regulations

- Run full
- Deliver best yields
- Operate at lowest sustainable cost

Tom met in small groups with all the frontline people, explaining the ideas of the new processes, what their personal roles would be, and what was expected of them. Even after everyone had heard his message, he kept repeating it, fearful that if he stopped, people might think he didn't mean it anymore. Tom also enlisted in this communication effort the managers who worked for him, making sure they understood the process story so well that they could teach it to others.

Tom also had to change the way people thought and behaved at Port Arthur. He realized that he had to use his managers to reach and shape the performers, but first he had to reshape the managers. To that end, Tom instituted a daily management meeting, held 365 days a year because an oil refinery doesn't shut down for weekends and holidays. This meeting is in essence a management counterpart to the operator team meetings that are central to both ESP and RCM. The foremen closest to the front lines sit in the center of the management meeting, with the higher-level managers arrayed around them to reinforce the notion, embedded in RCM and ESP, that it is the front lines who are the most important people in the refinery, and that everyone else's job is to support them. The content of this meeting centers on the discussion of processes and their metrics. Managers present process performance data, explain and interpret them, and describe what they have done as a result.

Tom used this meeting to force his managers to internalize the processes and to think in process terms. Tom himself attended these meetings every day he was in the refinery. If he hadn't, he would have been sending the message they were not important. When a manager exhibited the kind of thinking and behavior Tom wanted, it was reinforced. When a manager merely presented data, Tom would challenge that individual, demanding the data be explained and asking what had been done about them.

Leadership is not something that can be exercised by remote control. Top leaders have to be engaged, every day, or people will revert to old and deeply ingrained ways of thinking and behaving. As a result of Tom's hands-on involvement, process thinking has become institutionalized at Port Arthur. The devices he used to reshape Port Arthur have also been replicated across Shell.

Tom's leadership paid huge dividends. Port Arthur's unplanned downtime, which had been above 8 percent when he arrived, nosedived to 2.8 percent, the best in the world. Perhaps more importantly, the example that Tom had set has caused all of Shell's refineries around the world to adopt process transformation and the processes he devised. Tom himself is now leading transformation across all Shell's refineries on the Gulf Coast. His experience reminds us that a single determined individual, armed with the strength of a powerful idea and passionate about making it real, can change the world.

THE HARD PARTS

Leadership is about vision and commitment, but it is also about taking difficult and even painful steps to ensure your company gets to where it needs to be. Jim O'Brien demonstrated this as he led the transformation of Ashland.

If you think you've got problems, just imagine you had to face what Jim was dealing with in 2002. At forty-seven, he had just been appointed CEO of Ashland, a $5 billion conglomerate of oil and chemical businesses. Its best-known unit is Valvoline, the maker of a host of car care products. Unfortunately,

Ashland was about to lose its oil refining and marketing business, which accounted for about half the company's sales and
all its profit. That unit was to be bought by another oil company, according to the terms of a complex joint venture deal
the two firms had entered into some years earlier. Jim would
be left with a hodgepodge of miscellaneous businesses, from
road paving to water treatment, most of which were struggling
both operationally and financially. He may have wondered
why he had taken the CEO job.

Others in the company wondered whether Jim, a
twenty-two-year veteran of the company, would be able to
rise to the challenge. But Jim was not your typical CEO. He
grew up in a small town and worked his way through Ohio
State toting boxes in a warehouse, mixing ingredients on a
food company's production line, and laying railroad tracks
while living in a tent. He graduated from college on Friday,
got married on Saturday, and started at Ashland on Monday.
At Ashland, he worked as a controller, in marketing, and in
sales, while earning an MBA at night. He built the Ashland gas
station brand, spent six years as president of Valvoline, and then
was named CEO at the age of forty-seven. In other words, this
was not someone to shrink from a challenge.

Rather than dwell on the past, Jim focused on creating
the future. His vision for Ashland was as an integrated specialty chemical company, no longer a holding company for a
bunch of loosely affiliated businesses; in other words, a variety of products, but a single company. This would mean getting rid of many of Ashland's divisions and reconfiguring the
rest. In particular, it would mean eliminating duplications and
inefficiencies across the Ashland units in order to drive down
costs. A tall order, but Jim had a secret weapon up his sleeve:
end-to-end processes.

Jim had become familiar with the idea of end-to-end process while running Valvoline, which exhibited on a smaller

scale what he would later encounter at the parent company: a loose-knit conglomerate of fiefdoms, each with its own ways of doing business. This gave the head of every fiefdom a strong sense of pride, ownership, and autonomy, but it didn't do much for the performance of the company. Some units did things better than others, which is another way of saying that some units were doing things worse. There was no learning, no sharing of best practices, no economies of scale. Jim had encountered the process concept in his reading and realized it was a tool he could use to reshape first Valvoline and then Ashland as a whole.

Jim's strategy was even more ambitious than most process-based transformations. Not only would he use end-to-end processes to integrate functional organizations and drive out waste and non-value-adding work, but he would standardize these processes across all business units, so that they would work in a common way. To make sure that everyone adhered to these common processes, he decided to support them with a single instance of the SAP system—that is, the same software system would be used by every business. The benefits of process standardization can be prodigious. There are enormous cost savings from having a single computer system and a single set of training and support tools for a common process; it also allows the company to present a single face to its customers. But Jim wanted to go even further than that. Once processes are standardized across all business units, the individual processes can be withdrawn from those units and embedded in a centralized shared services organization, which can operate the processes on behalf of all business units. This leads to enormous economies of scale.

Many companies are now working on process standardization and centralization, but Ashland was among the first to see this potential and act on it. Jim's initial focus was on the company's supply chain processes, including order-to-cash, procure-to-pay, and plan-to-deliver (manufacturing). These together represented more than 50 percent of Ashland's costs and so were a great target of opportunity.

But the more ambitious the goal, the greater the change, and the greater the inevitable pushback from those who feel threatened by change. There is a widely believed fallacy that the greatest resistance to process transformation comes from the front lines of the organization. In fact, the biggest pushback comes from the most senior levels of the company, because those individuals have both the most to lose and the greatest opportunity to gum up the works. Divisional presidents at Ashland objected to what they perceived as an intrusion on their autonomy. Their first loyalty seemed to be to the power, oversight, and control they were accustomed to wielding. Functional heads in the supply chain arena who were given new and even larger jobs in the centralized supply chain process organization felt they were losing power; a senior divisional title and its appurtenances seemed to matter more to them than the content of their work and the contribution they could make to the company. Jim accurately compares the challenge he faced to the unification of Italy in the nineteenth century, getting the heads of the relics of medieval kingdoms to relinquish control of their narrow domains in support of the creation of a greater entity.

Jim first tried to persuade his senior managers to join him in the effort. He engaged them in designing processes so they could internalize the concept. He showed them the benefits that would accrue to the company. He tried to get them to focus "not on what you are but on who you are," on their contributions rather than their titles. While it worked for some, it did not work for everyone.

Jim told his senior team that he would give everyone two chances. The first time someone objected to what he was doing, Jim would listen and hear the person out—but would then expect him or her to get on board. If after that someone appeared to be struggling to adapt and seemed lost, Jim would provide help and support. But after that, Jim expected both commitment and results. Or else.

The eighteenth-century belle-lettrist Samuel Johnson famously declaimed that patriotism is the last refuge of the scoundrel, but he was wrong. Saying "We're different" is the last refuge of the scoundrel. Some divisional heads gave lip service to Jim's idea of process standardization but begged exemption from it because of their "unique" characteristics. Jim responded by announcing that he was shutting down all computer systems in the company other than the new SAP system, so everyone would have to comply with the new processes or get by with an abacus. Others objected that it was unfair to hold them accountable for financial results if they were dependent on someone else for their supply chain processes. Jim told them that he didn't care what they thought was fair, that he was making new rules and expecting them to work with the supply chain process owners to achieve the performance for which they were all being held accountable.

A year after Jim became CEO, only fifteen of the company's fifty top executives were still with the company. The rest could not adapt to Jim's vision and left, some voluntarily, but mostly not. Jim says this gave him no pleasure, that it was in fact the most difficult thing he ever had to do as a leader. He had known these people for many years and had worked for many of them; most were his friends. But his first responsibility was to the company. He owed it to Ashland's employees and to its shareholders to transform the company, and there was no place in the company for those who would not help him in this endeavor.

Jim's experience is far from unusual, and a willingness to take on senior executive resisters is the hallmark of a real leader. Many of the top managers of a company going through process transformation will not survive; it is too jarring to their sense of self. Typically we estimate that half the senior team will not make it. Unfortunately, this statistic is only mildly helpful, since it comes with a very high standard deviation. In some cases the fraction is much lower, and in others it is even higher than it was at Ashland.

Like virtually all other companies undergoing transformation, Ashland encountered some rough patches, when things seemed not to be working. Some orders were handled wrong by the new processes, freight costs seemed to be going up, and some of Jim's circle came to him and said this proved that the effort needed to be abandoned, that he had made a mistake, that he would destroy the company. Though Jim confesses to having had some sleepless nights, he did not let others see any doubts he may have had. He says that because he was intimately involved in the details of the new processes, he did not need to rely on anyone else's assessment of their potential. He made up his own mind that despite the difficulties, the approach would work and eventually pay off, and he pressed on. He cautions others following his path to anticipate that "things will get worse before they get better" and that they must maintain their commitment when it does.

Remarkably, considering the radical nature of the changes that Ashland was going through, Jim feels he should have implemented many of them even faster and earlier than he did. He believes that a leader who is creating a future needs to help people disconnect from the past, and that the longer one lets them live with one foot planted in the familiar, the harder it is for them to adapt to the new. The humorist Finley Peter Dunne coined the phrase "Politics ain't beanbag." Neither is leading transformation. It demands self-confidence, toughness, and a willingness to do whatever it takes to succeed—all qualities that Jim O'Brien evidenced.

FIVE KEY VALUES FOR A PROCESS CULTURE

Companies have many values within their corporate culture, but there are five key values that are essential to the process transformation effort: teamwork, customer focus, responsibility, change, and discipline.

TEAMWORK. Each person must recognize that his or her own work is only a part of a bigger plan. If you, as a leader, can help them internalize this perspective, they will develop a new set of attitudes toward their co-workers, valuing them as teammates with whom they share a common goal and with whom they must cooperate in order to succeed. People with these values will exhibit specific behaviors, such as taking care not to create problems for others working in the same process, even trying to help them, and working with them collaboratively to solve problems that arise. Despite all the platitudes about teamwork so prevalent in modern organizations, these behaviors are far from common today.

CUSTOMER FOCUS. To many frontline performers, the customer is only a rumor, an abstraction with no practical significance. Unless they have direct customer contact, they are unlikely to see how their own activities affect customers. Process, on the other hand, with its end-to-end orientation, is all about customers. If people subscribe to the process concept, they will recognize how their own work affects customers, and they will strive to work in ways that create ever greater customer value. The customer, not their manager, will be their guiding star. Instead of feeling that they have done their duty by carrying out the boss's orders, they will not rest until the customer's needs are met.

RESPONSIBILITY. The basic operating principle of hierarchical and fragmented organizations is to pass the buck: "It's not my fault that the customer did not receive the order, that the design is not ready on time, that costs are out of control. The other department didn't give us what we needed, they created problems for us, they messed things up. And if by some chance the fault does lie with me, then it's the boss's problem, not mine." A process environment does not tolerate such thinking. If everyone working in a process is focused on customers and results, then everyone shares responsibility and accountability, even if any one person lacks complete control over the outcome.

CHANGE. Transformation is massive change. If people in an organization fear change, if they regard it as an alien event, they are hardly likely to be receptive to, much less enthusiastic about, process transformation. A process culture recognizes that change and improvement are constants and becomes comfortable with and even eager for change.

DISCIPLINE. A real process has a real design, which is to be followed with discipline by everyone in the organization. A process design is not a microscopic specification of how each task is to be performed, but it does demand that people perform the right task at the right time with the right information. Too many organizations, lacking effective processes, create heroes, the individual who goes to extreme lengths to achieve the desired result. Done correctly, process doesn't need heroes.

If an organization is to succeed with process transformation, its culture needs to encourage teamwork, focus on customers, encourage personal responsibility, accept change, and value discipline. Unfortunately, few cultures are process-friendly. They value heroics and personal attainment, not teamwork; they encourage pleasing the boss rather than the customer; they promote shirking rather than accepting responsibility; they fear change; and they resent discipline. Sound familiar? The important question is how to change your culture from process-hostile to process-friendly

LEADING TRANSFORMATION

Every leader at every level has his or her own style. That's fine. Leadership needs to reflect your own personality and strengths. It can't be bought off the shelf; it comes with experience. Nevertheless, there are certain things that successful transformation leaders bring to their efforts. You will almost certainly want and need to use most of these in your own process transformation, albeit to varying degrees to accommodate your own style and your organization's needs.

EDUCATE. Education is one of the most important elements of transforming a functional culture into a process culture. If an organization doesn't understand what you are trying to accomplish and how, the people in it can't be expected to know and execute their roles in transformation. The educational process begins by creating process transformation leaders through the organization. That can be done through classes for senior leaders that include tutorials and workshops. Not only does attendance at those classes help senior managers learn the intricacies and language of process transformation, but it signals to everyone else in the organization that this initiative is important. Remember that the first thing an employee will ask when a big change is introduced is "Has the boss already seen and bought into this?"

Once you have a cadre of process leaders you can begin spreading the gospel more widely using your process leaders as teachers. Don't shirk the teaching duty yourself. The commitment of a senior leader to teach a class of people several levels below the top emphasizes the leader's personal commitment, demonstrates the importance to the organization, ensures that it is communicated correctly, and infects others with the your passion.

You and other leaders should adopt an approach of teaching by doing. One of the best ways to show people how end-to-end process can improve every aspect of an organization is to get them to make their own suggestions about how their process can be changed for the better. Not only does this approach create stronger buy-in and understanding, it can produce some genuinely significant payoffs.

SET AN EXAMPLE. We often cite the wisdom of "the two Alberts." Albert Schweitzer asserted, "Example is not the main thing in influencing others, it's the only thing," while Albert Einstein maintained, "Example isn't another way to teach, it is the only way to teach." Clearly, setting an example is a key part of process transformation. When Tom Purves attends and engages in the daily management meeting on process performance data at Shell's Port Arthur refinery, he is saying loudly and clearly that it is an important issue. When leaders stop hailing heroic behavior that saves the day in the nick of time and instead focus on what went wrong to require such behavior, people feel empowered to take the small steps that can avert a crisis—calling attention to a small problem that could become much larger. And when the CEO commits two hours a week to working the customer service lines, all the talk about customer focus becomes concrete. You may call that symbolic, but what is more important than symbols? The senior managers of an organization have all eyes trained on them, and how they behave gives others role models to emulate.

STRUCTURE THE WORK ENVIRONMENT. A bit of theological wisdom says, "Act as if you had faith, and faith will be given to you." For our purposes, it would be "Work as though you believed in teamwork (or responsibility or any other essential value), and a belief in teamwork will come to you." A slightly more scientific version of this idea was expressed by Timothy Wilson, a distinguished social psychologist at the University of Virginia: "One of the most enduring lessons of social psychology is that behavior change often precedes changes in attitudes and feelings." In other words, if we implement new processes that compel people to work in teams, they will begin to believe teamwork is important. If we implement new processes that force decisions down to the front lines, people will start to take personal responsibility.

CHANGE THE MANAGEMENT SYSTEMS. Measurement and reward were part of the old system, and they must of necessity be part of the new system. But you have to provide tools that manage processes and reward people differently. They have to be aligned to explicitly emphasize the values we are trying to encourage. At Rich Products, sales and marketing teams used to be compensated on achieving their annual sales goals, while functional leaders had their bonuses based on company profitability and functional productivity goals. Now 80 percent of all managers' bonuses are based on the same figure: company profit. The other 20 percent reflects the results of improvement initiatives in which each is involved. It is hard to imagine a blunter way of saying that we are all in the same boat and we need to make it an even better boat. Michelin is now explicitly assessing the degree to which a manager cooperates with peers by polling people from other organizations with whom that manager interacts.

DEMONSTRATE COMMITMENT. It is easy to preach about something when it costs you little; it is quite something else to demonstrate you are committed to it despite significant costs. In the mid-1990s, Matthew Thornton Health Plan, one of the country's first HMOs (and now part of Anthem Blue Cross Blue Shield), undertook a major effort to improve customer service. It did so by implementing a new process in which customer service representatives would immediately answer customer questions about coverage, rather than promising to get back to them. The new process was designed, implemented, and launched with great fanfare, only to encounter a major problem in its first week. A customer service representative assured a customer that he was covered for an upcoming expensive procedure, but the CSR was wrong. When the bill eventually came in, the company faced a difficult choice. The company's contract with the customer did not require the company to pay the bill, despite the CSR's assurances to the customer that it did. But such a decision would have made a mockery of the values of customer first and process discipline that the company's leaders were espousing. So they took a deep breath, paid the bill, fixed the process, and retrained the CSR. Did this cost them a lot of money in the short term? Absolutely. But in the months after this incident, everyone we encountered at Matthew Thornton felt compelled to tell the story of the errant CSR. And in the following year and a half, the company doubled in size. The commitment to the new value system allowed the new process to work, and the business results followed.

ARTICULATE DESIRED VALUES. This seems so obvious that it would hardly be worth mentioning. But too many managers behave as though this were the only thing they need to do in order to reorient their company's value system. Inspiring speeches, corporate value statements, and laminated wallet cards by themselves do not shift what people believe; by themselves, they only induce cynicism and laughter, as managers demonstrate both how far out of touch they are with the organization's real values as well as their naiveté in thinking that speeches will dislodge them. Articulation of desired values is valuable only as an adjunct to the other techniques we have just reviewed to make explicit what the others are trying to achieve. An additional caution here is to avoid using generic and widely used phrases. Strive to express your values in clear and dramatic ways. At Ashland Oil, for instance, CEO Jim O'Brien succinctly expressed what he expected in the phrase "Ashland first." People were to put the needs of the company as a whole ahead of the concerns of their functions or business units. This served as a clear expression of what he was trying to accomplish and explained the intent of changes in processes, rewards, and all the rest.

Those are the fundamental things that every leader must do in varying degrees and in their own way to ensure the success of a process transformation effort. But there are many smaller things that play a role, too. Here are just a few:

- Think like a salesperson. Like a good salesperson, ask yourself constantly what others in the company need and what you can do to help fill those needs.
- Remain open-minded. Don't assume that you, in your role of leader, will have all the good ideas. If you demonstrate a willingness to listen and ask others for their opinions, you will learn more than you ever thought you could.
- Take a personal risk. Don't let the chance of failure stop you from taking a chance. There's little profit or gain from a sure thing.
- Give others credit. Building the depth of goodwill needed to accomplish something as sweeping as process transformation requires a lot of credit sharing. Remember Harry Truman's take on giving credit: "It is amazing what you can accomplish if you do not care who gets the credit."

DOS AND DON'TS OF LEADERSHIP AND CULTURE

- Do be sure the top leadership fully understands all that is involved in implementing process and the gravity of the change the organization is about to undertake; this isn't about flow and organization charts.
- Do ensure that the leaders can relate process initiatives to business goals and that mistakes and innovation are encouraged and expected.
- Do prepare the leaders for the fact that they may have to make some tough personnel decisions.
- Do encourage each committed leader to help recruit other leaders.
- Do make it clear to the leaders that process is a way to run the business, not just a quick fix to some crisis or problem.
- Do be brutally candid about what your organization's culture is, looking at past successes and failures of large-scale initiatives to understand the organization's strengths and weaknesses.
- Do understand your organization's capacity and appetite for change so that you don't overwhelm people with too much change too fast.
- Do understand that culture is a by-product of leadership and that if the leadership doesn't change, neither will the culture.

- Don't assign the responsibility of process to a leader who isn't well respected by the organization, including peers and subordinates.
- Don't expect change overnight.
- Don't allow friendships, including among peers, to get in the way of making tough decisions for the greater good of the organization.

- Don't set incremental or uninspiring targets that waste all the effort that goes into process design.
- Don't overlook the need to sustain process beyond the initial rollout. Institutionalize the language and culture of process.
- Don't be impatient.
- Don't forget to train new people in process and to recruit leaders and process owners with process experience.

CHAPTER 6

Governance and Expertise

KEEPING PROCESS ON COURSE

A t this point, you may think you're all set to go with process-based transformation. You are blessed with at least one passionate, knowledgeable, and committed leader, and your organization's culture, if not entirely comfortable with the values of customer focus, personal accountability, team-work, discipline, and change, is at least getting there. Nothing ahead but clear sailing, right?

Wrong. To shift the metaphor, you are walking into a field full of land mines and surrounded by machine gun nests, illustrated by nine situations we present below. These situations—involving issues of information, alignment, and expertise—encountered by real but anonymous companies will give you an idea of what happens when the rubber meets the road of process transformation.

Information Issues
- One transformation project team selected a software vendor to support their process, while another team, working on another process, selected a different one.

The two systems used incompatible data formats, meaning that basic customer data could not be easily exchanged between them.

- The team redesigning the customer service process decided to eliminate the role of the customer service representative, moving toward customer self-service via the Web and voice response units. The team redesigning the sales process, however, put more responsibility on the customer service representative for outbound telemarketing. In other words, one group was adding to a role being eliminated by the other.
- A CEO wanted a sense of where the transformation effort he had commissioned stood, but could find no one who could provide an overall assessment. Individual process owners could report on their processes, but no one had the big picture.

Alignment Issues

- The company commissioned several process design teams, only to discover there was no one in the company with more than a cursory knowledge of how to design a process or how to manage and achieve results through process.
- The process owner of order fulfillment asked the process owner of sales and operations planning (S&OP) to produce a more detailed demand plan, so that order fulfillment could do a better job at its own capacity planning. The S&OP process owner demurred, not seeing the virtue of burdening his process with increased work and cost so that another process could improve its performance.

Expertise Issues

- Two process design teams each put in a claim for a talented individual to assist in implementing their process.

By the laws of physics, however, this individual could only be one place at a given time.

- A company's process owners developed a long list of projects for improving their processes. Each one was cost-effective, but the aggregate exceeded the company's available resources. Warfare ensued as each process owner insisted that his or her projects get funding.

- A process design team developed a very effective new sales process but ran into a wall of opposition from the sales force and their managers, who claimed that process was a lot of bureaucracy, would slow them down, and was treating them like a bunch of mechanics rather than the artists they were.

- A company's cadre of process design and implementation experts did such a terrific job that they came to the attention of headhunters, and before long had all been wooed away, leaving the company bereft of the ability to conduct the next round.

How successful you are in implementing a process approach to work depends heavily on how committed you are to the goal. *Committed*, not just interested or involved. Think of a typical bacon-and-eggs breakfast. The chicken was involved; the pig was committed. Process done correctly is a complex system of many moving parts: design teams in different phases of design and implementation; decisions for changing metrics; understanding the voice of the customer and balancing that with the needs of the business; investing in new skills, knowledge, and technology to support performers; and strengthening the hand of the process owners.

Change is the common element. It isn't just changing work flow, but also changing the culture to become more team-oriented and self-directed. The lives of performers change dramatically in terms of the work they do and the way they are measured, rewarded, hired, and developed. Managing all this change requires a commitment to a different way of work and a different way of running the business.

Leadership and culture, as we saw in the previous chapter, form the foundation that allows process to happen. We need two other key ingredients on the structural side to drive process forward: governance and expertise. Your organization must be set up to accept and sustain all the changes necessary to make process work through knowledge and alignment, and it must contain sufficient expertise in process at every level to ensure that the concept is understood and used correctly. This chapter explains how to set up your organization to execute process.

The situations described above are all too common and not minor inconveniences. At the least, they are serious problems that can dramatically increase the costs and delay the benefits of your program. At the worst, they can derail it altogether. You need to find ways of addressing or avoiding these problems that fall into three different, albeit related, categories.

The *information issues* arise when multiple groups work on different projects but no one has the big picture of everything that is going on. One group will inadvertently step on another's toes; two groups will make decisions that are individually sensible but collectively foolish; there is no mechanism for managing the effort as a whole rather than as individual projects.

The second category is about *alignment issues*. Here different groups may in fact be aware of what the others are doing, but they don't care, because they view themselves as being in competition for resources, attention, priorities, and the like. The final four center on *expertise issues*. Process-based transformation is not for amateurs or improvisation. You need people, now and in the future, who can manage the full range of issues tossed up by this endeavor.

The solutions to these three types of issues, while different, are interrelated because they are all at heart issues of governance and expertise. Governance is about structure: who is supposed to do what, and what authority they have to get it done. So we describe the responsibilities for each of the roles that are critical parts of governing a process organization: the chief process officer, the process program office, the process council, and the experts.

CATALYSTS

While no one has a formal title of "catalyst," more than likely you know the type: the person who gets the ball rolling on an initiative. For our purposes, a catalyst is simply one who sees the power and possibility of process—that the company can do better if it reorganizes the way work is done—and finds an opportunity to promote it, whether by talking to certain leaders and getting their attention or simply by starting some redesign work, getting results, and then going to the leaders.

They are often the unsung heroes of an organization, the people who derive more satisfaction from seeing results than claiming credit for them. They are usually at a fairly senior level or at least have some influence over senior leaders. They also have business savvy, have a deep understanding and commitment to their organization, and are well connected in terms of established rapport with all levels of management. They start by targeting the right leaders and influencers in the organization to engage and eventually enlist in the process movement. By speaking the leader's language and understanding the leader's goals and issues, the catalyst is able to show the leader how process can help the company reach business goals. Catalysts, such as Tom Purves of Shell (see pages 159–165), provide leaders with the information necessary to understand process, help with understanding the different constituencies and their reactions to process, and essentially coach the leader to be an effective role model to lead the process charge. They also work with the leader to solicit and engage other respected, influential leaders.

So what happens to the catalyst when the leaders become engaged? Often she becomes the chief process officer, our next topic for discussion.

THE CHIEF PROCESS OFFICER

The CPO is the organization's point person for process-based transformation, the leader's right hand in this domain. The leader has the passion, the authority, and the vision, but someone has to translate these into action and that person is the CPO, the leader's chief of staff for process. Through the process program office, to be discussed shortly, the CPO manages the effort, assuring its integrity and its progress. However, the CPO has other roles as well, including selling the program and the concepts on which it is based across the organization.

In Chapter Five, we met Jim O'Brien, Ashland's CEO and the leader of its transformation program. Now let's meet Rick Music, who recently retired as Ashland's chief process officer. Armed with a degree in chemistry, Rick joined Ashland in 1973 and eventually became the CFO of Valvoline when Jim was president of that unit. When Jim started to drive process transformation in Valvoline, he asked Rick to run the effort for him, and when Jim became CEO, Rick went with him. Rick retired with the singular title of vice president for enterprise optimization and served as a member of Ashland's senior management team.

The process program office reported to Rick, but that was only part of his responsibility. One of Rick's roles was, in his words, to "teach, coach, reprimand, and even nag the company's senior managers toward understanding and acceptance of the 'new' Ashland." Rick's attention never wavered from process-based transformation. He connected with other executives, helped them internalize what process is all about, and assisted Jim in determining who was getting it and who was not.

When CPOs first began to appear, their roles were largely confined to managing the process program office (PPO) and helping the leader advocate for process. But now CPOs wear many hats, reflecting the role of process throughout a company's operations. Rick, for example, also oversaw Ashland's IT organization, which made a great deal of sense. IT is not an end in itself but a mechanism for improving business performance. In an enterprise focused on using process transformation to boost performance, IT should be deployed in support of processes. Thus it can be very helpful to have the IT group report to the executive in charge of the process transformation, rather than, as is typical, to the CFO.

IT, however, is not all that resides in the CPO's portfolio. Anders Wester, the CPO of Tetra Pak (see pages 235–239), is also in charge of the company's measurement system and its strategy efforts, a sensible combination. Strategy is only a paper exercise unless it is executed, and the means of its execution are processes; at the same time, process transformation is useful only if it is deployed in support of the business strategy. And we have already seen that metrics are an essential component of the process effort, and that process metrics need to be linked with and derived from enterprise key performance indicators (KPIs).

Some people hear the title "chief process officer" and assume that the process owners report to the CPO. They don't. The CPO is a staff role, advising the leader, supporting the process owners, coordinating the work of their design teams, and overseeing the program as a whole. To be effective, the CPO should be a peer of the process owners, so that they will respect and trust him, but positioning them below the CPO places them too far down in the organization. Remember, process owners need to have authority and clout, which means they need to be very senior indeed. Jumping to the conclusion that the process owners report to the CPO is a vestige of old-fashioned organizational thinking, in which the only way to get things done is by wielding a stick over one's subordinates. The CPO is a classic instance of an executive who exercises influence without having great power. This is not as hopeless as it may sound. In 1935, when the French foreign minister suggested to Stalin that he encourage Catholicism in the Soviet Union in order to please the pope, Stalin's dismissive response was "How many divisions does the pope have?" Last we checked, both Stalin and the Soviet Union have been consigned to the dustbin of history, while the papacy endures. Influence even without power can be commanding.

But wielding this command requires the right individual. A successful CPO builds relationships with key constituencies across the organization, as part of an effort to get them to see that process is not a private agenda but a tool that will help them. The CPO is at least half salesperson, promoting the transformation agenda and enlisting executives in it. This demands persuasiveness, knowledge of the business, patience, and in-depth knowledge of process. It also demands the ability to leverage people's enlightened self-interest, helping them see that compromise will redound to their benefit. Though it is rarely stated in official job descriptions, CPOs need nerves of steel and lots of experience herding cats to do their jobs well.

Brigadier General S. Taco Gilbert III is the kind of person we think of when we think of the ideal CPO. Taco graduated with honors in engineering from the Air Force Academy, studied in China and at Harvard, and is an expert in national security strategy. He has piloted massive Air Force tankers and cargo planes and has commanded refueling squadrons and air-lift wings. He is also six foot five and has the body mass index of a marathon runner. To make matters worse, he is funny, engaging, and completely unimpressed with himself, perfect attributes of a CPO, the role he held as the first director of the Air Force's AFSO21 office. (The Air Force loves acronyms; AFSO21 stands for Air Force Smart Operations for the 21st Century.)

Though the Air Force doesn't have competition in the commercial sense, its leaders have recognized that the twenty-first century is not the same as the world for which the Air Force was created in the 1940s. New challenges, from asymmetrical warfare to counterterrorism to peacekeeping, have emerged. Combine this with congressional budget pressure, an aging fleet of aircraft, and higher jet fuel prices, and the Air Force leadership decided the service had to reinvent itself. Taco Gilbert was ordered to make it happen.

Easier said than done. Taco had to deal with a legacy of success, a highly balkanized organization with powerful four-star generals protecting their turf (and don't forget, they have aircraft and missiles), and a legacy of unsuccessful efforts in the past with TQM. Not the most auspicious environment. Nor, as a one-star general, could Taco order the four-stars to do anything. Instead, he had to persuade them, and his persuasion strategy had three parts:

- Aggressive early interventions with the senior leadership cadres across the Air Force—not just the four-stars, but the three-star and two-star generals who actually get things done. Taco organized one- and two-day seminars on process transformation to clarify the concepts, help the generals see their application to the Air Force, and respond to their concerns.

- Extensive educational programs at all levels of the organization, from how to be a process owner to what a base or squadron commander needs to know about process and how process affects individual airmen.
- Early successes. Even prior to the formal launch of AFSO21, various experiments and small-scale applications of end-to-end process change had been undertaken in the Air Force. Taco highlighted and publicized these to demonstrate that the ideas worked in practice. Additional quick-win projects were commissioned in order to have an ongoing steady stream of results, both to maintain commitment and to silence doubters.

Taco had the wisdom to realize that he had to build a foundation, that process transformation was not going to be fully accomplished in his tenure as CPO. He worked to change the thinking of the Air Force, to build a cadre of process experts in his PPO (the AFSO21 office), and to build enough momentum so that the effort would take on a life of its own. And it has. The Air Force has dozens of success stories with process transformation; process is no longer an ad hoc program but a standard part of doing business, and the AFSO21 effort endures, even after Taco himself moved on to another responsibility.

The CPO can do a lot through persuasion and education, but not all the problems confronting process transformation are susceptible to such approaches. Inconsistencies between process teams involving IT and job design arise, for example, because process design teams lack information about each other's work, and so make choices that create inconsistencies and incompatibilities. These problems can be dealt with by ensuring that teams do know what each other is up to, and by mediating compromise between them. That's a reasonably good summary of the role of the process program office, our next topic.

THE PROCESS PROGRAM OFFICE

The PPO is a company's nerve center for process transformation. It needs to consist of people we might describe as process consultants, people who can bring both expertise and independence to the redesign of processes. But the PPO is more than just a collection of individual consultants. As a body, they concern themselves with relationships and interconnections between processes. At Ashland, for instance, the customer acquisition (sales) process and the order-to-cash process were stepping on each other's toes. The company was experiencing customer complaints about invoice accuracy, and each of these processes was blaming the other for the problem. The problem, in fact, lay in the gap between them because of functional boundaries that were not integrated. There was not an organized way for a customer service representative (who created invoices while working in order-to-cash) to learn of special terms that a sales rep (working in order acquisition) might have negotiated with the customer.

No one in either of these processes had the elevated point of view needed to even recognize this issue. The two members of the PPO assigned to deal with this problem both had enough knowledge of these two processes and independence from them to identify the real nature of the problem. Once recognized, the two processes were able to modify their individual designs to make sure this critical information jumped the barrier between them. In a similar vein, salespeople were happy to tailor payment terms to every customer, seeing this as a way to increase customer satisfaction; they did not realize, however, that the proliferation of payment terms greatly complicated the work of the order-to-cash process and increased the likelihood of error and the customer dissatisfaction that errors breed. The members of the PPO served as the bridge to link the two processes and communicate to customer acquisition the impact of their decisions on order to cash and on customers.

Focusing on end-to-end processes helps people see past their narrow functional environments to recognize the impact of their work on others involved in the same process.

The PPO also has a role as integrator when the work of one process impinges on the work of another in areas such as work flow, job design, and technology platforms. Sometimes the members of the PPO will be the ones to recognize overlaps and conflicts and bring them to the attention of the relevant process owners and their teams. More generally, however, the PPO should be facilitating interactions and dialogue between these two groups so that these issues never arise in the first place or, if they do, are recognized and addressed by those directly involved.

In some areas, the PPO needs to go beyond the roles of consultant and integrator and in fact be the source and enforcer of standards. Every individual process design team should exercise its creativity and imagination in designing its process; however, this creativity should not extend to the techniques and methods they employ to do so. It is simply wasteful to have every design team invent or choose its own methodology. Far better to have the PPO invest energy and money to select or develop a methodology for the company as a whole, which every design team will use.

For example, in an organization that embraced Six Sigma, each business unit was given the freedom to select its own supplier of this tool. Unfortunately, the curriculum from each supplier varied so greatly that inconsistent results and application created great frustration, prompting the company to put the PPO in charge of the methodologies. The PPO also needs to be the owner of the company's official list of processes and subprocesses, including their definitions, inputs, outputs, and the connections and relationships among them. Without such oversight, a company's processes can take on a distinctly Alice in Wonderland character, meaning whatever a person wants them to mean.

Similarly, the PPO should be the return address for the communications program that informs people in the company about the transformation program and its progress. Coordination is not enough here. Different groups may use different terminology, have conflicting messages, and release their communications at the same time—leading to massive confusion. It is far better for the PPO to handle these communications, ensuring that they fit together through uniform vocabulary, consistent themes, and a managed schedule. It isn't efficient for every process team to develop the specialized expertise needed for internal communications. Let the PPO do that and use it on behalf of all process efforts.

Finally, the PPO needs to be the program manager of the transformation effort, overseeing the entire portfolio of change projects. A project is a focused set of activities, of defined duration, that creates a specific result. One project might be to develop a new design for order-to-cash, another to implement an information system to support the customer service process, a third to solve execution problems that arise in the product development process. Each process owner oversees the projects that relate to his or her individual process; the PPO oversees all of them, across all processes, including:

- *Master work plan and schedule.* The PPO maintains the overall schedule for the full range of projects, so that progress of the entire program can be tracked and relationships between the schedules of individual projects can be identified.
- *Monitoring progress.* The PPO tracks the performance of all projects, measuring results and identifying those that are on schedule and those that are not. In particular, the

PPO needs to recognize impacts of one project's schedule changes on others.

- *Quality assurance and audit.* The PPO makes sure that projects are being conducted as they should be and that the results they are claiming are in fact being achieved. The PPO may also need to recommend that a particular project be terminated because it is unlikely to achieve its stated goals. This is a particularly important role. In many organizations, projects, once started, can live forever, even if they are destined for failure, in a kind of "undead" zombie-like state.

- *Resource management.* The PPO is the clearinghouse for the resources different projects require, ensuring that critical resources are available when projects need them and rebalancing resources across projects.

- *Budget.* The PPO maintains the master budget for the transformation effort as well as the overall human resources inventory.

- *Best practices and lessons learned.* The PPO is a clearinghouse for the experiences of individual project teams, so each one doesn't have to painfully rediscover what others have already found.

A phrase popular in Washington and Wall Street advises, "If you want a friend, get a dog." Our version is, "If you want a friend, don't join the PPO." The PPO is not likely to be popular among the project groups doing the actual work of transformation. "Process police" is one of the more polite names we have heard used for the PPO. Project teams resent their oversight—who likes to have someone looking over your shoulder?—and dismiss them as corporate overhead and bureaucracy. It is—shockingly!—not even unheard of for project teams to mislead the PPO about their progress. There are three keys to avoiding these traps and having a successful PPO:

- *Keep it small.* The larger the group, the more resentment the PPO creates and the more prominent a target it makes. Remember, the goal is to change the culture and have everyone in the organization understand process. If the PPO becomes too big, any process work will be seen as the responsibility of a department or function and will soon be seen as overhead.
- *Make it user-friendly.* A good PPO imposes as little overhead on project teams as possible, relying on informal communications rather than formal documents. It also provides value to project teams, in the form of guidance, support, and help in problem resolution, in exchange for the information it asks for.
- *Staff it well.* The PPO is not a training ground for junior analysts. It needs to be peopled with individuals who will be respected by the project teams for their experience, their business acumen, and their process expertise. It is particularly important that PPO members have excellent communications skills, by which we mostly mean listening, facilitating, and consensus building (rather than giving presentations). This is a place for high-performing individuals who have the mind of an engineer and the style of a diplomat.

THE PROCESS COUNCIL

There may be problems that neither the CPO nor the PPO can solve. For example, if two processes are contending for a limited resource, such as a talented employee, or if one process needs another to make changes that aren't necessarily in the latter's interest, merely sharing information won't work. In such situations each process team will attempt to optimize the performance of its individual process and won't be overly worried about the other process or the impact of their choices on that other process.

The CPO, no matter how persuasive, is unlikely to make much headway in dealing with these issues because they are classic win-lose situations. If you get the talented person on your team, I don't; if you make the expensive change to your process that I request, my performance will improve but not yours. We need a different kind of solution for a different kind of problem, and that solution is the process council.

The goal of the process council is to address the needs and concerns of the enterprise as a whole, rather than those of individual processes. There is no other venue for doing this. The process owners are focused narrowly, and the CPO doesn't have the authority. The process council is a solution to the "tragedy of the commons," where everyone is focused on their narrow concerns but no one is concerned with the collective interest.

The two problems we started with—to which team a particular individual should be assigned, and whether one process should make changes to help another—should be restated and thought through in terms of what is best for the company as a whole, not in terms of what is best for one process or another. In which team can the individual in question make the greatest contribution to the performance of the company as a whole? Do the benefits that one process gets exceed the costs that the other process must assume? Rather than position these questions as conflicts between two processes—which will inevitably lead to a loser and a winner—they need to be seen as questions about what is best for the company as a whole. It is unrealistic to expect every process owner to internalize such a broad perspective and willingly sacrifice his or her interests on its altar.

Process councils come in many shapes and forms, but we can describe its membership as consisting of the process owners and key business unit heads and functional leaders; the chair of the council is the leader, and its secretary is the CPO. The process council is the ultimate decision-making body for the transformation program, deciding on budgets, priorities, and strategy, and serving as the ultimate arbiter for conflicts and issues that arise. It would be at a process council meeting that the two process owners vying for the same team member would present their cases and the decision would be rendered based on what is best for the company. But how do we ensure that these noble and high-minded sentiments are actually followed and that process council meetings don't degenerate into food fights? That's why the leader sits in the chair. Her role is to represent the enterprise, to remind everyone of the larger vision and goals for the transformation program, to speak for the customer, who is interested in the results delivered by the company, not by just one process or another. In short, the leader needs to turn the process council into a team. This is not as straightforward as it may sound. Executives, as a rule, are all in favor of teamwork as long as it does not involve them. Putting the enterprise before the individual is a radical reshaping of most executives' value systems. This is why the cultural realignment we talked about in Chapter Five is so important. The process council is both a system whose effective operation depends on that shift in values as well as a mechanism for accomplishing it. By forcing process owners and other council members to work together as a team, by compelling them to think and decide in terms of what is best for the company as a whole, the leader can reshape their style, weed out those who are unable to comply, and get the rest to adapt to a new mode of managing and decision making.

Shifting people's reward systems is an invaluable tool in promoting this shift in perspective. Getting a process owner to do what is in the best interests of the company at the expense of his or her process may feel like an elaborate form of sui-

Governance Structure

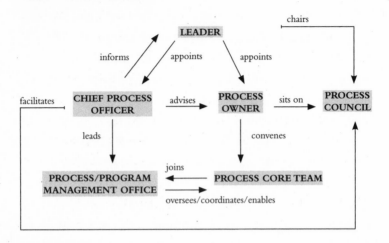

cide if the process owner's compensation is solely based on the performance of his process. Holding process owners accountable for their processes is an invaluable means of focusing their attention, but we don't want to focus their attention too narrowly. We need to counterbalance this focus with a concern for the enterprise by linking a part of their rewards to enterprise-wide performance and the progress of the transformation program as a whole. Does this set up some degree of internal conflict, of competing priorities? You bet. That's the real world, and the reason a governance structure is so critical.

If the leader has already whipped the executive team into shape and gotten them aligned around doing what is best for the company as a whole, then her actual presence on the process council may be less critical. At Ashland, for instance, Rick Music chaired the process council as Jim O'Brien's surrogate and together with key process owners made the tough decisions in terms of what was best for the company. Not all these decisions were manifestations of conflicts between process owners, but in the end they all related to processes.

For instance, one of the company's units wanted to purchase a software module to support a process in a way that was tailored to the unit's special needs—but could not do so without the council's approval. (The fact that Rick controlled the IT organization made it a lot easier to enforce the council's decisions in that area.) The council had to balance the benefit this module would bring the unit against the increased maintenance cost with which it would burden the company and the fact that it would introduce a variation on the process in this unit. Ultimately, the council decided against it, and the unit had to (reluctantly) comply.

It is important to understand how the process council and the process program office relate to each other. The simplest way to explain it is that the PPO is the staff group that supports the council. The council sets policy and strategy, while the program office manages its execution. The program office tracks the progress of projects in the portfolio but doesn't have the authority, stature, or perspective to decide which projects belong in it in the first place. That's the council's job. The council needs to translate the leader's vision of transformation and the company's critical strategic business needs into an overall strategy for transformation: which processes will be addressed, with what goals, with what priority, through which projects, and with what resources. The program office has the responsibility for seeing to it that this strategy gets carried out effectively and for keeping the council informed about progress and problems.

Doing what is best for the company as a whole is a great slogan and goal, but how does the process council actually make that assessment? It is wise for the council to have a formal structured mechanism (dare we say process?) for evaluating proposed projects.

For an example of such a system, let's return to Ashland. Rick Music and his council assessed each project in terms of six criteria, ranking each on a scale from a low of 1 to a high of 9.

- Customer satisfaction: the degree to which the project delivers results that make a material difference to customers
- Strategic alignment: the extent to which the project impacts performance goals for the company as a whole
- Benefits: scale of the net financial benefits the project will deliver, whether as income growth, direct cost reduction, or working capital reduction
- Compliance: whether the project is needed to support a regulatory or legal requirement, immediate or pending
- Complexity of implementation: length of project, scale of resources required, number of people in the company affected by it
- Transferability: the applicability of the project to other processes or parts of the company

Each of these criteria was given a relative weighting factor, and the individual weighted scores added up to create an over-all grade for the project. While many of the individual assessments are inevitably subjective, this approach at least provides an organized framework for discussing alternative projects. It also gives the council a way to communicate the rationale behind its decisions, especially to disappointed process owners.

The process council is the integration mechanism of last resort, the way to deal with the thorniest and most difficult issues that can't be resolved any other way. Among its duties are:

- Establishing overall transformation strategy
- Setting process boundaries and scopes
- Determining priorities

- Allocating scarce resources
- Resolving conflicts involving process owners and other senior managers
- Sponsoring improvement projects and initiatives
- Promoting ongoing process education efforts
- Assessing the progress and maturity of each process
- Ensuring that the multiplicity of projects and initiatives combine to achieve the goals of the enterprise

Ultimately, it is the process council that has accountability for the success of the transformation program; its members must exercise their authority in pursuit of this goal and enforce their decisions.

We need to stress that we are giving you a framework, not a blueprint. There are fundamental issues that need to be addressed in a process transformation program to ensure that the effort doesn't implode: someone needs to support process owners and their teams; someone needs to ensure that projects work together as well as individually; someone needs to manage the overall portfolio of projects; someone needs to represent the leader and the program in the halls of the mighty; there needs to be a way of setting priorities, managing interfaces, and resolving disputes involving processes and process owners. The mechanisms we have outlined for meeting these needs are the PPO, the CPO, and the process council. It's up to you to decide how you make these mechanisms work in your enterprise

EXPERTISE

No organization will ever make the transition to process without expertise. It starts small, with the first process owner and the first redesign team. They will make mistakes, and it will seem time-consuming and sometimes perhaps even fruitless. But the process owner and redesign team are learning the whole time. Their experiences will become the foundation upon which others will build similar efforts, figuring out what works and what doesn't, learning not only how to redesign processes but also how to convince others of the power of process. Not everyone working in process can or will become an expert. Many will pass through a redesign and then return to their former jobs. They will understand process, but they won't be experts. The people who become experts are a special breed. They're the ones who can't sit still, who have resumes filled with changes in jobs, positions, and companies. They hate routine and will always be looking for an opportunity to do something new and interesting. And that's the beauty of process. It will provide people like that with a lifetime of new experiences and learning. A typical comment: "This is the best job I've ever had. There's no routine, I learn something new every day, and I understand the company better."

Let's look first at some of the attributes necessary to become a process expert. Then we'll explore where to find these people.

Expertise Ingredients

Creativity. This is perhaps the most fundamental attribute for a process expert, yet it is also the one most likely to be in short supply in your organization. Companies claim that one of their goals is to foster creativity, but when you press them on how they do that, the answers are usually pretty lame. They confuse innovation, creativity, and entrepreneurial skills, which many lack, with being able to adjust to changing circumstances or produce customized products. The latter are great skills, but they aren't particularly innovative or creative. And even when a company does have some creative people, one of two things often happens. First is that someone with a great idea runs headlong into the bean counters, with their insistence on cost-benefit analysis and return on investment. If the person can't provide the requisite numbers before even attempting to implement the idea, it dies aborning. At the other extreme companies encourage creativity, but don't discipline it. People go wild producing complex procedures and processes, and then they keep changing them. There is no repeatability and the processes are not stable. Yet another problem is that companies believe that creativity should be applied only to their products or services, not to how they do their work. And that, of course, is exactly where creative talents are tapped to redesign processes.

But the sad fact is that most companies using traditional processes are geared up to stymie creativity. People rise through the ranks by doing things the way they were taught, and they, in turn, insist that employees coming along behind them do things that way, too. It's the old refrain "This is how we've always done it." Even if the company tries diligently to hire creative people, most of those who truly do have a creative spark will soon become discouraged and look elsewhere, perhaps starting their own venture or joining a smaller, more nimble company.

Ability to drive change. We know that transitioning to process work creates enormous change in an organization. Indeed, almost certainly there is no other change initiative, short of a merger, acquisition, or bankruptcy, that comes close to shaking up an organization as much. One executive likened it to one of life's most important events: "The last time everything changed so radically and so quickly was when I got married!" Almost everyone who thrives in this tumultuous environment must be able to *handle* change. But the real experts in process must go beyond that and *drive* change. Not only do they become apostles of process, but they have to be able to demonstrate how and why process is a better way and worth the effort to achieve.

Change drivers can be hard to find because the skill of driving change is part technical and part psychological. Most people are resistant to change because they are afraid of what will happen to them. Ten percent of their concern is logical: the change may indeed result in an environment less favorable to their skill sets than the old way of doing things. But largely their fears are emotional. Change drivers can do a lot to ease that anxiety by being able to explain why the change is happening, how it will take place, and what the benefits will be. The change drivers have to give people a reason for thinking that the change will be better for them. Often that means conjuring up a simple vision of the better future that lies on the other side of change that appeals to a wide audience. Complexity is the enemy of clarity when it comes to formulating and presenting that vision. One company made its point by simply stating, "We want to become the supplier of choice."

The ability to drive change is an important skill for everyone involved in the redesign, from the individual team members to the process owner, the leader, and even the top executives in the company. They must be able to communicate what the process redesign is all about, and that communication has to be frequent and in many different forms. The design team, for example, can hold periodic "lunch and learn" sessions in different departments to explain what they're doing, or they can invite people to join them for a team meeting. If that kind of communication doesn't occur, it's perfectly understandable how the rumor mill can get cranked up—"There's a roomful of a dozen people and they're planning how to get rid of our jobs!"—as the process redesign gets under way.

Ability to deal with complexity. As we've often noted, the transformation to process has many moving parts, and it can seem or even be complex. As the process transition moves forward there will be simultaneous demands to design new processes, implement completed designs, and sustain the processes that were created earlier. Worse, you don't ever finish because you'll need to redesign processes again and again as your organization matures and as markets and competition change. Process experts at every level must be able to juggle multiple demands in different time frames and across multiple functions. They can't be easily flustered, must be able to shift gears instantly, and must have a grasp not only of what they will be doing today but also of what they should be doing a year from now.

We always recommend that the members of a design team should be assigned to the team full-time, although we recognize that not every company will have the luxury of pulling their best and brightest off their regular jobs for six months or more. But in either case the members of the design team will have built-in conflicts between their redesign tasks and their regular jobs. The full-timers will keep in touch with their former group and will be hearing about how things are changing and who's getting promoted. When the design gets tough— and it will get tough, there's no question about that—even the most dedicated will have a tendency to want to revert to what was comfortable and what they were good at. Part-time teams will have a tougher go of it, particularly the team members drawn from the process that is being redesigned. Think about what they're doing: the first half of the day they're working in a process, and the second half of the day they're trying to destroy it!

Certainly every design team, process owner, and leader would love to see a perfect design emerge from the team. But that will never happen. The experts have to deal with reality, and that reality comes in many forms. There is no company whose employees have the perfect skill sets, that has the perfect technology, whose departments are perfectly aligned, and that has an unlimited budget and no time constraints. The design team must deal with whatever skill sets and technology the company has, it must stay within a budget, and it must move quickly to score some early successes and build confidence in the new process. Then there are the political facets of the change, ranging from turf wars to overcoming pet projects that don't fit into the process design. The process owner and the leader will play an important role in helping the design team overcome political obstacles.

FINDING YOUR EXPERTS. Obviously, becoming a process expert isn't for amateurs. As you think about these requirements for being a process expert you're probably enumerating in your mind the people who might fill the slot—and you're probably still counting on one hand. It's true, these kinds of people are rare in most organizations. That's why there will be a strong temptation to hire a consultant to handle process implementation. Don't give in to that temptation! A consultant might be helpful in certain facets of implementing process, but the whole point of undertaking process is to change your organization's culture radically and irrevocably. If expertise isn't institutionalized within the organization and culture, your company will simply become an annuity for a consulting firm and the process initiative will fail when you tire of paying the consultant.

You're going to have to be a little creative yourself in finding the right people, those who have the right attitude and aptitude and the right blend of cognitive style and temperament to become process experts. First, take a hard look at your organization's culture to find the places that really do encourage creativity, perhaps marketing, R&D, product design, or maybe engineering. Hopefully there will be one or more hotbeds of creativity, but don't count on it. You may have to let the creative cream rise to the top over time. As people see the innovation that is part of process work they may volunteer to become involved, which tends to indicate they're the kind of people you want. Remember that back in the 1960s there were no IT departments and very few degrees in computer science. Yet as computers quickly spread through business and industry the "techies" began to come out of the woodwork. People who were captivated by the intricacies of programming and mastering new hardware and software could be found in virtually every part of a company. They were the first "geeks," and they became the first employees in newly formed IT departments.

Be imaginative about where to look for budding expertise. One very large company, starting down the process journey, did some extensive evaluations of its own culture, and senior leaders were dismayed to realize that the company actually *discouraged* new ideas, new thinking, and change. As a result, the company didn't have the kind of people it needed to become process experts. But part of the evaluation included reviews of exit interviews with employees who had left the company. One of the big reasons that people left was the active discouragement of creativity and new ideas. When the company contacted some of these people to talk about why they left, they found the former employees eager to return if they could make a difference by doing things differently. Perfect! The ones who returned were put into process roles where they not only thrived but also made a huge difference in business performance. And, true to form, as the advantages and innovative nature of process began to become evident, employees interested in driving change came forward and volunteered, too.

How many experts you will need depends largely on the culture of your organization and its ability to accept change, the goals you set for process implementation, and the urgency to achieve the goals. As we noted in the design chapter we generally recommend that the design team itself consist of seven members, plus or minus two depending on the size of your organization. That's the core team, the people dedicated to redesigning the process. Two-thirds of those members should come from deparments directly affected by the process that is being redesigned. The remainder should be outsiders who can bring a fresh perspective.

The outer ring is comprised of subject matter experts, such as in human resources, information technology, finance, legal, and strategy. But don't be shy about inviting in customers and suppliers to serve as advisors. After all, as you change your processes you will be affecting their processes, and who knows more about what will work for your customer than the customer?

GETTING EXPERTS UP TO SPEED. Once you find your potential experts, or at least figure out how to find them, what do you do with them to be sure they're effective in their new roles?

The first step logically is to begin training them in the intricate arts of process. A robust training program will include the basic techniques—process, design, and continuous improvement—but will also encompass a wide range of other skills, including project and program management, business knowledge, change management, negotiation, communication, root cause analysis, and presentation skills. Some emphasis should be placed on teaching consulting skills because these people will act as internal consultants to the organization. Of course that raises the logical question of who will teach them these things. The answer is to use your imagination. Big companies will have internal training departments that can develop the necessary curriculum. There are outside experts, including Hammer & Co., the pioneer in process work, who can serve as teachers. But the training can be as simple as assigning books or articles for the team members to read, starting with this one and with *Reengineering the Corporation*. We were gratified to find when we hired Mindy Woolf, a West Point graduate who had served in Afghanistan, that the outplacement firm used by the U.S. Army made *Reengineering the Corporation* assigned reading for officers transitioning to the "corporate world," as the Army calls it.

Keep in mind that it is vital that you have the leadership and the infrastructure to support a highly demanding and stressful environment. With the right support, your corps of experts will thrive. Without the right support, companies will experience a high rate of burnout with these dedicated individuals.

The single most critical element of supporting your experts is for them to know what you're going to do with them when the redesign is done and the new process is up and running. Just as NASA engineers had a very thorough plan for bringing each space shuttle back to earth long before it was launched, you must have a reentry plan in place for your experts. Remember that you are seeking the best of the best for your design work, not the people the company doesn't know what to do with. You're asking these people to step away from a place where they are highly successful and well regarded to take part in what will at first seem like a very uncertain venture. Why in the world would they want to do that?

The first part of the answer is that they will be taking on a new challenge that will be stimulating and intellectually rewarding. The second part of the answer is that they will be doing that with minimal risk because you can tell them what happens after they finish the redesign. Beyond that, you should hang a carrot in front of them. At the very least they will suffer no financial harm during the redesign, and if you're smart, there will be a symbolic pay increase to whet their appetite. They will also be learning new skills and will be exposed to many parts of the company that may represent inviting opportunities for the future. Let's suppose you want to entice a rising star in the supply chain process who has been working in materials. "Join the team," you can say, "and you'll be working not only in materials but also in inventory and purchasing management. When you finish the redesign you'll be an expert in all those areas. Before joining the team your next logical step was director of materials. But when you finish the redesign you can easily take over as a director of any of the other facets of the supply chain or even become the functional manager or process owner of the supply chain."

Another critical area for support arises as the design team is mapping out the existing process before undertaking the redesign. They will be working closely with people in the existing process and will invariably uncover a saboteur. It isn't their job to deal with saboteurs. Any confrontation between a saboteur and a design team member will prompt rumors and stoke fear about the changes that are coming. The team members need to know that when they come across someone intent on sabotaging the effort, someone in a position of authority will step in and take care of the problem.

A third area of support will come when the redesign runs into problems. That most likely will occur in the simulation or pilot phases and can be extremely discouraging despite the fact that the experts have been warned many times that the design will not be perfect and that problems will occur. The process owner and the leader need to interject themselves forcefully when that happens to reassure everyone that this was expected: "It isn't a problem. Let's just go back and fix it. Don't worry, we've got your back!"

There are other ways of supporting the experts, such as mentoring and coaching. Have the right people in place to be available to advise the experts. These mentors and coaches should be senior-level people so that they can remove roadblocks and make appropriate changes to support the process experts.

An integral part of supporting the experts is to institutionalize process. The experts will be absorbed in crafting new language and new approaches to work. That language needs to become part of the entire organization's vocabulary. Too often, companies underestimate the importance of a common language. While changing the language completely isn't necessary, it is important to infuse concepts and terms such as "voice of the customer" and "end-to-end process" into the company's working vocabulary. Without that understanding there is a strong temptation among functional managers to protect their turf and to say, "Fine, I understand process, but we can do it ourselves." Of course, anyone saying that doesn't understand process at all. Just don't overdo it. You don't need to introduce a hundred new terms; a dozen will serve well.

Titles are important as a symbol to many people, and process experts are no different. Consider formulating new titles for your experts, such as "certified process designer" or "process design master," that they can include on their business card. We ask only one thing: don't use the term *belt,* as in "green belt" or "black belt," in any way, shape, or form. That confuses process with Six Sigma, a mistake too many companies already make.

Finally, provide your experts with validation from a third party. In the simulation or pilot phases, bring in people from your quality assurance operation or from finance to take a hard look at the process and point out not only potential problems but also what the team has done well.

THE POLITICS OF PROCESS GOVERNANCE

Virtually every organization proclaims the importance of both teamwork and candor. Then they do nothing to encourage either. One of the most important functions of governance in a process organization is to expose political issues that threaten to undermine teamwork. It brings explicit attention to problems that many would rather be left alone. This level of candor is very uncomfortable for many people who may feel personally exposed. Conversations surrounding metrics, responsibilities, and ownership expose turf issues and frighten people who may think they will be personally attacked for presenting performance metrics that are falling short of targets. Thus it's useful to have some explicit rules of engagement to govern these kinds of necessary conversations.

Here's a list of some typical rules that have proven very useful:

- Speak openly and honestly.
- Highlight issues that we might encounter.
- Don't just point out the problems; provide solutions.
- When criticizing, do so constructively.
- Don't make it personal.
- Use facts, figures, and data whenever possible.
- Not everyone will agree with the decisions, but once the decisions are made everyone must support them.
- Egos will be challenged; it's best to leave your ego at the door.
- Performance issues aren't always about you; we need to find the root cause, and find a way to make you successful.
- For every negative, find something positive to say.
- Come prepared.

The most frequent causes of political problems in a process organization center on loss of control, loss of power, budget, and resources. More than one organization we have worked with have seen bureaucratic fights break out over the simple appointment of a caseworker because the position would cross functional boundaries and the functional managers couldn't work out who would pay for the person and whose budget would carry the headcount.

When a process owner is put in place, many functional managers see that person as someone intent on telling them what to do and "sticking their nose in my business when they don't have a clue." They fear that the process owner may be going to expose problems or issues and they fear retribution. They try to avoid it by claiming they will do process on their own, within their department or function only, and then adopting Six Sigma or some other system, completely ignoring the end-to-end needs of the organization and ultimately reducing the impact of any improvements that might be gained through process.

And maturity doesn't make the problems disappear. There is almost always a turf war when an organization reaches a maturity level at which the process owners start to manage budgets for things like IT. This creates a real sense of loss among those who previously were responsible for the IT budget. And over the long term there will be a steady and simmering resentment among some functional managers who see process owners as competitors for promotions and advancement.

Another common problem in implementing governance of process is the perceived conflict of redundancy with other internal groups that might use a similar model, such as IT. In most organizations, the IT department already has a review board in place that is responsible for managing the number of technology requests that come in from all the other functions throughout the business. IT's job is to take a functional request, determine budget and schedule, assign resources, and manage the development through successful implementation (or termination, when requirements or conditions have changed). Successful process organizations find a way to create a synergy between the two governance structures so as not to create redundancy, and to find a way to bring process and technology together. The challenge is to ensure that process comes before technology. A best-case scenario would be to have the CIO and the CPO run the process council together, as long as one thing is clear for both of them: process before technology.

DOS AND DON'TS OF GOVERNANCE AND EXPERTISE

- Do include all process owners for core, governing, and enabling processes in the initial governance structure so that they all understand how the process being redesigned will affect their processes.
- Do establish "rules of engagement" to foster rational and unemotional discussions of difficult issues when they arise.
- Do create a training curriculum for process experts that includes instruction in change management, negotiation skills, communication skills, and problem solving.

- Don't overdesign or overengineer the governance structure in a way that makes it look like another bureaucracy instead of a value-adding structure to enhance process design.
- Don't overlook other governance structures in the organization that can provide support and resources.
- Don't forget functional managers as part of the governance structure and process.
- Don't create a permanent team of experts that loses touch with the day-to-day reality of operating the company.

PART II

CHAPTER 7

Pulling It All Together

So now you know the elements that constitute a high-performance process organization. It's easy to understand, straightforward, and logical, but difficult to implement. You know that making the transformation is complex, with many moving parts. You know that it will require much time and effort and that it will be disruptive, creating massive change in the way your organization does its work. You're prepared for all of that. But where do you start and how do you pull it all together so that you actually reap the rewards of the transformation? In short, how do we get there from here?

This section contains five case studies, two of companies that have been highly successful in transforming themselves into process-driven companies and three of companies that have failed despite earnest efforts. These cases provide considerable insight into how the transformation occurs and what can trip it up along the way. But before we get to the case studies, we can offer some advice about ways in which you can pull together the many interrelated parts of process transformation that you have been reading about in earlier chapters.

218 Michael Hammer and Lisa W. Hershman

KNOW THYSELF

The transformative journey to process begins with a little self-diagnosis. What are you trying to accomplish and why? Some of you picked up this book with the aim of cutting costs. That's fine. Nobody will complain if you succeed in cutting costs. But cutting costs alone can be a dangerous game. Focusing solely on improving costs may in the longer term also cost you gross profit because it not only doesn't *add* value to the customer but also inhibits your ability to *provide* value to the customer. Many companies adopting end-to-end process experience an increase in operating income as operating expenses decline as a percentage of that income. But just as important, in addition to reducing costs in response to economic factors and competition, they reduce costs by eliminating the work customers don't value or the companies don't need (waste). You boil down the work necessary to you but not to the customer (non-value-adding). You place more emphasis on the work the customer truly values, and then you charge them for it. That is the power of improving process.

Cutting costs is just one goal of transforming your business into a high-performance organization. But the fact is, if you implement process correctly, you will wind up accomplishing much, much more. Your business will become more creative, much more efficient, and much more competitive. Along the course of your journey you will learn a lot about your organization, some good, some bad. When we ask clients to describe their culture, they usually tell us what they think we want to hear or what they want it to be. Understanding the culture as it is, while potentially painful, will unlock the secrets of where to start and where to anticipate issues. You will discover hidden talent among your people, but you will also discover that teamwork and collaboration too often are just words, not reality. You will hear some painful criticisms of your work

from customers you thought were delighted with your performance, but you will also cement their loyalty as well as win
new customers.

But doing your work faster, cheaper, and better must have a
more profound goal, and that goal is making your current and
future customers happier with your product or service. Process
looks outward, not inward. It's all about listening to the voice
of the customer. You may think you're doing that. After all, you
may not be experiencing any crisis, your revenues and profits
may be rising, and your customer retention rates are good. But
we guarantee you that no matter how well you think you're
serving your customers, you are falling short in something.
That you don't know where it is tells us that you're not a process company. You may have lots of procedures, but procedures
aren't the same thing as process.

Like every other company, you will have your own assumptions about your customers' impressions, and it's fine to start
your self-analysis there. Talk to your salespeople, your billing
department, your customer service reps, and even the truck
drivers making deliveries. You'll be amazed at the depth of
their customer knowledge. Go to the data, examining trends
in things such as returns, warranty costs, and receivables (happy
customers pay on time, unhappy customers don't). And look,
too, at the performance of your main competitors—who's up
and who's down, and why. Much of this you will already know,
but nevertheless go through the exercises to see if any new
information turns up to change your assumptions. Either way
you'll know more than you did before.

But no matter how accurate your assumptions seem, you
must have customer validation of those assumptions. So go to
the source: ask your customers what more they need from you.
You can do it with surveys, you can invite the heads of your
five best customers to come in separately and give you presentations about what you're doing right and what you're doing

wrong (seek out the latter, not the former), or you can solicit the same information from your oldest and newest customers. One caution: don't rely solely on the sales force's advice or that of others who are in constant contact with the customer about whom to invite for these discussions; they'll invariably load the deck with their happiest customers. The devil is in the details, so don't be afraid to push your customers to reveal even seeming trifles that might be a source of dissatisfaction. The more you listen to the voice of the customer, the better able you will be able to pinpoint how and where to begin the transformation to process.

YOUR ORGANIZATIONAL CULTURE

The other big piece of your self-diagnosis examines the nature of your culture. In the broadest terms, you will have either what we call a "mandate culture," in which direction comes from the top, or you will have a "cowboy culture," which permits and even encourages making changes on the fly. If you perceive your organization to have a mandate culture, you probably will want to begin your process journey at the enterprise level, as this type of organization usually has a sense of comfort around structure. But be forewarned: you may think you have a mandate culture, but if you have departments that are allowed to ignore mandates or people who decide whether or not they implement what the top brass wants done, you probably have a "cowboy" culture or a very weak version of a mandate culture, and you're going to have to deal with those problems if you're going to succeed in doing process work.

In a mandate culture, there is strong leadership directing the company. The leadership's motivation to undertake the process journey can stem from a crisis, or simply from frustration at the top levels. It may be nothing more than a vague sense of stasis, that the company is doing okay but isn't excelling or isn't gaining market share. Recall the Michelin example (pages 76–83). Michelin wasn't facing a crisis, but over time the company grew increasingly concerned about its growth and competitive posture. Senior leadership's concern was acted on and Michelin was launched on the path to process.

A cowboy culture is quite different. In this kind of culture, people are impatient. They want to see results they can believe, they want them fast, and they need them to help them succeed. To win over the various cowboys in this culture, you're going to want to start small so you can produce results quickly and prove the viability and benefits of process. A cowboy culture is more likely to start the process journey as a result of a specific customer complaint or problem. Fixing that problem through process provides the quick results that can win over the cowboys and keep them from exercising their pocket vetoes to kill the initiative. But if your organization is a cowboy culture, be careful. Because cowboy cultures tend to encourage initiatives, you can fall prey to initiative overload and mistakenly turn the transformation to process into just one more initiative to try. That won't work. Your goal must be to make process the umbrella for all the other initiatives. If a particular initiative contributes to the transformation to process, fine; keep it and modify it to become part of the process work. But if an initiative isn't appropriate for a process organization, dump it or table it. It takes up too much valuable time and energy that can be more profitably devoted to process transformation. View pulling the plug on an initiative that isn't going to contribute to the process transformation or end results not as a failure but as a victory.

No matter which kind of culture you have, it is important from the outset that process transformation have a leader to advocate and defend it. The leader must have influence in the organization, possess a deep-seated interest in improving the process, and be willing to take a risk. The leader will be responsible for engaging the necessary resources and driving the communication about process. The leader will appoint the process owner, who in turn selects the team and sets the target that the redesign team will strive to hit.

SETTING PRIORITIES

You will have many choices about where to begin your process redesign work. There are three types of processes: *core*, which is work you do that the customer will pay for; *enabling*, which supports the core processes, and *governing*, which makes sure the trains run on time, that resources are correctly allocated, and that the organizational structure is optimized for process work. Most companies will want to start their process journey with a core process that will have an identifiable and significant impact on your customers. That's where the information you gleaned about and from your customers will show you the path to choosing the process you need to redesign. You don't typically start with an enabling process such as HR, although if it's an HR person who sees the need and benefit of process and becomes the catalyst, that's fine. In any case, you will certainly enlist such enablers as HR, IT, legal, and finance. Finance is particularly important since it can help the team figure out how to capture the as-is and to-be performance data necessary to document the performance of the new process. It's also politically valuable to have finance sign off on the new metrics since that minimizes the tendency for potential critics to rationalize the improvements as a result of "the economy picking up" and to deny credit to the design team and the new process.

How long it takes to accomplish that first redesign depends a lot upon the size of your organization and how ambitious and well-supported the redesign initiative is. A dedicated, full-time redesign can produce results within four weeks, although a more likely time frame is two to four months. Keep in mind that the longer it takes to produce results, the more likely it is that support for the initiative will wane. And you will have results to report along the way. Getting rid of waste is a big first step and should be communicated and celebrated as soon as those steps are successfully removed.

Don't expect that first redesign to be perfect. It won't be. There's too much to learn about process design to avoid making at least some mistakes. Indeed, you want to find as many mistakes, issues, or problems as early as possible. That's why you will do a simulation of the process before you actually launch it. The whole object is to benefit your customer, and you don't want the customer to suffer as a result of your early mistakes. Fix whatever problems the simulation reveals and then run another simulation. Chances are that minor flaws were hidden behind the bigger problems of the original design and the second simulation will reveal those flaws. If by the third simulation you're still finding significant problems, you might begin to consider going back to the drawing board and either trying again from scratch or redesigning a portion, depending on what your root cause analysis reveals. Doing process work can be a little confusing or disconcerting at first, but if three simulations haven't solved most problems or don't have you trending toward your goals, your design may be fatally flawed.

When the simulations indicate your design is functioning well, it's time to test it in the real world. But not at full

scale! Rather, you will want to do several pilot runs in a very
well-monitored environment. At this stage you are actually
affecting your organization's internal systems—the processes
that connect to the redesigned process and those that take
its output—and customers are beginning to see the results.
It is important to monitor customer reaction from the start,
perhaps on a daily basis initially and then weekly as time goes
by and everyone's confidence in the new process grows. Customer feedback often reveals some minor hiccups, but that's to
be expected. They can be fixed with some running tweaks. If
you have done the design well and tested it through simulation, you shouldn't be getting any big surprises in the pilot
phase. The pilot runs should ramp up in complexity and scope,
going from a small-scale test of how well the redesigned process
works internally to how well the people involved are working
in a process environment, whether their new job descriptions
are useful and correct, and, looking ahead, how well the new
compensation system will work. Overall, you are looking for
two things in the pilot process: that the process is capable of
achieving the goals you set and that the process is stable, yield-
ing predictable and consistent results through trending data.

When the pilots show that your redesign is both capable
and stable, you're ready for the full-scale rollout. As the process
ramps up, the needles should begin moving toward the target.
You don't have to hit the target in the first month or even
the first quarter, but you must be making measurable progress
toward it. If you aren't, something is wrong with the process,
the implementation, or with the initial target.

When your process achieves its target, it's tempting
to declare victory and celebrate. Just keep the party short.
There's more work to be done. When your initial process
is running well, it's time to begin looking at the processes
that feed into it and those to which its output goes. That's

when things start getting complicated. When you first set up the new process you had to design it so that it would take the input from traditional processes and produce an output that could be used by yet another traditional process. Now that changes. Your challenge is to modify the initial process so that it will be compatible with redesigned processes both feeding into it and accepting its output. At a minimum, then, your initial process will have to interact with four different processes: the traditional input and output and the designed input and output. It's pretty easy to see how these multiplying redesigns can create lots of complexity. That's why we have the governance processes, what we call the "air traffic controllers" of the process transformation. Your initial process had at least a minimal and informal version of governance in that the leader and process owner secured the resources, organized the team, and oversaw the redesign. When people start competing for resources and design talent to overhaul multiple processes, governance has to be sophisticated enough and sufficiently formalized to make sure the decisions about which processes get redesigned, when, and by whom are the right decisions.

SKIDDING OFF THE PATH

Because the transformation to high-performance process work takes time and effort and involves complexity and change, it's easy to make mistakes that severely undermine the benefits that flow from a well-honed process organization. The last three case studies, of companies we're calling Four Acres, Hattaway Inc., and Acme Specialties, provide some graphic examples of what can happen, but we can identify and summarize the most likely failure modes organizations may encounter.

FAILURE TO RECOGNIZE THE SCOPE OF CHANGE. Too many people think that process redesign amounts to changing flow charts on paper and boxes and lines on the organization chart. They completely underestimate all the things that are required to implement an end-to-end process and how long it will take. Process transformation is akin to changing the tires on a moving car. When you begin the transformation you truly are thinking outside the box. But if you do it right, process will create an entirely new box, one that is far more efficient and innovative than the old box. One of the major symptoms of the failure to recognize the scope of change is when a company renames its functional managers and begins calling them process owners when nothing else has changed. They fail to recognize that process is not about the span of control of a functional manager, but about the span of influence of the process owner. The process owner doesn't control the resources but influences how they are allocated. A company that fails to recognize the scope of change will never take all the steps necessary to become a high-performance process organization. Making the transformation is a multiyear process, and there will be confusion and complexity.

CRISIS RESPONSE. Process often offers a solution to a major crisis. We estimate that at least 60 to 75 percent of the companies that initially set out on the path to process do so because of an issue that threatens the organization's profitability or, worse, its very existence. Process has an amazing ability to fix big problems. The trouble is, once the big problem is fixed and the crisis has passed, there is a temptation to revert to the old ways. It's easier to quit innovating and changing the way the organization does its work and simply "do it the way we've always done it." The key is to keep forcing change until process becomes institutionalized and it is more difficult to go back than to keep going forward.

INDIVIDUAL CHAMPIONS. This problem arises when a leader high in the organization is the champion of the transformation to process. As Jim O'Brien, chief executive of Ashland, learned, even the compelling logic of process isn't sufficient to sell it to some entrenched executives who fear the change in their status and power. He had to get rid of thirty-five of the company's top fifty executives and bring aboard new people who understood and endorsed process. If you're the process champion in your organization and you don't get a buy-in from people above or below you and can't or won't get rid of the naysayers and skeptics, it's likely that process in your organization is doomed. But don't get complacent about the future of process even if the CEO herself endorses and supports it. If she leaves, it's very possible that the board won't fully understand process and what it has already done for the organization. If the board doesn't seek out a new CEO with a successful experience in process, it is likely that the new CEO, seeking to put her brand on the organization, will either fail to support the process journey sufficiently or will simply dump it in favor of a more traditional and (for her) comfortable way of working.

STARTING AT THE WRONG PLACE. Given the nature and scope of the changes inherent in process, there is a strong tendency among leaders to get the framework or the infrastructure to support it in place before actually beginning to do process work. But excessive planning can be deadly because it delays the actual start of the transformation and creates at least the impression that this is just another bureaucracy. General George Patton long ago recognized that "a good plan that you act on today is better than a perfect one tomorrow." Process has to produce noticeable results quickly to gain a foothold in the organization. Resist the temptation to start big. That will take too long to produce results. Better to start small and show tangible benefits in order to secure longer-term support for the transformation.

USING OLD METRICS. Your company has had a set of metrics in place for years. For whatever reason—mostly because their paychecks and bonuses are tied to those metrics—a lot of people are reluctant to give them up and are even more reluctant to have to perform against entirely new measures. But the old metrics won't tell you what you need to know to implement process. Without new measures of progress and success, your efforts to introduce process will flounder as people continue to do what the old metrics reward them for doing. Metrics in organizations are a lot like laws: new ones keep being added, but old ones stay on the books even when they are no longer relevant. But in process work the old has to go to make way for the new. Metrics drive behavior, and keeping the old measures around is tantamount to keeping the old behaviors around, too.

ACCEPTANCE OF FAILURE. Inevitably there will be missteps on the path to process. But failure should not deter you from continuing on your journey. Failures are learning opportunities. It's better to make your mistakes early before they become expensive.

SHIFTING TO COLLABORATION. Process requires, not encourages, collaboration. When people say they don't like process, they really mean they don't want to share power. You're asking people to work out of their comfort zone and outside their silo, and there will be some or even many who can't or won't do that. When good people threaten to leave rather than adjust to process, don't be tempted to try to keep them. They may have been good performers in the old system, but they won't succeed in the new one. Either they will break the process or the process will break them. And while the transformation to process requires persuasion and diplomacy, it also requires an iron determination to eliminate sacred cows and resisters. Leaders need to be one-third visionary, one-third communicator, and one-third leg breaker. As Al Capone put it, "You get further in life with a kind word and a gun than a kind word alone."

CHAPTER 8

Tetra Pak

A BUSINESS TRANSFORMED

It was the mid-1990s and the Swedish company Tetra Pak had a big problem. For years it had been on a spectacular growth trajectory. Sales of the aseptic packaging equipment and materials it had pioneered soared as dairies and beverage companies scrambled to offer consumers products that tasted fresh but needn't be refrigerated. Like many rapidly growing companies, Tetra Pak did not operate systematically. It was so busy keeping up with demand that it had neither the time nor the patience to develop discipline and systems. But now growth was slowing and competition was growing. Something had to be done.

The symptoms of an out-of-control company were everywhere. Customers, once grateful that Tetra Pak would take their orders, were growing more demanding. The sales force would try to mollify customers by promising to make packaging products that simply couldn't be produced because of their unusual shapes or configurations. Customers demanded two-week lead times for ordering packaging materials, but Tetra Pak took six weeks to process orders. Customers wanted a single point of contact with Tetra Pak, but the company was too fragmented to do that.

Reengineering the Corporation had been published a few years earlier and the concept of process design and redesign had been talked about a lot. More than a few executives in Tetra Pak's global organization believed it made sense to run their operations on process lines, and over the next few years there were multiple attempts to redesign parts of the organization. But the efforts lacked any central coordination and were not designed on an end-to-end basis. Over time, they weren't sustained as they failed to produce the kinds of efficiencies people had hoped to achieve.

Then in 2000, in an attempt to gain control over its systems, Tetra Pak rolled out an enterprise resource planning effort using SAP software. As part of that new initiative, the company made a corporate-wide commitment to reengineer its processes. Two attempts failed for lack of resources, but the third attempt was backed by ample financial, human, and consulting resources and began to gain some traction in the company. For a few years process got a lot of attention, but it still was being done through a variety of theories and methodologies, and by 2003 it had started to drift again. But the seeds of change had been planted.

THE U.S. INITIATIVE

While the United States was far from the largest of Tetra Pak's markets, process redesign had some notable initial success there, mostly as a result of the efforts of Johan Rabe, probably the only graduate of the University of Virginia to serve as a captain in the Swedish army. Born in Sweden, he spent his youth in Indonesia, where his father worked for Volvo. He was sent to the United States for high school and college and

then did his mandatory stint in the Swedish army. After fulfilling his military obligation Johan went to work for Tetra
Pak and in 1999 found himself in the position of customer
service director just as customers were becoming much less
enamored of the service Tetra Pak provided. Burdened by the
many customer complaints, Johan, on the advice of a friend,
learned the techniques of end-to-end process transformation
and immediately recognized the potential to reengineer the
order fulfillment process so that it could be handled by a single
individual. He envisioned that single individual working with
customers to design the packaging they wanted, ensuring it
both met their needs and could be made, taking the order for
the necessary equipment and supplies, planning and scheduling the order for completion, scheduling transportation to get
the machinery to the customer on time, set it up in the customer's location, and finally bill the customer.

Johan's vision was a far cry from what was really happening in Tetra Pak's U.S. operations. The work he imagined
being handled by a single person was, in fact, being handled
by many people in different departments. The inevitable mis-
understandings and handoffs created delays, confusion, complexity, and all the other malfunctions so typical of fragmented
organizations.

Johan knew that theoretically he could streamline the order
process in a way that would transform the company's operations. But there was a hitch: Johan didn't have the authority
to make that happen. He had control over the customer service representatives who took orders, but not over the other
departments that played roles in the dreadful process. He
couldn't compel other departments to do anything. Nevertheless, he decided to push ahead.

While Johan didn't have the authority to *command* his peers,
he thought it might be possible to *persuade* them to do things
his way. He encouraged the head of the finance department to

cede responsibility for forecasting to him and thus free finance from what was regarded as an annoying burden. He persuaded logistics to move shipping coordinators out of the warehouses to sit with his own customer service reps so that they would have an earlier view of customers' transportation needs. He promised production that if it gave his department more influence over production schedules, he could reduce the number of burdensome rush orders directed to production. Then he went to the head of the sales group and told him that sales would be hit with a surcharge every time there was a rush order. Johan had some support from his peers and even from his boss, who approved an increase in the skill requirements and pay for a new breed of customer service reps who could do business the way Johan had envisioned it. Before long, Johan's guerilla efforts began to bear fruit. Costs, lead times, rush orders, and customer complaints all decreased, and customers even started praising the new way of doing business. Still, Johan knew that while he had gotten the transformation ball rolling, he simply didn't have the leverage in the organization to take it much further. That's when Dennis Jönsson stepped into the picture.

Many managers effectively operate their businesses by remote control on the basis of data and reports. But that wasn't Dennis Jönsson's style. Since joining Tetra Pak in 1982 and serving in Sweden, Panama, and Mexico, he had run his organizations with firsthand knowledge. He spent lots of time with customers, listening to their complaints and ambitions. He walked through the plants, kept careful tabs on orders and scheduling, and made sure Tetra Pak's equipment worked as advertised in the customers' operations. It's easy to imagine, then, Dennis's reaction when he arrived at his new post as president of Tetra Pak's U.S. operations and asked a simple question: "What is the on-time delivery rate for the product development pipeline?" No one knew!

Dennis knew that if you asked a simple question and

couldn't get an answer, something was very wrong. And indeed, there was a huge problem. Upon investigation it turned out that only 13 percent of orders were delivered on time. Johan had just begun his efforts to turn customer service into an end-to-end process, and that got Dennis's attention. The president began spending a lot of time with Johan, developing his own understanding of end-to-end processes. Using Johan's end-to-end methodology, the company quickly saw on-time delivery of orders soar to over 80 percent. Dennis provided additional funding and support for Johan's process work and was making plans to extend it to other parts of the U.S. operations when in 2001 he was promoted to head of Tetra Pak's Carton Ambient business unit, the largest in the company.

Dennis took Johan with him to Carton Ambient, where they pushed process transformation through various parts of the division even as similar efforts in other parts of the company were floundering. But because Carton Ambient had extensive ties to other parts of Tetra Pak, Dennis persuaded the CEO to put transformation on the corporate agenda. Dennis was taking a chance, but despite some of the skepticism from his peers he won the group over and Tetra Pak began its journey to process-centered transformation. In 2006 Dennis Jönsson became CEO and process transformation was baked into the company's DNA.

BRINGING DISCIPLINE TO PROCESS

In 2003, as the latest corporate-wide process initiative began to drift off course, Tetra Pak named Anders Wester to the role of chief process officer. It was his job to figure out how to bring a sense of discipline and order to the multiple process efforts that were going on throughout Tetra Pak. Anders didn't know it then, but he was embarking on a three-year journey.

Anders's first move was to end the "process for the sake of process" mind-set that seemed to dominate Tetra Pak's many process initiatives. He set out instead to create a strong and explicit link between process work and Tetra Pak's strategic objectives. In the simplest sense, Tetra Pak had three strategic priorities: focus and grow the core, emphasize cost-driven innovation, and drive operations and performance. Suddenly there was a very good reason for everyone, not just the process acolytes, to pay attention to process.

As Anders explains: "If you say, 'We're doing this process stuff that improves the strategic objectives,' someone can either agree or disagree with the method, but if you disagree about our strategy, then we have a big problem. It's very, very difficult for executives to take on that debate."

Once everyone knew that process was an integral part of Tetra Pak's strategy, education about what exactly process is became the priority. That education began at the top with 250 senior executives. In small groups the executives attended a "process academy" that Tetra Pak set up in conjunction with IMD, the Swiss graduate business school. The three-and-a-half-day seminar immersed the executives in process design. As part of the course the executives had to draw up a plan about how they would embrace and implement process in their own areas. On the final day each executive had to present that plan to the CEO. "It created a lot of buy-in and a lot of understanding at the executive level," Anders said. When the last of the executives finished the academy training eighteen months later, Tetra Pak had reached the tipping point that marked the beginning of full acceptance of process.

In retrospect Anders is convinced that the entire company bought in to the idea of process only because the CEO was fully committed. "It may start at the grassroots level, but eventually you have to have the CEO say, 'This is the way we're going to run the enterprise,'" Anders said. One of the CEO's most visible tasks in the beginning of the process journey is to publicly name the process owners and explain their role as full-time designers of the process transformation. The CEO's imprimatur gives the process owners the clout they need to go into the organization asking questions aimed at figuring out the best design.

Anders also found that there is a strong temptation to try to overhaul the entire company in one fell swoop. But that would be overwhelmingly complex and would certainly doom the redesign to failure. Instead, he said, the focus should be on a few core processes that have a direct and visible impact on the company's strategic objectives. For Tetra Pak that meant hurting some feelings. While Tetra Pak was floundering with multiple process efforts, it had set up a process council that was intended to bring people from diverse functions together in support of process design. But it became clear that too many voices and opinions were impeding progress. When Tetra Pak decided to focus on only a few core processes, the number of people on the process council was slashed. Human resources, for example, was told it was no longer welcome.

"When we started out we had all these initiatives going on and there were too many people at the table at the same time trying to do too many things without any real prioritization. When we decided to focus on a just a few core processes we had to say to some people, 'You're not invited to the process council anymore. You are less important than others.' We certainly wouldn't win any popularity contests by doing that, but for the sake of achieving progress it had to be done."

During the initial design phase of the corporate-wide effort, the process owners had no responsibilities other than creating the design. They left their high-level executive posts to devote all their time to the design. As Anders said, "It can't be done on the night shift." But as Tetra Pak began to implement the initial design, that changed. Process was grafted onto functional responsibilities in an organizational design that enabled process work to be done in what amounted to a functional organization. Tetra Pak now is built around functional capabilities, but work gets done through processes.

"Process owns the P&L," said Anders, "but function is where people sit. There's a great deal of overlap in terms of process responsibility and organizational responsibility. The downside of that is that the process owner often has to step outside his functional responsibility and that is difficult to do, because in their operational role they have a lot of confidence and they have command and control, which is not true in their process responsibility."

Tetra Pak also found that it could not become so caught up in the implementation of process through executive fiat that it forgot about the people on the line. It would have been easy to underestimate the people side of implementation and skip over it. Instead, Tetra Pak executives understood that they had to get people excited about process design, both intellectually and emotionally. Process design at its core is very logical and very easy to learn for someone with a good education and a good head on his shoulders. But getting him to connect with it at a more emotional level is more difficult.

"People are complicated," said Anders. "You have to train them and it takes time to change their attitudes. You have to win their hearts as well as their minds."

The right measures are critical to the early success and evolution of process design. Tetra Pak realizes today that it made a big mistake early on when it failed to build a master database as it was implementing its enterprise resource planning system with SAP. It was difficult to see the benefit of such a broad-based data repository in the early stages of planning, but its value became painfully and expensively obvious as process design and business transformation matured.

Getting the metrics right is too important to just improvise.

Rather, Tetra Pak applied much time and effort in the early stages to setting baselines and definitions. It isn't always clear at first which measures drive the objectives, and only thorough discussion and testing can produce the needed results. The key is to listen to goals and objectives, then ask how they can be measured. Adding the element of measurement to a goal or objective makes it more tangible. Keeping the metrics simple is important, too. At the highest levels the critical metrics become part of the company's balanced scorecard, and everyone knows the CEO looks at that every quarter. Add to that bonuses based at least in part on those critical metrics and everyone tends to pay close attention.

THE JOURNEY NEVER ENDS

Today Tetra Pak is an exemplar of a process-oriented company, one that is often used in our process training as one company that really gets it. When Anders Wester was asked to address one of our classes in 2008 he entitled his talk "From Project to Way of Life" and had this to say: "There's good news and there is bad news. The good news is that this process stuff is actually very, very simple. Intellectually, it isn't rocket science. The bad news is that it isn't easy. Actually, it's very, very difficult to accomplish. And it takes a hell of a long time. I'm not a very patient man but I've been humbled in terms of what we have achieved through persistence because it takes a very, very long time, but it is worth it. Everyone asks, 'When are you there?' I think we're there because we know that we're not thinking about it anymore. It just becomes how we do things and how we approach a problem. Our people now talk about 'Is it an execution problem or a design problem or do we need to redesign the process?' When you're having those conversations routinely, then I think you're there."

Nevertheless, when one of our research groups in 2009 polled Tetra Pak and several other process-oriented firms about their use and acceptance of process, the answers it got back indicated that while Tetra Pak may "be there" in terms of making process a central focus of its discussions about planning and execution, the company believes it has much further to go. On the PEMM scale of 1 to 4, with 4 best, Tetra Pak rated itself 1 on customer focus, 2 on attitude about change and teamwork, 3 on leadership awareness, 3 on governance accountability, but 2 on the definition of metrics, and just 1 on uses of metrics.

Why would a company that seemingly has mastered the use of process and is widely admired as a leader in the field rate itself so critically? Because the journey never ends. The more you learn about process, the more ways you find to make it useful and the more sophisticated you become in your recognition of the nuances and subtleties of things such as governance and metrics. The leaders of Tetra Pak realize there is more to do and that "being there" is simply another way station on the journey to excellence.

CHAPTER 9

Gamesa

CREATING A COMPANY-WIDE PROCESS CULTURE

For many years Gamesa had been Mexico's foremost producer of cookies and other sweet snacks. A family-owned company founded in 1921, it was, as were many others, very hierarchical. Employees were directed in their jobs by supervisors who had supervisors supervising them and yet more layers of oversight above them. That strict control served the company well in the early years as it grew through acquisitions and boosted its sales through wholesalers and supermarkets to capture about a third of the market for snacks by 1990. But when PepsiCo acquired the company in 1990 the old management methods weren't working so well. Gamesa wasn't innovating and it was focused on its own costs, not the value of its products. The quality of its products was inconsistent, and its manufacturing processes were inefficient; its employees were paid poorly, worked in dreary conditions, and were unengaged and uninterested. Perhaps worst of all, Gamesa's customers, ranging from wholesalers and big retail chains to tiny street bodegas, were unhappy with Gamesa's service and

241

products—and so were the consumers who were the ultimate buyers of Gamesa's products.

As PepsiCo pushed for improved performance, Gamesa's executives struggled to find a new way forward. The company's fragmented bureaucracy was one big problem. There were too many bosses with too many constituencies to appease, and people at every level seemed to have no focus. No one seemed to know what to do to drive improved results. The dispirited workforce was equally problematic. Gamesa had a long history of conflict with the union that represented its workers. Annual contract negotiations took months. Workers had no voice in the factories and felt disconnected from their jobs. Indeed, the union told its members to not even try to improve things at Gamesa. "Leave your head in your locker and bring your body to work" was the union's advice. It was clear to workers and bosses alike that all Gamesa wanted was the workers' labor, not their thinking. And given Mexico's traditional forty-eight-hour workweek, most employees wound up working six days each week, sometimes with overtime, leaving precious little time to spend with family in a country that is defined by close family ties. Some of the work was seasonal, too. Many Catholics in the predominantly Catholic country deemed Gamesa's snacks a Lenten sacrifice and sales tumbled each year at the onset of Lent, leading to layoffs and reduced hours. Clearly Gamesa was a troubled company.

Then Juanito took over as boss.

Salvador Alva, Gamesa's chief executive officer at the time, knew the company needed to make radical changes, from its culture to its production methods. But he also knew that to pull off such a bold move he would have to find a powerful but simple theme that would align everyone in the company, from the senior executives to the maintenance workers on the night shift. So far that unifying theme had eluded him. Then one day in 1996 Salvador was strolling through a marketplace in Monterrey, where Gamesa is headquartered, deep in contemplation about what could be done to get Gamesa back on the path to growth and financial health. As he rounded a corner the CEO spotted a young boy sitting on the curb eating a Gamesa cookie. The scene struck him vividly: this was Gamesa's customer! In Monterrey, a snack or treat isn't just a snack or treat. It's an important part of a child's daily nutrition. The CEO quickly made his way over to the boy and asked his name.

"*Cómo te llamas?*"

"*Me llamo Juanito.*"

At that moment Juanito became the answer to Gamesa's problem. No longer were there too many bosses. Here was the new boss: the customer embodied by young Juanito. Now Salvador had his rallying point. He set out to convince everyone, from his top staff to the employees in the factories, that what Gamesa needed to do was focus all its efforts on the customer. His message: the customer needed and deserved a quality product at a reasonable price. If Gamesa could consistently provide that product, it would succeed. The vision was simple: to become the favorite convenient, nutritious, and fun food company. In order to delight the customer Gamesa would change everything about the way it did business. From that point on, Salvador proclaimed, nothing that Gamesa did would have any value unless it added value for the consumer. Juanito would define value, not the CEO or anyone else working at Gamesa.

Easily said, not so easily done. Salvador knew that changing an entire culture and the ways it did its work would be a monumental task that would take years. He decided early on that adopting a process approach to work would ultimately be the only way to achieve the results the company needed. Still, the implications of becoming a process organization seemed staggering. Functional silos would have to yield to end-to-end work, with Juanito and other customers at the end of the process. But before that could happen, the company would have to undertake a total revamp of its labor relations in order to tap the expertise and energy of its workforce, a daunting task given the history of ill will between management and labor. Salvador assumed that if the workers understood that their mission was to delight and nourish Juanito, they would have valuable ideas about how to do things better if only management would listen. But that was just part of solving the problem. The workers would also have to trust management, and management would have to earn their trust. Given that challenge, Salvador formulated a simple guiding principle: employees don't care how much management knows until they know how much management cares.

Building a trusting relationship with its workforce, while perhaps difficult, would be merely the first giant step in a long journey. Eventually would come massive changes in the organization of the work and the workers. How fast that might happen and what shape it might take wasn't entirely clear, but by emphasizing process as the organizing principle Salvador was confident that a new and more efficient shape would emerge for the business.

The first hurdle was to persuade skeptical workers that the company that had long scorned them as anything other than manual labor was really intent on changing that relationship. After all, this was the company that had shown in innumerable ways how little value the workers had as human beings. Long hours and low pay were just part of it. There were the primitive and dirty bathrooms, the lack of eating facilities in the factories, and little or no company support for recreational activities. In a soccer-obsessed culture Gamesa refused to field a company team to compete in corporate leagues.

Since Gamesa's management was embarking on a process journey, it decided to create a process to solve the problem of hostile labor relations, called Winning the Confidence of the People. The key to the process was to tell workers that the company wanted to change the relationship it had long had with them, but that it would be the workers' ideas that changed it, not the company's ideas.

"We will not tell you how to change it," the leaders told employees. "That will be your job. We will listen to what you have to say. We are going to put the business in your hands."

Just more words? The workers clearly remained skeptical. But then management began holding large meetings and asking for ideas about what needed to change. An initial reluctance to speak up for fear of retaliation eventually faded, and the employees began to suggest first dozens and then hundreds of ideas for improving relations with management as well as working conditions. Some were directly work-related: supervisors came in for much criticism for harassing the workers on the line. Other suggestions were aimed at working conditions, with the sordid state of bathrooms in the factories high on the list of complaints. And the soccer aficionados got their two pesos in: Gamesa needed to provide a practice field. Underlying everything else, of course, were calls for better pay and hours.

With literally thousands of ideas from workers, it was up to Gamesa's executives to sort through and implement them. Without that final implementation the workers would become convinced that it was all just another management ploy to get more from them without any cost. But Gamesa had told the employees at the outset that it was putting the business in their hands. True to that promise, it called on the employees for more ideas about how to make work more efficient so that the cost savings or additional profit could fund their ideas. And sure enough, the ideas were forthcoming.

Cost savings paid for half the new soccer field and the company contributed the other half. It didn't happen overnight. Indeed, it took several years for the Winning the Confidence of the People process to mature. But the signs were unmistakable: the company and the workers were starting to trust each another.

Perhaps the clearest sign of that growing trust came as Gamesa's management pressed the workers for their ideas about making the company more profitable: "What do we have to do to make the business more profitable so that we can pay you more and invest in growing the business?"

The unequivocal answer: "Let us do our work without interference." The workers had long felt that supervisors needlessly interfered with the way work got done, slowing things with overly stringent requirements in some cases and heedlessly speeding up other things with resulting losses in quality. "We know best how to do our jobs, so you should let us do them the way we know," the workers said. But was that too risky? After all, Gamesa would be turning over to the employees such critical aspects of the business as quality control, safety, and maintenance. The employees really would take ownership of the business if that happened.

Again, the transformation took time and required a strong and consistent leadership. José Luis Prado, Gamesa Quaker CEO since 2002, said: "It required consistency and congruency," but eventually the workers adopted a businesslike approach to their jobs. Quality, safety, and maintenance standards actually improved even as the number of supervisors in the factories steadily declined. Over time, most of Gamesa's facilities reached the point at which there was one factory director, a few facilitators from human resources, engineering, and supply chain, and the remainder were frontline workers. Some night shifts had no one in what could be called a supervisory role.

The cost savings were obvious and Gamesa was becoming a more profitable company. And, as "owners of the business," the workers quite naturally wanted their share. Negotiations between the company and the union became more amenable as the workforce realized that Gamesa was serious about changing labor relations. One of the crowning achievements of the new relationship between management and workers was a new system of variable pay, an unprecedented concept in Mexican industry. Employees' salaries were tied to a set of metrics that were completely up to the teams to accomplish. Variable factors such as efficiency and quality were controlled by the self-managed teams of frontline employees. They knew their metrics and they met at the end of every shift to analyze performance and to plan the improvements that would yield them more pay. It sounds like a management initiative, but it is in fact an example of employees managing themselves without supervisors.

Pay had been only one of the workers' big complaints when Gamesa set out on its process journey. The other was the long hours spread over six days of the week. As the workers learned the intricacies of their new roles as owners, they decided there was a better way: they proposed going to four 12-hour days. Management agreed to try it if the workers determined and managed the staffing issues—shift coverage, vacation schedules, sick time, overtime needs, training, resource needs, and, above all, meeting production requirements.

The culture at Gamesa was changed forever. Feeling more like partners with the company's managers, the workforce took on greater initiatives. For example, they pointed out to leadership that their handicapped workforce was being unfairly overlooked for advancement. Working together, they came up with a development and training plan to give handicapped workers a chance to prove themselves and move into managerial roles. They also found a way to take care of displaced workers during seasonal slumps, thus acknowledging and giving back to those who sacrificed for the sake of the company.

The results that built over the years were amazing. As the process redesign matured, Gamesa was able to reduce its supervisor-to-worker ratio to just 1:55 from 1:12. Compensation shifted from flat-rate work to a 100 percent variable system with zero base pay. The new pay structure, based largely on process performance, included income divided among team members based on the type of job they held. Business results included volume increases of 50 percent, labor cost reductions of 12 percent, yield increases of fifteen points, a doubling in quality, and an increase in take-home pay of nearly 160 percent.

THE LONG JOURNEY

The transformation of Gamesa's labor relations alone would have been achievement enough for the company to rest on its laurels. But the transformation to process is relentless. It requires much detailed work, but it also requires bold insights into how to do things differently. For example, before beginning its transformation, Gamesa was a cost-driven company. The price of its products in the marketplace was based on the costs of producing the cookies and snacks. That sounds logical enough, but that measure proved useless when Juanito and the customers he represented were put in charge of the company. The new pricing strategy that drove process reorganization became what the company called "the added-value number." It wasn't difficult to find that number. All you had to do was go to the consumer with the product and ask, "What should the price of this product be?" Working backward, the company had to figure out how to make the product so that the price identified by the customer yielded a profit to Gamesa.

Of course, as economic and marketplace conditions change over time, so, too, must the price. And that means constant innovation in its processes. But for Gamesa, it is always the customer who sets the price of its products.

Structuring the transformation to process work is another constantly evolving struggle. The initial vision of a revitalized and renewed Gamesa was of a holistic transformation that swept through the entire company, turning it into a totally process-centric organization. But that goal proved much easier to envision than achieve.

Certainly Gamesa's intentions were right. It appointed process owners and devoted teams to reengineering processes, beginning with the innovation process. To emphasize how radical the changes were to be, the senior executives, who also served as process owners, were given new titles. The vice president of marketing, for example, became the process owner for the Captivating the Consumer process and the direct reports to her or him became the team members of that process. The title changes had the desired effect of sending a powerful message throughout the company: *We are serious about transforming the company.* And there were some successes, mainly in creating a culture that understood the concept of process.

But as time passed, it became evident that Gamesa was far from achieving the vision of a corporate-wide transformation that had set it off on its process journey. Instead, efforts were piecemeal, and the single most important thing limiting progress was that the processes Gamesa devised did not, for the most part, cross functional lines. What had happened was that Gamesa had merely added process titles to functional responsibilities. The functions remained mostly in their silos, and the company failed to gain the full benefits of end-to-end process work.

Process transformation often moves slowly, and it took several years for Gamesa's leadership to recognize that fact. To get the company back on the course to total transformation, José Luis Prado decided to begin in 2005 with a reorganization that would turn Gamesa into what senior management deemed a "multidimensional organization." One dimension of the new organization would be the existing functional roles for knowledge, expertise, and talent management. A second would bring together the company's four business units, who, as a group, would take ownership responsibility for consumers, the Juanitos of the world. The business units would run Gamesa's portfolio of brands, and focus on innovation and deep knowledge of consumers and Gamesa's competition. The third dimension was the creation of customer teams who, again as a multifunctional group, would take ownership responsibility of Gamesa's direct customers, the wholesalers and retailers who got Gamesa's products into the hands of the consumers. The customer teams specialized in one of three market segments: wholesale, supermarkets, and tiny "mom-and-pop" stores. Finally, there would be process owners guiding the move into process work. But process was not stressed in the second phase of Gamesa's transformation. While process would eventually be at the heart of the multidimensional organization, it was critical that Gamesa first achieve the reorganization before imposing process on the entire company.

This second phase of Gamesa's transformation was aimed at achieving a set of five priorities—"Must-win Battles" in Gamesa's parlance—that encompassed the entire organization. Four of the priorities directly engaged Gamesa's four business units—snacks, convenience foods, healthy snacks, and international—and sought to establish clear market dominance in their respective categories. The fifth battle was to achieve new capabilities and new levels of productivity through process, although end-to-end process was not yet emphasized.

Only after the reorganization had matured did Gamesa embark on the third phase of its transformation journey with a focus on process work. That phase began with a "Total Company Transformation Agenda" and the appointment of a chief transformation officer as part of the company's executive committee. As José Luis Prado, said: "The aim is to bring science to the art of management." The title of "process owner" was formalized, and the process owners were appointed for various processes: captivating the consumer, trade development, customer service, planning and management and organization, and talent. Each process owner was given the responsibility for delivering consistently effective end-to-end process performance by redesigning, improving, and managing their own end-to-end processes. "Faster, Better, Leaner" became Gamesa's governing mantra. Faster meant anticipating and getting ahead of change, better meant improved performance through synchronized and connected process, and leaner called for making more with less to fund future growth.

To implement the third phase of its transformation, Gamesa established a process council, a multifunctional team of leaders, including the process owners, who reported to Gamesa's executive committee. It also created new executive roles under the process owners. "Business architects" served as internal consultants to help manage processes and process improvement, "organizational architects" made sure the organizational structure had in place the proper roles and coordination to support processes, and the "IT architects" were charged with ensuring that the right information technology was available to support processes. Taken together, the changes represented an enterprise architecture approach that embraced every process and change in the company.

The results over three years were startling. Cycle times were reduced, with some products going from idea to market in just four months. Customer service achieved record levels even as inventories were reduced to new lows. Forecasts became more accurate, costs fell, and productivity doubled. Miguel Galvan, Gamesa's chief transformation officer and leader of the company's process council, noted that by the end of 2010 Gamesa will have risen from Level One in the PEMM model to Level Three, no small accomplishment. Most important, the third stage of Gamesa's transformation created the conditions for the company to make a quantum leap forward in coming years. But to do that, it must push harder in some areas, particularly in the role of the process owners.

"We need to mature the role of the process owner," Miguel explained. "Sometimes the functional managers are concerned about the process owners making decisions that affect the functional managers. The last mile of implementing process governance is for the functional leaders to recognize that changing the process goes beyond their boundaries and is the responsibility of the process owner to bring end-to-end benefits to business performance. So we are giving the process owners the formal authority to decide about process improvement investments and make operational trade-offs among functional managers."

Gamesa's customers also will play a more important role going forward. The company intends to integrate its customers into its own planning process, seeking insights and ideas about how better to serve its ultimate boss, Juanito, and the other consumers who enjoy Gamesa's products.

CHAPTER 10

Four Aces

COMING UP SHORT

When Kevin, the executive vice president of operations at Four Aces Manufacturing, and Glynn, the vice president of sales, were golfing with the newly appointed CEO of one of Four Aces' biggest customers, Zorba Technologies, they got an unanticipated earful.

"Look, I'm new on the job and I'm not here to beat you guys up, but everybody I talk to in my company complains about late deliveries and screwed-up billing from Four Aces," he told the shocked executives. "Your product quality is great, but your prices are going up faster than your competitors'. This isn't a threat, but I'm going to be keeping a lot closer eye on these things in the next year, and you need to know that I'm not guaranteeing you'll keep our business."

Visions of disaster loomed before the two chagrined executives. Kevin spent the rest of the day stewing about what he had heard on the golf course. "Why the hell didn't we know this earlier?" he kept asking himself. "We sure have lots of data and we go over it every month, but this never came up."

He called Glynn on Sunday and told him how unsettled he

253

was over the conversation. "I like surprises, Glynn, but not that kind. It was embarrassing. What's your take on his complaints, and how can we fix them?"

Glynn assured Kevin that it was nothing more than Four Aces experiencing some growing pains combined with Zorba having a new CEO who was a former operations guy. The new CEO was looking at things the last CEO hadn't much cared about. But then Glynn mentioned that perhaps Four Aces might want to beef up a bit.

"I'm telling you, Kevin, I could use some more resources. Perhaps we assign a few folks to hand-hold Zorba until the new guy gets used to the way we do things at Four Aces. You really need to talk to the operations team, too. Those guys can never seem to get anything out the door on time. Maybe they need to hire some more folks, too."

While more resources sounded okay since the company was growing, Kevin silently noted something that Glynn had said: "Until the new guy gets used to the way we do things." *Hmmm*, Kevin thought. *Does Glynn really believe that? Does he operate that way with all our customers? If so, how does that translate to his sales team? And how is operations involved?*

Kevin couldn't relax with these thoughts running through his head. *Have the fortunes of company growth made us arrogant? Are we forgetting the customer? What will Four Aces be like in five years if we continue this way?*

Kevin decided to forgo the football game that afternoon and spent the rest of Sunday searching the Web for ideas about what could be done to fix things. He found several articles and books that pointed out the fallacy of simply throwing resources at a problem. An excerpt from a book by Fred Brooks titled *The Mythical Man-Month* put it simply enough: "If you want to make a late project even later, throw people at it." Kevin wasn't convinced more resources was the answer. He also came across a new term: "voice of the customer."

Kevin knew time was of the essence, and he wanted to prove to the Zorba CEO that he was listening and that he was responsive to customer input. With Glynn's comments haunting him, he sensed there was much more to learn. He could feel it: this was big and it was important.

Monday morning rolled around, and Kevin started to dive into other customer data. His hunch was right—there were lots of other data that pointed in the same direction. On the surface, the issues wouldn't have been apparent. But since he was looking for something specific, it became like putting together a puzzle with a common theme. He was worried and optimistic all at once. Thank goodness the issue had surfaced, but what had Four Aces suffered unknowingly until now?

Kevin had several options for action, among them understanding how the sales, delivery, pricing, and billing activities worked and how they were linked. After a few days of following the process himself, he determined that a total overhaul of the company's order-to-cash process was necessary to get a handle on the late deliveries and bad billing. After doing some research into how process redesign could bring more discipline to Four Aces' operations and the connection with the voice of the customer, Kevin prepared a pitch for the executive committee to let him assign Roger, a rising young star, to do a process redesign of the order-to-cash process.

"What you say makes a lot of sense," said Four Aces' CEO, "but it sounds complicated. If Roger can pull it off, that'll tell us a lot more about just how good he really is."

Roger took on the new assignment enthusiastically. He knew the top brass had a good opinion of him, but he hadn't really had the chance to stretch himself in his other jobs. Moreover, he had a great deal of respect for Kevin and could sense Kevin's deep anxiety. Roger wanted to help, and this looked plenty challenging. It also fit well with his analytical abilities.

Roger started by sitting down with several of the top

executives to pick their brains about how their departments worked and to try to outline some bold targets and metrics for reaching them. Each executive voiced his or her support for what Roger was doing and gave him a great deal of information. The chief financial officer was known for not supporting anything other than reductions in costs to improve performance. Roger knew he needed to win him over first. The CFO told him that adding resources wasn't in the budget and that he thought the problem was with sales.

"Nobody really keeps an eye on that team, and they're a bunch of cowboys wheeling and dealing and not paying attention to margin, only gross revenue," he told Roger.

The director of operations was also critical of sales, but for a different reason: "They have no idea what 'capacity' means and they're out-selling as much as they can. That's great for the company, but I'm measured on labor utilization and costs as well as equipment uptime and unit costs. They never tell us ahead of time when a large order is coming. We see it in the system and then my materials team has to expedite materials in to make a delivery time that is way beyond our published cycle times."

The head of sales and marketing had sharp words for operations. "Nice folks, but clueless. They spend all their time running around picking inventory, and the new supervisor on the floor has all these new ideas that are killing us. If you ask me, that's where you need to spend your time making changes."

Finally, the chief information officer weighed in with a complaint about the finance group: "They keep telling me the order entry system has an issue and it keeps generating invoices with calculation errors. I told them there is nothing wrong with my system—their problem is garbage in, garbage out. I can't help it if they can't get the pricing and quantities straight and put them into the system incorrectly. You need to spend your time in finance and straighten them out.

And just to give you a heads-up, my team is very focused on the big next-generation project, so they need to be used sparingly. I won't tolerate any compromise on that systems implementation."

All that was great information, but it was also a bit disconcerting for Roger. "This gets complicated fast," he said to himself. "If it's going to work, we're going to need an infrastructure to support that much change. I've also got to be sure I address each of the senior executives' concerns or they won't back me."

For the rest of the year Roger devoted himself entirely to working out a sophisticated foundation for the transition to process. He found the people he wanted to do the redesign, worked with their leadership to have them on the team full-time, and put them through extensive training with outside consultants. He also sat down with HR to devise a new compensation scheme for the people whose jobs would change radically when the redesign was implemented, and negotiated with IT for the information systems that would be necessary to capture and analyze the new metrics that would support the new targets and measure the progress toward implementing the redesign.

Finally Roger felt comfortable that everything was in place to support the redesign effort. For the first four months of the new year the team worked on the redesign. The people selected for the design team came from different backgrounds and were chosen in part for their collegiality, and they seemed to really enjoy the work. Roger was impressed with the number of new ideas they had, and he did his best to incorporate them all. This could be a real game-changing moment for him and Four Aces. This went beyond the redesign. It was exciting. The team worked well and produced a design that looked great on paper.

Nevertheless, when Roger presented the redesign to the

executive committee, he encountered some unexpected oppo-sition. The IT vice president said his people were complaining about being diverted from more important work to devise software that measured things that had never been measured before and which didn't really matter.

"Look, we're already doing Six Sigma, we've seen some improvements using it, and we've got the software and metrics we need to keep going that way," he told the committee. "We don't need another layer of quality control on top of that."

Then the chief financial officer weighed in, noting that Roger had already exceeded the budget for the redesign and there was no evidence that the company was getting any pay-back. And even Kevin, who had urged the company to try process, complained that he was getting hassled by managers who had been cajoled into giving some of their best employ-ees to the redesign effort. The managers were getting impa-tient and wanted those people back doing the jobs they had left to work on this "temporary" project that had already taken more than a year.

HR supported the managers' complaints with evidence that the training and temporary personnel budget had sky-rocketed to backfill for those on the redesign team.

"Roger, I know you've worked hard on this for over a year now, but we're going to have to see some results very soon if we're going to continue down this path," the CEO told him. "Our customers know we're working on this and they're wondering when they'll start seeing the changes we've prom-ised. We'll take another look at it next quarter, but if we don't see any results, then I think we need to look at other options, such as a reorganization. With the cost overruns, that may be the quickest way to offset the financials so we won't blow our earnings call."

Roger knew there was no way he could get the process redesign up and running in three short months. Hadn't he

made it abundantly clear just how big the order-to-cash process was? It would take at least six months and more like a year
to do the necessary simulations and pilot runs, fix the inevitable glitches, and get the process running smoothly. But he
decided to keep that information to himself. It would be too
disheartening to his team to know that the executive committee was unhappy and voicing doubts.

But, of course, things like that never stay secret. Roger's
secretary, who had come from one of the areas that was part of
the redesign and who had lunch every day with her old team,
mentioned her concern about Roger and whether or not it
was a bad move for him to take on this project. "I can tell you
this much—the executive team is not happy and is growing
very impatient."

Word soon began to filter down to the team members that
the project was doomed. Fearful for their own careers, two
team members asked to be released from the team. Despite
his efforts to convince them otherwise, Roger realized that
by keeping them on the team he really might be jeopardizing
their futures. He didn't want to do that, so he allowed them to
go. When they left, the rumor mill really cranked up. He tried
to replace the two team members who had left, only to find
that those interested in being part of the initiative had deserted
him. The process redesign was nicknamed the "Only to Crash"
project, playing off the order-to-cash term that Roger had
so successfully socialized. The remaining team members went
through the motions of trying to test the redesign, but their
morale was falling and they argued about how to fix glitches
rather than brainstorming solutions.

When the executive committee met three months later,
Roger had to tell them that he really hadn't been able to make
much progress toward launching the process redesign. "As you
know, I've lost some team members and need to replace them,"
he said. "It doesn't make sense to keep going on the redesign

without representation from some of the departments that will be affected. Once I have the replacements I think we can have the process up and running within six months."

"Roger, we don't have six months and we can't keep breaking people loose from their jobs to work on this," the CEO said. "I'm telling customers that we're close but that we need to do some fine-tuning before launching. You need to make a concerted effort to get it working by the end of the year, and we'll make a decision then on whether to pull the plug or implement it."

Thoroughly demoralized, Roger bowed to the inevitable. He did what he could to provide good performance reviews for his team members in the hopes they could return to their old jobs, but he also updated his resume, trying to put the experience of the last two years in the best possible light, and began looking for another job.

Roger's approach to implementing the order-to-cash process looked fine on paper: put the enablers in place to support a high-performance process, design it, implement it, and realize the benefits. But Roger made some all-too-common mistakes: he tackled a project that was simply too large by attempting to implement the entire redesign all at once; he focused on getting the enabling processes and infrastructure in place, not on getting results driven by the core processes through design, metrics, and those performing the work. And he failed to gain the support of key players, including the chief financial officer and the head of IT. Roger was too ambitious, and he was thinking and implementing linearly when he needed to be thinking and implementing elements simultaneously. The delay in producing results increased skepticism and anxiety while decreasing commitment and resources, and process died an unnecessary death.

CHAPTER 11

Hattaway Inc.

THE BAND-AID

Hattaway Inc. is a big company with a high percentage of market share in the specialty metal-forming business. Much of the company's spectacular growth over the past decade was the result of mergers, acquisitions, and consolidation as it rolled up many smaller players in the industry. In 2008, as the global economy tanked, Hattaway stepped up its acquisition pace, grabbing at bargain prices a half dozen small companies that were in danger of failing. Each of the acquisitions brought something great to the table: customer base, proprietary methods, seasoned employees. All would add to strengthen their current market position. Hattway's CEO, Don Barkley, was confident that the company could maintain its dominant position in the industry.

As Don was enjoying his Sunday paper and a cup of coffee on his deck, his cell phone rang. Don didn't like being disturbed on Sunday mornings, so he let the phone take a message. When he looked at the screen an hour or so later he saw the caller was his CFO, Natalie Jackson. As he listened to her voice mail he realized she sounded awful. "Don, I need to talk to you right away."

Don felt bad for her. She must have lost a loved one or had some terrible family news. Natalie never called and never complained—she just handled things. That's why she was at the top of Don's succession plan. So imagine his surprise when Natalie informed him that she'd just gotten word that Hattaway's arch-competitor, Axon Forming, the second-largest player in the industry, had announced an all-cash offer for Marinko Metals, the third-largest player. At first he thought it must be a joke, but that couldn't be. Natalie was all business, all the time. His stomach turned. He felt as if his world had just come crashing in on him. Thoughts of the upcoming board of directors meeting immediately came to mind. What a game changer!

"What in the world are we going to do, Natalie?" Don asked with a groan.

"Unfortunately, Don, our hands are tied. We've spent too much on small acquisitions. We can't possibly raise enough cash to match Axon's offer."

Suddenly it looked as if Hattaway, even with the successful acquisition of the other companies, was destined to become number two in the industry it had long dominated. The company, started by Carl John (CJ) Hattaway, had never been in a number two position. Don did not want his legacy to be associated with bringing the family business down. CJ's grandson was a board member, and Don needed to think of something quickly before that board meeting.

Hunkering down in a defensive posture, Hattaway started looking for ways to defuse the new competitive situation. The first thing it did was a thorough customer analysis. The results weren't good. In its quest to grow through acquisitions Hattaway hadn't paid much attention to how well it was retaining customers from the smaller shops that it had gobbled up. It had focused on the acquisition of new, large customers and didn't bother measuring the retention of those smaller players. When all was said and done, keeping the small customers would have been three times more lucrative than the big customers. Hattaway's new customer segmentation scheme looked at each individual customer in terms of revenue generation. Since the smaller shops had a lower revenue rate, they were placed in the "silver" category, while the big customers were given the top spots in either the "gold" or "platinum" categories. The smaller customers didn't garner the same level of attention paid to the bigger customers. If Hattaway was ever going to have a shot at regaining the top spot in the industry, that had to change. Keeping existing customers happy would have to be the new priority.

That's when Mark Eldridge, the vice president of sales, stepped forward and volunteered to oversee an effort to redesign the Acquire and Retain Customer (ARC) process. He made a persuasive case that the redesign would provide Hattaway with a more focused approach to customer satisfaction and retention. With few other solutions apparent, Don agreed to let Mark give it a shot. Don asked Mark to put together a PowerPoint presentation to outline the plan and to make the concept simple enough so that he could explain it to the board of directors. The funding was secured, and Mark was given the green light to move ahead quickly.

Mark himself had been focused on getting new customers, not retaining old ones, so the new approach required him to shift gears in a major way. But he acted rapidly to convene a project team, and within four months a new design was developed and rolled out. It was an enormous success, both operationally and financially. Don had Mark present the results to the board and even brought in two customers to give their personal accounts of the positive impact the changes had brought about. Customers liked the way they were being treated, retention numbers improved, and some former customers returned to Hattaway. It looked as if Hattaway had a chance to regain its leading market share in the next few years. As a reward for his extraordinary efforts, Mark was promoted to chief marketing officer. Also, key players on the design team were promoted, and the sales staff began earning large bonuses. The entire company sighed in relief.

But a year later things were different. While many employees loved working in a process organization and were performing better and hitting their targets, there were others who weren't happy. Many of them were supervisors who had thrived in the old system, getting their work done and leaving at 5:00 p.m. to go home. The newest members of the management team, who came from the acquisitions made in previous years, were the most upset, as a more "normal" workday had been promised to them as part of the acquisition package. Now, under the new process, they had to stay later to provide a transition for the shift coming into work. And the targets they used to hit had changed. The new goals were not nearly as easy to accomplish and some of the supervisors were falling short. They really didn't like it when they were warned by a process owner, who used to work under them, that they had to shape up. The supervisors began sandbagging the system, backsliding to their old ways. In order to look as if they were supporting process, they came up with their own pet projects for their departments and labeled them "redesigns." They stopped including the process owners in their efforts and made presentations that touted their successful improvements, threatening the credibility of the process owner role.

Since the role was never made official and the expectations and measures were never communicated, the process owners had little to fall back on. As an informal group, they attempted to talk to individual executives, but to no avail. They struggled to maintain their focus and started spending more time in their "day jobs" than focusing on the process owner role.

The crisis had passed and the CEO allowed the behavior because he wanted to keep his management team happy. New designs came more slowly and didn't have the impact that the first big push had produced. As the company reverted to its old ways some of the employees who enjoyed and were thriving in a process environment became discouraged and left. Some were hired by Axon Forming, which immediately started to educate the entire company about process and how to thrive in a process-led organization.

Today Hattaway is still aiming to regain the top spot in the industry, but the gap between it and number one is widening, not shrinking. Don decided to take the bonus he was offered for pulling the company out of the crisis and head for an early retirement. Natalie was offered his position, but given the environment, she turned it down. Don is helping her connect with potential new employers. Without process, Hattway is just another company struggling to survive.

Hattaway's experience is typical of how companies fail when they adopt process to meet a crisis and don't implement any infrastructure or enterprise elements (leadership, culture, governance, expertise) to sustain the work. Some people become genuinely engaged in process work, but others do so grudgingly, acceding to it for the time being because it seems the senior leadership sees it as a way to solve the crisis. Once the crisis is past, the impetus to continue process slows. The people who had been doing process work because they had to, not because they wanted to, begin to undermine the transformation, arguing with process owners. Without the crisis as a motivator, the senior leadership becomes less determined to push ahead with the changes involved in process transformation, and this lets the dissension continue to simmer. Over time the process effort dies a lingering death.

It could have been different. Had Mark, as a leader of process, engaged more leaders, created more expertise beyond just the design team, worked with HR to formalize the process owner role, and implemented a governance structure to align with the strategy, Hattaway might have been able to sustain its early process successes. A process-managed enterprise needs to address *both* the process enablers and enterprise capabilities, and focusing too much on one to the exclusion of the other can be costly. The key: process enablers *attain*, enterprise capabilities *sustain*.

CHAPTER 12

Acme Specialties

THE BEST-LAID PLANS

There's something to be said for learning from failures. Of course, it's always better to learn from someone else's failure, not our own, so let's take a moment now to see how one company with the best of intentions went abysmally wrong in executing the transition to process. We'll just call the company Acme Specialties Corp. to avoid embarrassing anyone.

Acme Specialties was somewhat unusual in that the CEO made the decision to implement process, becoming, in effect, both the catalyst and the leader. The CEO was known for his amiable and consensus-driven style and not for single-handedly mandating what the company would do and how it would do it. Still, he instructed his direct reports to have a process improvement goal as part of their balanced scorecard and then assigned a leader to spearhead the entire effort through skills enhancement, methodologies, and coordination. The person he chose for that role, Emmitt Campbell, did not have enough duties to fill his plate full-time as the result of a reorganization.

There was more to recommend Emmitt for the job than just some spare time. He was well known in the company, was a quick learner, and had a technical background with extensive sales experience. He was an excellent presenter, adept at taking complex topics and simplifying them so they could be understood at all levels of the organization. His business acumen was superb.

But there were some hints of problems, too. Emmitt was arrogant. Every conversation centered on him and what he had accomplished. Seldom did he credit his teams. His peers didn't like him at all, although they had little choice but to tolerate him. While he possessed great aptitude for learning, he did not have the interest to learn more than what was needed to sell a concept. To top it off, he was a bit on the lazy side.

That laziness, though, wasn't such a bad thing. It compelled him to hire Bill Smith, a business and process expert, to be the chief process officer and do most of the heavy lifting associated with the process transformation. Bill, who came from the outside and had Fortune 50 business experience, was accepted by this difficult culture very quickly despite the fact that the majority of the people at the company had long tenure and generally looked askance at outsiders. They described their culture as having the "antibody effect," meaning that they would surround and devour any new people or ideas.

The initial plan was to create a large department, somewhere around eighty people, to facilitate the work around the world. But that idea immediately ran into a lot of pushback from the senior leaders running the business units, and it was scrapped in favor of a much smaller corporate process team. Despite the small size of the process team, they were given a very audacious cost-saving goal and put to work.

Focusing first on awareness, they invested in training for the top fifteen hundred people in the company. It took quite a while to development the curriculum and then teach it to those fifteen hundred people. While that was going on Bill, the

new CPO, saw opportunities to get smaller process redesign
initiatives started, and at some risk he seized the opportunity
and got the ball rolling. The first small-scale redesign was a
huge success, and momentum began to build. The CEO of the
external customer who benefited most from that first project
came in to speak to Acme Specialties' senior leaders, sharing
his amazement in the performance turnaround and announcing more business for Acme Specialties.

Riding the crest of that first success, Bill sat down with
Acme Specialties' chief financial officer to work on a plan to
measure the impact of the planned initiatives. The definitions
and formulas they devised would be used when determining the effect any particular redesign was having. Bill insisted
that his own corporate process team be measured by the
bottom-line savings it achieved. Should the team reach the
audacious goals set earlier, they would be richly rewarded.

As the process started to build momentum, Emmitt, the
process leader, convinced the CEO that at the next executive meeting he would introduce the concept of the process
owner. After the meeting, process owners were assigned for
each of the core, governing, and enabling processes in each
geographical region. They were told that Bill, the CPO, was
the person to contact if they had any questions.

That's when the first signs of trouble cropped up. Unfortunately, Emmitt never fully understood the concept of the process owner. He simply assigned functional leaders to process
owner roles. The process owners were encouraged to start ini-
tiating redesigns and to populate a scorecard when the results
started to come in. The process leader congratulated himself
on ticking off another box in the transition to process.

But when Bill learned who had been named process owners, he got a little nervous and began calling around to the new
owners. Only a few voiced much interest in what a process

owner's responsibilities really were. Most indicated that they would just wait until they went through the process training and go from there.

Excitement at the grassroots level began to grow, and department managers and directors began to initiate redesigns in their areas. Because there was only a limited number of resources available full-time to work on the redesigns, a backlog started to build. Bill received a call one day from a business leader requesting that the process office figure out a way to manage all the projects. Bill was delighted, and before long a governance council was started in one of the business units. It took a while for the first meeting to happen, due to busy schedules, but eventually the reviews became quarterly.

Acme Specialties had the ingredients for achieving industry changing breakthrough performance. Some things it did very well, and other opportunities were squandered. Let's explore each element needed for successful implementation and see what happened.

LEADERSHIP AND CULTURE

Acme Specialties was fortunate to have a CEO willing to try something different. And while a process leader was assigned to run the global initiative, the *right* leader was not selected. Regardless of how well a person drives process and performance, any important initiative that is aimed at significantly changing the way a company operates or its culture should never go to a leader who is not well regarded in the organization. Even though the process leader had accomplished many things in his career, the "path of destruction" he left behind him in the course of achieving those goals was so significant that he would never get corporate-wide support. The CEO actually knew how people felt about the process leader—he had received the process leader's 360-degree results, which were candid and damning—but because he personally liked him, he made the assignment anyway.

The mandate from the CEO was a good attempt, as mandates from him were rare. His own personal style was such that the heads of the business units were given a great deal of power and autonomy and were never managed toward a common goal. In fact, the business unit presidents were known for arguing and public jabbing, even though they tried to veil the criticisms with humor. Unfortunately, because there had been only a few mandates from the CEO in the past and little or no follow-through or consequences, the CEO's staff knew that they could easily prove why it was not going to work for them and be given some degree of exemption. Some just figured they would ignore it until it went away.

Bill showed a great deal of promise, considering his acceptance into the tough culture, but results were limited. While Bill was hired to help change the culture, the leadership team did not give him the public support he needed to bring about that change. The message sent to Bill was a Catch-22: *Your job is to change the culture here, but make sure your changes fit into our existing culture.* In just a few years, Bill's level of frustration became unbearable. It was clear that the leadership expected everyone else's jobs and behaviors to change, but would not change any of their own.

CHOOSING PROCESS OWNERS

Acme Specialties assigned process owners in all of the global geographies and at different levels of influence, but it either chose the wrong people or didn't invest the selection with any authority. In human resources, for example, the role of process owner was given to three people in the course of just one year.

The first process owner delegated her duties to someone else and then fired that person a few months later. The third person selected was laid off after being in the role for about four months. The message came through loud and clear: the head of HR wasn't taking the assignment seriously. And although the process leader complained about it to the head of HR and the CEO, both ignored the situation. It was evident that the leadership team did not understand the role enough to implement it the right way. They knew that cross-functional responsibility was required, but indicated that "they didn't work that way," then modified the role to fit the structure.

Timing was also a significant issue. Bill assigned process owners and convened design teams before training was complete and before any experts could be trained. The process leader did not tell Bill what he had planned for the executive meeting, and so Bill had to scramble. Assigning process owners and convening design teams took about five months. Unfortunately, by that time any excitement had worn off and the organization did not believe the process owner role was important.

Finally, the head of HR did not want to add the process owner role and title to the company's compensation and job description system. She said she had reviewed the number of job titles and pay bands in the system and that Acme Specialties actually needed to reduce the number rather than add any more. She also said that because the process owner role was "experimental," she didn't want to change the system until it was proven that it was going to remain a legitimate role in the company. When Bill produced a job description complete with responsibilities and authorities, he was told that it was not in the HR-approved format; plus HR was undergoing a change in technology support, and so this was not a good time to make changes. Bill tried to explain that this thinking was completely backward and showed the vice president for HR how making the necessary process changes before technology would actually save time and money in the long run. But she shrugged him off. "We have a solid plan and a budget that has been approved by the leadership team. We don't have the time or the budget to experiment with this new technology implementation."

While a significant stretch goal was set for Bill in terms of savings, he was the only one who had the goal assigned to him. There was no alignment with the functional leaders, with the process owners, or with Acme Specialties' key performance indicators. There was no willingness to examine existing metrics and make changes. There was also no balance between voice-of-the-customer goals and voice-of-the-business goals—all process efforts were focused on improving costs and cycle time. Despite the fact that customers came to headquarters to extol the virtues of process redesign, the leadership at Acme Specialties refused to acknowledge that redesign efforts could translate into growth. Some of the top executives openly compared process management to much narrower tools such as Lean and Six Sigma. Process, they said, was only about efficiency and effectiveness.

Establishing definitions of progress and methods for measuring it was a big positive. It framed the debate for understanding what was considered acceptable in the design initiatives and what wasn't. Bill socialized the definitions and got stakeholder buy-in from around the world. Unfortunately, when things started to go well, certain influential leaders wanted to take personal credit for the improvements and would not give credit to accomplishments that were the result of process.

DESIGN, PERFORMERS, AND INFRASTRUCTURE

Those working on the design teams were really having fun. They had a chance to innovate and implement some of their own ideas that they had wanted to try for several years. Even those who were not on the team but who were solicited for input felt a renewed sense of importance, as their ideas were being heard and considered. One group went rogue and decided they knew a better way to design, but they eventually came to the CPO desperately looking for some help. They had too many on the team and therefore were suffering with having too many opinions and never getting to consensus. They'd also gone down a rat hole of trying to make Six Sigma the only tool they used but weren't getting the results they wanted. Luckily, the CPO got them back on track and the design was a great success.

The performers working in the newly designed processes were happy. They enjoyed working as teams, and self-directed work teams began to spring up all over the organization. And even though HR was reluctant to make permanent some of the changes to the way compensation was structured, those measured on process performance in addition to their other measures were excited about the difference they were able to make—to the customer and to their own bank accounts.

When it came time to implement an Enterprise Resource Planning (ERP) system in one of the business units, the leader of the business made a very public announcement that process was going to come first. The design teams were ecstatic, and the head of the process organization for that business unit quickly realigned the existing design efforts to fit the plan for the ERP system. Then they waited for the call—but it never came. The new generation of leaders for the organization was put in charge of the ERP implementation, and while they agreed to put process first, it was conditional—it would have to be on their terms. Designing for the business they wanted to have in the future was difficult, as most of them were tenured and were comfortable with the way they had always done things. Thus, the first of the onboard terrorists were identified but allowed to do things their way, due to the aggressive budget and schedule for the ERP implementation.

GOVERNANCE AND EXPERTISE

It was brilliant not to start the process initiative by building the governance structure first. Given Acme Specialties' culture, starting with the structure would have made it feel bureaucratic and not relevant considering there wouldn't have been any quick results. Instead, the CPO allowed the backlog of process requests and initiatives to build up purposely so that the governance structure was the business's idea. And while the start was slow and the governance council didn't meet often enough, it was a good beginning. The experts, once they were trained, were dedicated full-time, and that was an enormous plus for the organization.

ACME SPECIALTIES TODAY

In the first three years of process, there were many millions of dollars in audited (by the finance organization) bottom-line savings that had been realized. Despite the stretch goal being achieved within a few million dollars, Bill was given a very poor rating for not hitting the goal exactly. When he asked the process leader if he thought he could ever really hit it, the process leader replied, "No—I never even thought you'd get as close as you did. But you still didn't hit it." Bill left the company for a much better opportunity. The ERP initiative failed, and millions of dollars were lost. The people who'd been excited about process left the company in droves when they saw that Bill left and that the onboard terrorists were allowed to stay and were never dealt with. And while the stock price is holding steady, the realization of breakthrough performance on a company-wide level never happened. At Acme Specialties process is now analogous to process improvement at the individual department levels. Managing by process and achieving breakthrough performance is dead.

PART III

CHAPTER 13

Modeling Process Maturity

YOUR GUIDE THROUGH THE JOURNEY

As more and more organizations strive to harness the power of their business processes, the need for an implementation road map has become critical. After reading the previous chapters, it should be clear that redesigning and managing processes deliver dramatic improvements in cost, quality, speed, and service that can, in turn, yield strategic advantages. In industries that range from consumer goods and heavy manufacturing to health care, government, and nonprofits, and in processes ranging from order fulfillment to human resource management, process management and redesign are no longer seen as quick fixes for a crisis, but instead have become fundamental parts of the business.

But a process effort is not a minor undertaking. End-to-end process management and redesign do not just change processes, they change *everything*. This book explains in detail the nine critical high-level organizing principles that can transform a mediocre company into a high-performance process organization. We have emphasized throughout that becoming a process organization is about integrating all nine levers into the way your company does its work. We have found that while companies understand the need to make many changes in order to harness the power of process, they are often uncertain about what exactly needs to change, by how much, and when. That uncertainty leads to confused planning, lack of integration, much debate, lots of errors, rework, and delays in achieving the transformation to process.

After studying companies undertaking the effort to become process-oriented organizations, both those that succeeded and those that failed, Michael Hammer devised a model of process transformation that will serve as a road map to your own efforts to do things faster, cheaper, and better. The model, described in more detail below, lays out the standards for four levels of maturity in both the five process enablers and the four enterprise capabilities that are necessary to achieve process success. The Process and Enterprise Maturity Model (PEMM) applies to any organization in any industry, and it doesn't specify what any particular process should look like. Rather, it identifies the characteristics that any organization should have to succeed in implementing process transformation. A company can apply PEMM to all its processes and can develop processes unique to its own needs.

Before we explain PEMM and how to use it, a few critical notes are in order:

- A process enterprise cannot be created overnight. It must be realized over an extended period of time. Most organizations cannot redesign all their processes simultaneously. Implementing a new process is usually a complex and costly effort, and most companies do not have enough human and financial resources to undertake numerous projects simultaneously. Realigning all aspects of the enterprise with end-to-end processes (metrics, rewards, responsibilities, development plans, compensation, etc.) will also have to be done gradually.

- The extended nature of the process transition poses a real challenge for executives embarking on the process road. They must address such basic questions as where to start, how fast to go, how to maintain momentum, how do the process goals support the overall business strategy, how resources will be allocated, and the like. The PEMM is a tool to help companies and executives navigate their way through these issues. The PEMM does not attempt to provide answers to these questions; rather, it is a framework for thinking through and resolving them.

- Process is an integrated approach to getting work done. You cannot pick and choose among the nine principles and expect to succeed. All nine principles must be addressed to realize the full transformational benefits and the ability to sustain them. For example, you cannot design a process, appoint a process owner, and train the process performers without having the right process metrics in place to measure the process. If your organization measures performance the way it always has, it will reward people for focusing on narrow functional goals, not outcomes, and process won't live up to its promise.

- Ideally, process will become the way in which the entire company gets its work done. However, it is unlikely that all parts of a company will adopt processes at the same time. Often, especially in large companies, process transformations start in a business unit, a plant, or a geographic region. It's important to understand that process only works when it moves across functions, and the business unit is typically the smallest organizational unit in which that can happen. A functional department will not, by definition, be able to undertake process on its own because it can't do cross-functional work, and attempting to impose process on a stand-alone functional department likely will be a disaster.

- You don't need to reorganize your enterprise by process.

Most organizations committed to process maintain their functional organization, but manage by process. This means that your departments will likely remain intact, but such elements as budgets, job definitions, performance measurement systems, workflow, and department goals, to name a few, will need to change. Don't make the mistake of changing only certain aspects and ignoring others. For example, senior executives might encourage managers to create a cross-functional process, and then be tempted to prevent the managers from changing the measurement system appropriately to align with process. It is true that process work incorporates functional departments, but the relationships and alignment among those departments undergo fundamental changes in process work.

THE PROCESS AND ENTERPRISE MATURITY MODEL (PEMM)

With those caveats in mind, let's look at how the PEMM works. It is a model designed to measure how well the organization is adopting the nine principles of process. Five of those principles we describe as process enablers are Design, Performers, Process Ownership, Infrastructure, and Metrics. The remaining four are enterprise capabilities: Leadership, Culture, Expertise, and Governance. While the process enablers are focused on process design, execution, and *making* the change, the enterprise capacities are focused on supporting and *sustaining* the change, so that it becomes "business as usual" or the way people work. The term *enterprise* refers to the scope of the organization undertaking the transformation effort, which can be an entire company or one or more business units. While we evaluate process enablers in a separate chart from enterprise capabilities, you nevertheless should think of them as a whole.

In the model, each principle has four numerically designated levels of maturity, ranging from what we might call "just getting started" to "best in class." More formally, we can say that a process rated P-1 on the chart is both reliable and predictable, i.e., it is stable. The P-2 level indicates that a process delivers superior results because the company has designed and implemented it from one end of the organization to the other. At the next level, P-3, a process delivers optimal performance because executives can integrate it, when necessary, with other internal processes to maximize its contribution to the company's performance. Finally, in the rarefied realm of P-4, a process truly is best in class, transcending the company's boundaries and extending back to suppliers and forward to customers. Similarly, enterprise capabilities can be rated at four equivalent maturity levels, E-1 through E-4.

For each principle, the model provides two or more ways to measure the degree of maturity in an organization. If, for example, we look at how the maturity of Performers is measured, we find separate measures for knowledge, skills, and behavior. For each of those measures, the model provides narrative explanations of what performers should exhibit at each level of maturity.

Notice that at the right side of the Processes and Enterprise charts are four cells for each facet of the principles. Those cells are where you actually rate the maturity of that aspect of process. We encourage people using the PEMM to signify the "as is" position of your organization using a stoplight—or red, yellow, green—method for a high-level assessment. To use the model, simply read the statement in the appropriate box and decide how accurately it reflects the state of your process. If the statement is largely true or at least 80 percent correct, color the appropriate cell green or write 80+ in it. If the statement is somewhat true, or between 20 percent and 80 percent correct, color the cell yellow or write 20–80 in it. If the statement is largely not true, or less than 20 percent correct, the cell is colored red or you write −20. The score itself doesn't particularly matter. Rather, it serves to give you insight into where to focus or where to start.

Let's use the Performers example again. Let's say you're trying to introduce process into your own organization and have explained it to the workforce several times. To assess the maturity of the Performers, you first think about how well they know the process they execute and how well they can identify the key metrics. Have they heard your explanation and understand it pretty well? Color that P-1 cell green. How about their skills in problem solving and process-improvement techniques? Okay, but not great? Better color that cell yellow. Now comes the tough one: To what extent are the performers actually demonstrating their allegiance to process and not to their functional department and boss? Not very well, right? Color that cell red. The result is that you now know where you're making progress in introducing process to the performers and where you need to do a lot more work.

While the PEMM is very useful in determining where you need to focus more effort in any given process, the real value lies in its ability to coordinate your progress in process transformation across the entire spectrum of the nine critical principles. The PEMM should be used to achieve a balanced and synchronized approach to process transformation. Remember the old saw about a chain being as strong as its weakest link? That's true of process, too. Therefore, you want to use the PEMM to discover how mature your overall organization is in achieving the nine principles, where the weaknesses are, and in what order they should be addressed. Let's say, for example, that after six months of undertaking process transformation

you go down the list evaluating maturity in each of the various facets of the nine principles. In the Process Enabling chart, you find that most of the cells come up green or yellow, but two come up red. You need to pay a lot more attention to those red flags and also undertake some work to turn the yellow cells green before you can accurately proclaim reaching Level 1. You might be tempted to score your processes enablers significantly higher than you score your enterprise capabilities because of resources, time, or even level of understanding of the processes over the enterprise as a whole, but you would just be kidding yourself. Because the principles are so intertwined, you simply cannot have Level 3 processes in a Level 1 enterprise. A Level 1 enterprise, by definition, cannot support Level 3 processes.

Finally, use the PEMM for communication and education. The concepts of process and process enterprise represent very different ways of thinking about work and organizations than those with which most people are familiar. Even when these concepts have been introduced and explained to people in an organization, they often do not truly comprehend what these notions mean and entail. In particular, there are key concepts and lessons that must be widely appreciated but can be difficult to communicate. A failure to comprehend them can make an organization feel either complacent or hopeless about the challenges it faces. They can be difficult to communicate because they entail a sophisticated appreciation of the impacts of processes on an enterprise and of what is involved in making process a reality. The PEMM can be helpful in getting people to understand and internalize these important messages. The key lessons that need to be communicated throughout an organization are:

1. **There is a lot to be done.** Many people underestimate what is involved in moving to processes. They think that

convening process redesign teams is all that is required.
They need to appreciate what a process-based enterprise
actually entails.

2. **There is a path.** Conversely, some people who do
   appreciate the magnitude of the process transition may not
   understand how to negotiate it. They need to recognize
   that it is possible to succeed at this endeavor.

3. **It doesn't have to happen all at once.** It is natural
   to think that the move to process must be done
   instantaneously. Understanding the evolutionary nature
   of the transition allays anxieties, creates reasonable
   expectations, and prepares people for a long journey.

4. **An accurate assessment is critical.** Many organizations
   are overly optimistic about their capability in the process
   sphere. It is important to deflate any undue confidence,
   which is usually due to a lack of understanding of process
   and therefore inaccurate interpretation. An accurate
   assessment is critical, because any overconfidence will
   impede the effort in various ways, such as underfunding
   or insufficient priority, which can quickly turn into deep
   pessimism when the going turns out not to be so smooth.

Keep in mind that the PEMM is a granular model. That
is, it captures the maturity of each individual process in an
enterprise as well as the maturity of the enterprise itself.
Each of these is expressed in terms of the maturity of a number of different elements (such as leadership knowledge and
process-owner authority). This raises the very real possibility
of inconsistencies in which the maturity of some elements
(or a process or enterprise) may be very different from that
of others, even elements associated with the same enabler or
capability. For instance, it may be that Leadership Knowledge
is at E-3, but Leadership Style is not even at E-1. This occurs
because organizations may not have had available during their

process work the kind of framework that the PEMM provides, so they neglected to put adequate energy into certain areas. It is not a cause for alarm. Often, more energy needs to be expended on certain processes or areas than others. The PEMM will highlight these discrepancies and enable leadership to determine where the gaps are and the appropriate action to take to rectify the issues.

PEMM AT WORK

When an organization begins redesigning its business processes or attempts to rise from one level to the next, it is imperative to conduct a maturity analysis. In 2001, when Tom Purves, whom we met in Chapter Five, took over as the manager of the Motiva refinery in Port Arthur, Texas, he and his leadership team used process-based techniques to redesign two core processes, Ensure Safe Production and Reliability-Centered Maintenance, to improve the refinery's performance. Purves was determined to take the process enablers in those areas from P-2 to P-3.

They began by setting up two separate evaluations of the process enablers and enterprise capabilities, one by process owners and senior executives, the other by frontline workers. While the two groups had different opinions, a joint discussion resolved those differences. Nevertheless, Purves and his team found that several enablers were at the P-3 level but also rated performers' knowledge and the use of metrics for goal setting at P-2. Using that information, the team launched efforts to increase the understanding of processes by performers, to use a more structured approach to setting performance targets, and to create a program-management office. The result was further improvement in operations. For example, Port Arthur's alarm rate, a key metric of the Ensure Safe Production process, soon ranked the lowest in Shell's manufacturing system, and the mean time between failures of key equipment shot up. Those changes contributed significantly to the refinery's bottom line, and Tom Purves is now Shell's vice president of manufacturing operations for the Americas Gulf Coast.

When many people hear the word *process,* they immediately think of flowcharts and boxes on paper and continuous improvement. As we've shown throughout this book, end-to-end process thinking is much more. Using the PEMM and addressing all nine elements is the way to drive transformational business results. And you don't have to wait until you reach Level 4 to see truly remarkable changes; you can realize improvements all along the way. Using PEMM can give you insight into the state of your process enablers and show you what needs improvement.

But companies do not live by process alone. High-performance processes require supportive environments in order to sustain the changes and succeed. The more successful your organization is at developing its enterprise capabilities, the more effective any end-to-end change will be. And done right, these changes won't be incremental; they will drive game-changing and breakthrough innovation and results in efficiency, effectiveness, and growth. Faster, cheaper, better. You really can have all three.

The Process and Enterprise Maturity Model (PEMM)

How Mature Are Your PROCESSES?

		P-1	P-2
DESIGN	**Purpose**	The process has not been designed on an end-to-end basis. Functional managers use the legacy design primarily as a context for functional performance improvement.	The process has been redesigned from end to end in order to optimize its performance.
	Context	The process's inputs, outputs, suppliers, and customers have been identified.	The needs of the process's customers are known and agreed upon.
	Documentation	The documentation of the process is primarily functional, but it identifies the interconnections among the organizations involved in executing the process.	There is end-to-end documentation of the process design.
PERFORMERS	**Knowledge**	Performers can name the process they execute and identify the key metrics of its performance.	Performers can describe the process's overall flow; how their work affects customers, other employees in the process, and the process's performance; and the required and actual performance levels.
	Skills	Performers are skilled in problem solving and process-improvement techniques.	Performers are skilled in teamwork and self-management.
	Behavior	Performers have some allegiance to the process, but owe primary allegiance to their function.	Performers try to follow the process design, perform it correctly, and work in ways that will enable other people who execute the process to do their work effectively.
OWNER	**Identity**	The process owner is an individual or a group informally charged with improving the process's performance.	Enterprise leadership has created an official process-owner role and has filled the position with a senior manager who has clout and credibility.
	Activities	The process owner identifies and documents the process, communicates it to all the performers, and sponsors small-scale change projects.	The process owner articulates the process's performance goals and a vision of its future; sponsors redesign and improvement efforts; plans their implementation; and ensures compliance with the process design.
	Authority	The process owner lobbies for the process but can only encourage functional managers to make changes.	The process owner can convene a process redesign team and implement the new design and has some control over the technology budget for the process.
INFRASTRUCTURE	**Information Systems**	Fragmented legacy IT systems support the process.	An IT system constructed from functional components supports the process.
	Human Resource Systems	Functional managers reward the attainment of functional excellence and the resolution of functional problems in a process context.	The process's design drives role definitions, job descriptions, and competency profiles. Job training is based on process documentation.
METRICS	**Definition**	The process has some basic cost and quality metrics.	The process has end-to-end process metrics derived from customer requirements.
	Uses	Managers see the process's metrics to track its performance, identify root causes of faulty performance, and drive functional improvements.	Managers use the process's metrics to compare its performance to benchmarks, best-in-class performance, and customer needs and to set performance targets.

P-3	P-4	P-1	P-2	P-3	P-4
The process has been designed to fit with other enterprise processes and with the enterprise's IT systems in order to optimize the enterprise's performance.	The process has been designed to fit with customer and supplier processes in order to optimize interenterprise performance.				
The process owner and the owners of the other processes with which the process interfaces have established mutual performance expectations.	The process owner and the owners of customer and supplier processes with which the process interfaces have established mutual performance expectations.				
The process documentation describes the process's interfaces with, and expectations of, other processes and links to process to the enterprise's system and data architecture.	An electronic representation of the process design supports its performance and management and allows analysis of environmental chances and process reconfigurations.				
Performers are familiar both with fundamental business concepts and with the drivers of enterprise performance and can describe how their work affects other processes and the enterprise's performance.	Performers are familiar with the enterprise's industry and its trends and can describe how their work affects interenterprise performance.				
Performers are skilled at business decision making.	Performers are skilled at change management and change implementation.				
Performers strive to ensure that the process delivers the results needed to achieve the enterprise's goal.	Performers look for signs that the process should change, and they propose improvements to the process.				
The process comes first for the owner in terms of time allocation, mind share, and personal goals.	The process owner is a member of the enterprise's senior-most decision-making body.				
The process owner works with other process owners to integrate processes to achieve the enterprise's goals.	The process owner develops a rolling strategic plan for the process, participates in enterprise-level strategic planning, and collaborates with his or her counterparts working for customers and suppliers to sponsor interenterprise process redesign initiatives.				
The process owner controls the IT systems that support the process and any projects that change the process and has some influence over personnel assignments and evaluations as well as the process's budget.	The process controls the process's budget and exerts strong influence over personnel assignments and evaluations.				
An integrated IT system, designed with the process in mind and adhering to enterprise standards, supports the process.	An IT system with a modular architecture that adheres to industry standards for interenterprise communication supports the process.				
Hiring, development, reward, and recognition systems emphasize the process's needs and results and balance them against the enterprise's needs.	Hiring, development, reward, and recognition systems reinforce the importance of intra- and interenterprise collaboration, personal learning, and organizational change.				
The process's metrics as well as cross-process metrics have been derived from the enterprise's strategic goals.	The process's metrics have been derived from interenterprise goals.				
Managers present the metrics to process performers for awareness and motivation. They use dashboards based on the metrics for day-to-day management of the process.	Managers regularly review and refresh the process metrics and targets and use them in strategic planning.				

How Mature Is Your ENTERPRISE?

		E-1	E-2
LEADERSHIP	Awareness	The enterprise's senior executive team recognizes the need to improve operational performance but has only a limited understanding of the power of business processes.	At least one senior executive deeply understands the business process concept, how the enterprise can use it to improve performance, and what is involved in implementing it.
	Alignment	The leadership of the process program lies in the middle management ranks.	A senior executive has taken leadership of, and responsibility for, the process program.
	Behavior	A senior executive endorses and invests in operational improvement.	A senior executive has publicly set stretch performance goals in customer terms and is prepared to commit resources, make deep changes, and remove roadblocks in order to achieve those goals.
	Style	The senior executive team has started shifting from a top-down, hierarchical style to an open, collaborative style.	The senior executive team leading the process program is passionate about the need to change and about process as the key tool for change.
CULTURE	Teamwork	Teamwork is project focused, occasional, and atypical.	The enterprise commonly uses crossfunctional project teams for improvement efforts.
	Customer focus	There is a widespread belief that customer focus is important, but there is limited appreciation of what that means. There is also uncertainty and conflict about how to meet customer needs.	Employees realize that the purpose of their work is to deliver extraordinary customer value.
	Responsibility	Accountability for results rests with managers.	Frontline personnel begin to take ownership of results.
	Attitude toward change	There is growing acceptance in the enterprise about the need to make modest change.	Employees are prepared for significant change in how work is performed.
EXPERTISE	People	A small group of people has a deep appreciation for the power of processes.	A cadre of experts has skills in process redesign and implementation, project management, communications, and change management.
	Methodology	The enterprise uses one or more methodologies for solving execution programs and making incremental process improvements.	Process redesign teams have access to a basic methodology for process redesign.
GOVERNANCE	Process model	The enterprise has identified some business processes.	The enterprise has developed a complete enterprise process model, and the senior executive team has accepted it.
	Accountability	Functional managers are responsible for performance, project managers for improvement projects.	The process owners have accountability for individual processes, and a steering committee is responsible for the enterprise's overall progress with processes.
	Integration	One or more groups advocate and support possibly distinct operational improvement techniques.	An informal coordinating body provides needed program management while a steering committee allocates resources for process redesign projects.

E-3	E-4	E-1	E-2	E-3	E-4
The senior executive team views the enterprise in process terms and has developed a vision of the enterprise and its processes.	The senior executive team sees its own work in process terms and perceives process management not as a project but as a way of managing the business.				
There is strong alignment in the senior executive team regarding the process program. There is also a network of people throughout the enterprise helping to promote process efforts.	People throughout the enterprise exhibit enthusiasm for process management and play leadership roles in process efforts.				
Senior executives operate as a team, manage the enterprise through its processes, and are actively engaged in the process program.	The members of the senior executive team perform their own work as processes, center strategic planning on processes, and develop new business opportunities based on high-performance processes.				
The senior executive team has delegated control and authority to process owners and process performers.	The senior executive team exercises leadership through vision and influence rather than command and control.				
Teamwork is the norm among process performers and is commonplace among managers.	Teamwork with customers and suppliers is commonplace.				
Employees understand that customers demand uniform excellence and a seamless experience.	Employees focus on collaborating with trading partners to meet the needs of final customers.				
Employees feel accountable for enterprise results.	Employees feel a sense of mission in serving customers and achieving ever-better performance.				
Employees are ready for major multidimensional change.	Employees recognize change as inevitable and embrace it as a regular phenomenon.				
A cadre of experts has skills in large-scale change management and enterprise transformation.	Substantial numbers of people with skills in process redesign and implementation, project management, program management, and change management are present across the enterprise. A formal process for developing and maintaining that skill base is also in place.				
The enterprise has developed and standardized a formal process for process redesign and has integrated it with a standard process for process improvement.	Process management and redesign have become core competencies and are embedded in a formal system that includes environment scanning, change planning, implementation, and process-centered innovation.				
The enterprise process model has been communicated throughout the enterprise, is used to drive project prioritization, and is linked to enterprise-level technologies and data architectures.	The enterprise has extended its process model to connect with those of customers and suppliers. It also uses the model in strategy development.				
The process owners share accountability for the enterprise's performance.	A process council operates as the seniormost management body; performers share accountability for enterprise performance and the enterprise has established steering committees with customers and suppliers to drive interenterprise process change.				
A formal program management office, headed by a chief process officer, coordinates and integrates all process projects, and a process council manages interprocess integration issues. The enterprise manages and deploys all process-improvement techniques and tools in an integrated manner.	The process owners work with their counterparts in customer and supplier enterprises to drive interenterprise process integration.				

Acknowledgments

I owe a debt of gratitude to all those who contributed their stories to this book, especially the Phoenix Consortium members and alumni. Their willingness to share their experiences was indispensable to portraying real-world applications of the power of process.

My deepest appreciation goes to Doug Sease and John Mahaney. To Doug, who was able to meld two different writing styles and a variety of stories into one great book with patience and his characteristic good humor. And to John, whose vision for the completion and publication of this work kept us going. Both of you are great professionals and good friends. To Bob Barnett, who, as always, provided us with wise counsel and effective representation. To Jack Grayson, whose contribution toward the book title made it perfect.

To the Hammer and Company staff, thank you for telling me about the journey through the past and sharing in our vision of the future.

I also appreciate the efforts of the Hammer children—Jessica, Alison, Dana, and David—in locating and organizing the core draft of this book and related materials during the difficult time of transition. Thanks to Joe Tischler for his sage advice to Hammer and Company and all its projects.

Last, my sincere gratitude goes to Phyllis Hammer for keeping this book alive and for believing in me as Michael did, trusting me to carry forward this incredible legacy.

—Lisa W. Hershman

Index

First-call resolution (FCR), 44–45, 88, 89
Four Acres Manufacturing (pseudonym), 225, 253–260
Frivolity, performance measurement and, 72–73

G

Galvan, Miguel, 251–252
Gamesa, 23, 241–252
General Electric, 38
General Mills, 39–40
General Motors, 4, 10
Gilbert, S. Taco, III, 188–190
Governance and expertise, 5, 23, 181–214, 225
  alignment issues, 182, 184
  catalysts, 185–186
  Chief Process Officer (CPO), 186–190, 195–197, 201, 214
  dos and don'ts of, 214
  expertise issues, 182–183, 184
  finding experts, 206–208
  governance structure, 198
  information issues, 181–182, 184
  ingredients of expertise, 202–206
  politics of, 211–214
  process councils, 195–201
  process program office (PPO), 186, 187, 191–195, 199, 201
  support for experts, 208–211
  training programs, 208
Governing process, 19

H

Hammer & Company, 3, 208
Hammer, Michael, 1–3, 5, 6, 11, 280
Harvard University, 53, 54
Hattaway, Inc. (pseudonym), 225, 261–266
Health care, 36–37, 41–42, 47

Helseth Industries, 139–142
Hemingway, Ernest, 33
Hewlett-Packard, 50–51
Hills Pet Nutrition, 132
Hiring, aptitude/attitude approach to, 130–133
Hospital billing, 36–37
Hospital surgery booking, 41–42
Hospitalists, 47

I

Inanity, performance measurement and, 72
Industrial Revolution, 10, 11
Infrastructure (*see* Performers and infrastructure)
International companies, 10–11
Inventory, 39–41
  vendor-managed inventory (VMI), 53, 54

J

Job descriptions, 133, 142
Job interviews, 130–131
Johnson, Samuel, 169
Jönsson, Dennis, 234–235
"Juanito," 242–244, 248, 252

K

Kelvin, Lord, 79
Key performance indicators (KPIs), 83, 88, 187
Keyser, Janet, 110–113

L

Language, 211
Last promise date, 68–69
Laziness, performance measurement and, 71
Leadership, 5, 23, 153–179, 184, 222, 227, 229

About the Authors

MICHAEL HAMMER was a bold and revolutionary thinker, and the coauthor of *Reengineering the Corporation,* the most important business book of the 1990s. Named to *Time* magazine's first list of the twenty-five most influential Americans, the business world lost one of its rare geniuses when he passed away in September 2008. Dr. Hammer was also the author of *The Agenda,* as well as articles in *Harvard Business Review,* the *Economist,* and other publications.

LISA W. HERSHMAN is the CEO of Hammer and Company, the global leader in business education process methods. Hershman previously served as corporate senior vice president of operational excellence at Avnet, Inc., where she was honored with the 2008 Avnet corporate Chairman's Award. Hershman, whose career experience includes GE Aerospace, is a contributing columnist for *BusinessWeek.*